TANZANIA TAX LAW REPORTS

2004

VOLUME I

PUBLISHED ON BEHALF OF THE GOVERNMENT OF THE UNITED REPUBLIC OF TANZANIA
Mkuki na Nyota Publishers Limited
Dar Es Salaam

TANZANIA TAX LAW REPORTS 2004
VOLUME I

ISSN 1821 – 7117

ISBN 978-9987-08-041-0

Published under the Board Secretariat and Legal Services Department of Tanzania Revenue Authority through collaboration between the Ministry of Finance, Tax Revenue Appeals Board, Tax Revenue Appeals Tribunal, Faculty of Law of University of Dar es Salaam, Attorney General's Chamber, Tanganyika Law Society, and National Board of Accountants & Auditors.

Edited by the Tanzania Tax Law Reports Editorial Board
Published by Mkuki na Nyota Publishers Ltd.,
P.O. BOX No. 4246, Dar es Salaam, Tanzania. www.mkukinanyota.com
Printed and bound by Thomson Press (India) Ltd.,
P.O. BOX No. 705, Delhi-Mathura Rd. Faridabad – 121 007, India

SCOPE OF THE SERIES

These Reports cover appeals & applications decided in the Tax Revenue Appeals Board and Tax Revenue Appeals Tribunal

CITATION

These Reports are cited thus [2004]1TTLR

CHAIRPERSONS

1. The Hon. Mr. Justice A.F.K. Shangwa - Chairperson, Tax Revenue Appeals Tribunal
2. The Hon. R.K.B. Meela -Chairperson, Tax Revenue Appeals Board
3. The Hon. B.R. Mutungi - Vice Chairperson, Tax Revenue Appeals Board

CASES REPORTED

DIGEST OF CASES REPORTED

CASES JUDICIALLY CONSIDERED

Afrika Mashariki Ltd v Commissioner General (App 18/03), unreported

Attorney General v Said Juma Muslim Shekimweri (Civil Appeal 35/97), unreported

Attorney General v Wilts United Dairies (1922) 38 TLR 781

Cape Brandy Syndicate v Inland Revenue Commissioners [1921] 1 KB 64

Gunda Shubaya v CIT (1939) 7 ITR 20

IRC v Duke of Westminster [1935] All ER 259 (HL)

Iron & Steelwares Ltd v CW Martyr & Co (1956) 23 EACA 175

Jefarrali Ali v CTT 3 EATC 328

Kliman v Winkworth (1933) 17 TC 569

Mandatory v CTT 2 EATC 426

Marie Stopes (T) Ltd v Commissioner General (Comm Case 10/04), unreported

Nassor Athumani Gogo and Jessy Willium Lugiana and others v The Board of Trustees of

The Parastatal Pensions and Another (Misc Civil Cause 76/03), unreported

Nimrod E Mkono v Commissioner General (Tax Appeal 6/04), unreported

O'Brien v Associated Fire Alarms Ltd [1968] 1 WLR 1916

Osenton (Charles) & Co v Johnston [1942] AC 130

Rungwe Freight Tanzania Ltd v Tanzania Revenue Authority Commissioner General (App 1/2002), unreported

Russell v Scott [1948] 2 All ER 1 (HL)

Solomon v Solomon [1897] AC 22 (HL) X v CIT 2 CIT 39

Tanzania Air Services Limited v Minister for Labour, Attorney General and the Commissioner for Labour [1996] TLR 217 (HC)

TANZANIA
TAX LAW REPORTS
2004(1)

A **AFRIKA MASHARIKI GOLD MINES LTD v COMMISSIONER GENERAL**

TAX REVENUE APPEALS BOARD

DAR ES SALAAM

B

(CONSOLIDATED VAT TAX APPEAL: NO. 4 OF 2004; AND INCOME TAX APPEAL NO. 10 OF 2004)

7 January 2005

C BR Mutungi, *Vice-Chairperson*, J Karashani and I Dallushi, *Members*

Capital Gains Tax—Sale of shares in a foreign company outside Tanzania—Whether capital gains tax payable—Income Tax Act, 1973

Stamp Duty—Dutiability of share sale instrument—Shares in a foreign company sold to foreigners in a transaction taking place outside Tanzania—Whether
D *the transaction is dutiable—Stamp Duty Act, 1972*

The appellant company at the time of dispute had two shareholders, namely East African Gold Mines (the Australian company) and Godfrey Hugh Stewart. In 2003, a Canadian company, Placer Dome Inc went into a public takeover bid of the Australian company (East African Gold Mines Ltd) and bought the majority
E shares in the Australian company. Upon learning of this takeover, the respondent demanded payment of capital gains tax and stamp duty. The appellants argued that the Australian company had no shares to sell and did not receive any payment because it was the shareholders who sold out shares. Further that the shares were sold outside Tanzania, so the transaction was covered by Australian laws.

Held:

F (i) Shares in a foreign company not registered in Tanzania that are sold to foreigners outside Tanzania cannot attract capital gains tax in Tanzania.

(ii) A subsidiary company cannot be treated as an automatic agent of a holding company for purposes of raising a tax assessment. There must be an express appointment of an agent.

(iii) Shares sale instruments in a sale of shares in a foreign company that
G takes place outside Tanzania cannot attract Stamp Duty in Tanzania.

Appeal allowed

Case referred to:

Cape Brandy Syndicate v Inland Revenue Commissioners [1921] 1 KB 64
Gunda Subbayya v CIT [1939] 7 ITR 21
H *IRC v Duke of Westminster* [1935] All ER 259 (HL)
Jefarrali Ali v CTT 3 EATC 328
Mandatory v CTT 2 EATC 426
Solomon v Solomon [1897] AC 22 (HL)
X v CIT 2 CIT 39

Dr Luoga, for the appellant
Mr Songoro, for the respondent

6 December 2004:

Dr Luoga, for the appellant: Before we proceed with submissions there are two intertwined appeals: No. 4 of 2004 and No. 10 of 2004. They arise from the same transaction and address similar issues of facts. The same could be consolidated with leave of the Board as they were previously consolidated for application for leave Nos. 17 and 18 of 2003.

Mr Songoro, for the respondent: I have no objection to the consolidation.

Board: There being no objection, let the two appeals be consolidated and form the appeal under cover of appeal No. 4 of 2004.

Dr Luoga: After consolidation we propose first to submit what the appeal is all about, the basis of the appeal, issues for determination by the Board and the position of the law in Tanzania. Thereafter, we will sequentially submit our submission on capital gains tax and stamp duty.

Your Honour, the appeals are challenging assessments raised by the respondents against the appellants in respect of stamp duty and capital gain tax. Both appeals relate to assessments which were raised in respect of shares that were acquired by a Canadian company called Placer Dome Incorporation (Placer Dome Inc) The appellant is a Tanzanian registered company holding a certificate of incorporation No. 23446. The certificate is appended (appeal No. 4 of 2004 statement annex AMGMH 1) and we pray that this be tendered as exhibit.

Mr Songoro: I have no objection.

Board: Admitted and marked P1.

Dr Luoga: Previously the appellant was registered in the name of East African Gold Mines Limited, but the name was changed to Afrika Mashariki Gold Mines Limited and it was discovered later that there was another company by the name of East African Mines Limited. The change was authorized by the Registrar of Companies as per annex AMGM 2 which is appended as an annexure in appeal No. 10. We pray the same be tendered as exhibit.

Mr Songoro: No objection

Board: Admitted and marked P2.

Dr Luoga: Your Honour, the appellant has two shareholders as per para 4 of the statements of appeals No. 4 and No. 10. These are first, East Africa Gold Mines Limited of Australia which holds 1,184,464 ordinary shares in the appellant's company and this is the majority share holder. The second shareholder is Mr Geoffrey Hugh Stewart holding one ordinary share. The record attesting to the records of the Australian company is annex AMGM 4. We pray that the copy be tendered as exhibit.

Mr Songoro: No objection

A

Board: Admitted and marked P3.

Dr Luoga: The shareholding pattern in the appellant company still remains the same and there have been no share transfers or sales to date. Your Honour, at the time of filing these appeals, the official records showing the status of share
B holding was the annual return which is required to be filed by the appellant in compliance of ss 108 and 347 of the Companies Act (Cap 212). This was appended as annex AMGM 5 in both appeals. We pray the same be tendered as exhibit.

Mr Songoro: No objection.

C

Board: Admitted and marked P 4.

Your Honour, while waiting for the hearing date of appeals, an official search was carried out at the registrar of companies, particularly in response to the respondent's statement and in order to apprise this Board with information of the current status. It was found that the annual return of year 2003 was filed on
D 17 March 2004. This was not appended. We shall pray for leave to file before tendering it in evidence.

Your Honour, in the course of the year 2003, the Canadian company placer Dome Inc. went into a public take over bid of the Australian company East African Gold Mines Limited. Placer Dome successfully bought the majority shares in the Australian company from more than 20 shareholders. These are
E found as AMGM 13 in appeal No. 4. I pray to tender it as exhibit.

Mr Songoro: No objection.

Board: Admitted and marked P5.

F Dr Luoga: The fact of purchase is reflected in annex of Tanzania Revenue Authority 8A submitted by the respondent.

The acquisition of these shares took place in Australia in accordance with the laws of Australia. The acquisition was widely published as pointed out by the respondents in their statement of response. Immediately, the memo of acquisition of the shares came to the Regional Revenue Officer Musoma, and the Regional
G Revenue Officer at Samora. Letters were issued to the appellants. The Regional Revenue Officer Musoma issued a letter demanding to be furnished with a copy of contract of sale of the shares for purposes of raising the capital gains tax under s 13 of Income Tax Act, 1973. The letter of demand is annex AMCM 6, appeal No. 10, of which we pray to tender as exhibit.

H Mr Songoro: No objection.

Board: Admitted and marked as P 6.

Dr Luoga: The Regional Revenue Officer, Dar Es Salaam, also issued a letter of demand, demanding to be furnished with the particulars of the same for purpose of stamp duty, AMGM 6 appeal No. 4 of 2004. We pray to tender the same as exhibit. A

Mr Songoro: No objection.

Board: Admitted and marked as P 7.

B

Dr Luoga According to the explanations given by the appellant to the respondents it was alleged that the appellant had sold their shares. This came out emphatically in annex AMGM 7 in appeal No. 10 of 2004, which we pray to tender as exhibit.

Mr Songoro: No objection.

C

Board: Admitted and marked P8.

Dr Luoga: In another dimension, annex 7 in appeal No. 4, provided the same explanation urging further that the sale by the Australian company of its shares was actually the disposing of the share in the appellant company; hence they demanded that a capital gain tax be imposed on whatever gains realized D therefrom in accordance with s 13 (1) of Income Tax Act. They also demanded that the appellant pay stamp duty under s 5 of Stamp Duty Act as well as under item 60.

Your Honour, on the basis of the reasoning by the respondent in respect of capital gains, assessments were issued annexs AMGM 8, 9 and 10 in appeal No. 10. We pray that they be accepted as exhibit. E

Mr Songoro: No objection.

Board: Admitted and marked collection P9.

Dr Luoga: Your Honour, the amount of capital gain assessed in the three F assessments reflects the amounts reported as cash consideration paid to the shareholders of the Australian company as depicted in annex TRA 8 P.

Your Honour, two things are significant in this annex:

(1) The respondents subjected to capital gains tax the whole of the consideration paid by placer Dome Inc and not the capital gain contemplated in s 13 (1) of G the Income Tax Act.
(2) The assessments themselves, annex AMGM 8, were issued on 31 July 2003. The document bears no assessment number and it was issued to East African Gold Mines Limited, PO Box 422, Tarime. The assessment purports to assess capital gains of an amount of Tshs 257,040,389,040, thereby demanding Tshs 25,704,038,904 as capital gains tax at a rate of 10% H

Your Honour, annex AMGM 9 was also issued on the same date, 31 July 2003. This is marked as assessment No. 30F.77 and was issued to the appellant purportedly. The appellant was assessed to a capital gain of Tshs 257,040,389,040 and Tshs 5,704,038,904 and the same was demanded, being 10% of the purportedly assessed capital gain tax.

A After exactly 14 days, that is, 14 August 2003, the Regional Revenue Officer of Musoma who issued the two assessments issued assessment No. 30F.47. This was purportedly served on appellant Afrika Mashariki, but in the address it was written as East African Gold Mines (this was to another person) as attested by AMGM 10; again the same amount of Tshs 257,040,385,040 was subjected to tax at a rate of 10% thereby producing a capital gain tax of Tshs 25,704,038,904.

B All the three assessments are still in force to date. As such there is demand for capital gains tax first against Messrs East African Gold Mines Limited of PO Box 422 Tarime, a company which is nonexistent in the United Republic. The postal address in annex AMGM 8 is that of the appellant. We may not know whom the respondent refers to as East African Gold Mines Limited. We may only summarize that perhaps there was a clerical error committed by the Regional
C Revenue Officer, Musoma, and therefore the respondent, which might have been occasioned by the appellant's change of name. Your Honour, we are only assuming that because on the same day the appellants were served with assessment No. 30F.77, demanding more or less the same amount. The assessment implicitly assumes that the appellant sold shares and was paid money in consideration for the shares sold. There was no evidence of such sale as we will subsequently prove
D that annex AMGM 10 was served on the appellant as East African Gold Mines Limited the same does not make it clear which East African Gold Mines Limited was intended to be served because there is East African Gold Mines in AMGM 81 and another under AMGM 10.

Your Honour, it is clear that one transaction cannot be subjected to capital gains tax three times in the hands of three different persons. We may wish to
E presume through rationality that possibly annex AMGM 8 and 9 might have been abandoned or superseded by AMGM 10, but that presumption is not supported clearly by the action of the respondent who has not vacated any assessments and rejected the objection by the appellant that they are not assessable to tax.

Your Honour, the validity of the assessments is complicated by the shifting positions that the respondent took when the appellant was seeking leave to lodge
F an appeal application Nos. 17 and 18 of 2003, the respondent issued a confirming notice in respect to assessment No. 30F.7 against East African Gold Mines Limited and did not address the two other assessments. We pray to tender the confirming notice AMGM 11 appeal No. 10 as an exhibit.

Mr Songoro: No objection.

G

Board: Admitted and marked P10.

Dr Luoga: While confirming assessment No. 30F.47 the respondent did continue to demand from the appellant to produce the share sale agreement which shows that Placer Dome Inc did purchase the majority of shares in the Australian
H company. Your Honour, this demand was placed on the appellant while the respondent was fully aware that the share transaction took place outside the United Republic and that the appellant was not a party. Assuming that assessment No. 30F.47 was meant for the Australian company, that company would have been the proper person from whom to demand production of documents.

Your Honour, we assume that the Australian law is the same as the Tanzanian law in that share transfers are mandatory registerable under the Companies Act.

Should the law be the same in Australia, then information as to any transfers A
would have been obtained from the Australian registry and the respondent was required to effect service in accordance with requirements of ss 135 (2) and 63 of income tax and not simply dump the document with the appellant who at law under s 135 (2) does not qualify to receive service on behalf of the Australian company.

Your Honour, the respondent was apprised with information that would have B
guided him to pursue a proper line of inquiry but chose to ignore the information that was communicated. This is clear from the channel of the responses by the respondents attested through annex 13, 14, 15 and 16 in appeal No. 10. Clearly, the respondent was bent simply to collect money from the appellant. Annex 17 in appeal No. 10 is a notice of agency to the applicant's bank seeking to enforce collection. The question that arises by the conduct of the respondent is what C
would be the basis of assessment raised against the appellant if to-date the assessment they deemed confirmed is assessment No. 30F.47, which was not raised against the appellant. As may be the case, with annex AMGM 16 on 22 October 2003 having been petitioned to abandon assessment No. 30F.77 that was previously issued against the appellant, the respondent refused to vacate the assessment but more strangely the respondent put forward three (3) main D
arguments which have relevance to the assessment raised against the appellants.

The three arguments are the following:

(1) The Australian company has interest in the United Republic by virtue of the shares in the appellant company.
(2) The shares owned by the Australian company in the appellant company are E
the ones confirmed to have been sold to the Canadian company.
(3) The shares of the Australian company constitute financial assets which are subject to capital gains tax on sale as required by the Income Tax Act.

Your Honour, these arguments do not relate to assessment No. 30F.77 raised against the appellant. They probably address assessment No.30F.47 which we F
will address later.

For purposes of consistency, I pray at this juncture to bring forth the background of the stamp duty dispute.

Your Honour, the assessment to stamp duty has been issued directly against the appellants. We have submitted in exhibits annex AMGM 6 and AMGM 7 appended in appeal No. 4. It is insatiable that in the two exhibits the respondent acknowledges G
that the purported share sale transaction took place in Australia and the respondent clearly states that it was a sale between East African Gold Mines Limited and Placer Dome Inc. Strangely, no assessment is issued to either the purported seller or buyer, and the assessment is issued to the appellant basing on the main argument that the shares were sold in respect of property situated in Mara Region in Tanzania. The respondent based the claim on three (3) main assumptions: H

(1) They assume that the Australian company sold its shares. This assumption is faulty.
(2) They assume that the Australian company received payment from the Canadian company as consideration for the shares purportedly sold. This assumption is again at law faulty as we will submit later.

A (3) There is an implicit assumption that the Australian company realized a capital gain, which again is a very faulty assumption at law.

At this point it suffices to point out that the Australian company had no shares to sell and it did not receive any payment, because it was the shareholders who sold the shares and this transaction therefore would never have formed a basis for
B raising a presumptive assessment.

Your Honour, in the light of our submission on how the dispute arose as detailed in the statement of appeal and in the light of the respondent's response in both appeals, it seems that there are five sets of issues which are to be resolved. The first set comprises factual issues which are common to both appeals. The Board will need to establish the following: (a) whether there was any sale of
C shares, (b) which shares were sold (c) where the sale transaction took place, (d) who were the parties to the sale transaction, and (e) who received consideration in respect sale of shares for cash.

(2) The second is a set of factual issues in respect of capital gain tax against the appellant. Here, there are four issues. While the Honorable Board has to
D establish with clarity as to which East African Gold Mines Limited, the assessment order of 31 July 2003 (annex AMGM 8) was raised against; it is unclear whether it was East African Limited (Afrika Mashariki) or Australian East African Gold Mines. The Board will have to find whether the assessment was vacated or superseded by the subsequent assessments or whether it is still in force.

E

The Board needs to address assessment No. 30F.77 which was superseded by assessment No. 30F.47, or if it is still in force, and also establish which East African Gold Mines is referred to in assessment No. 30F.47.

(3) The third set is legal issues common to both appeals. (a) Whether the sale of
F shares if it is so established constituted a disposition of financial assets held in United Republic of Tanzania. Should the answer to that question be in the affirmative, then the Board will have to address as to whether such interest is an interest in the appellant.

(4) The legal issues specific to capital gains tax appeal No. 10 of 2004 are whether the appellant realized capital gains chargeable to tax. The alternative is whether
G there is any other person who realized the capital gains tax under the alleged transaction of sale of shares and who will be that person if there is any capital gains tax realized, whether the same is covered under s 13 of the Income Tax Act.

(5) The legal issues specific to stamp duty appeal No. 4 of 2004 are whether any instrument in the alleged sale of shares is a dutiable instrument under the Stamp Duty Act, 1972, and whether the appellant is the person under the law
H who is required to pay stamp duty under such alleged instrument.

The findings in respect to each set of issues will ultimately establish the validity or otherwise of raising any assessment against the appellant.

Your Honour, before submitting on the grounds addressing the issues we hereby beg to state the position of law in Tanzania in respect of capital gains tax and stamp duty.

In respect of capital gains tax, the law on the chargeability on capital gains tax A
is the Income Tax Act. As far as the present appeal is concerned s 13 lays down
the rules and procedure for the chargeability of capital gains to Income Tax Act,
under s 13 (1), as amended under s 13 of Finance Act, 1999. Provided that any
person who sells any financial asset owned by him in the United Republic, then
the difference between value of consideration for such financial asset sold and
much of the adjusted cost for such financial assets of the person that has not been B
claimed as deduction in respect of capital expenditure to such financial asset
under the Second Schedule shall be deemed to be capital gains income of such
person, accrued or derived from the United Republic in the year of income in
which the same takes place. Your Honour, under the same provision no person
can transfer or change the ownership before attaching a certificate of clearance
issued by the Commissioner certifying that capital gain tax has been paid or is not C
payable.

Your Honour, s 13 does not operate in isolation. It is subject to the provisions
in the charging provision, s 3 (1) of the Income Tax Act. The person to be
assessed must be a resident or non-resident person. In the case of a resident
person, he will be charged upon all the income which accrued to such a person
from worldwide sources. Ideally, if such a resident person owns financial assets D
in the United Republic of Tanzania he will be liable to pay tax. However, the
worldwide concept under s 3 (1) para (*a*) is restricted by the provision of s 13 (1)
in respect of chargeability of capital gains. The sale can only be chargeable to
capital gains tax if the financial asset is situated in the United Republic. This
restriction means therefore, that a resident person who owns financial assets in
the United Kingdom or Zimbabwe will not fall under the scope of s 13 (1) of the E
Income Tax Act.

In the case of a non-resident, s 3 (1) (*b*) subjects to income tax all the income
of such a person which accrued in or derived in the United Republic of such non-
resident person. Any sale of a financial asset not owned by him and any profit
arising therefrom cannot be held to derive in the source of the United Republic
according to the law. The first step in determining the chargeability to capital F
gains tax is to identify the seller of the financial assets as per s 13 (1) of the
Income Tax Act.

The second step is to ascertain the seller's residential status. If the seller is a
residential person then the third step is to determine whether the financial assets
are owned in the United Republic. If it is owned in the United Republic then the
fourth step is to calculate the capital gain as per formula given in s 13 (1) subs (*a*) G
and (*b*) of the Tax Appeals Act, 1973. If the seller is a non-resident person, then
the second step becomes imperative and at the third step to determine whether the
seller owns a financial asset in the United Republic.

Your Honour, the words "owned by him in the United Republic" as used in
s 13 (1) of the Income Tax Act, mean that the asset must be located in the United
Republic and not elsewhere. It follows therefore that if a non-resident person H
owns assets outside the United Republic, such a person is not chargeable to tax
both under s 3 (1) (*b*) as read together with 3 (2) (*e*), as well as s 13 (1) of the
Income Tax Act.

Your Honour, the provisions of the law as to the chargeability to capital gains
tax are very clear and unambiguous, and have to be strictly applied in line with
their clear plain meaning.

There is no room for entertainment or reading in anything in those provisions. The courts in East Africa have persistently applied the rule of construction which requires strict interpretation of statutes. The Board may kindly wish to make reference to *Jefarrali Ali v CTT* 3 EATC 328 and *X v CIT* 2 EATC 39 and the famous case of *Mandatory v CTT* 2 EATC 426. There are other cases decided in the England expounding on the same principle *Cape Brandy Syndicate v Inland Revenue Commissioners* [1921] 1 KB 64 at p 71 as well as the case of *IRC v Duke of Westminster* [1935] All ER 259 (HL). Let me turn to the law of stamp duty.

The law applicable is the Stamp Duty Act, and there are mainly four provisions applicable to the instant appeal.

(1) Section 5 (1) which provides that "any instrument specified to the schedule to the Act which is whether executed in Tanzania or if executed outside the United Republic, if it relates to any property in Tanzania or to any matter or thing to be performed or done in Tanzania". This according to the respondent should be read with

(2) Item 60 of the schedule (transfer of shares).

(3) Section 25, any chargeable instrument executed outside Tanzania shall be stamped within 30 days of its arrival in Tanzania.

(4) Section 40, which identifies who is the person carrying the obligation to pay the duty and in the case of transfer of shares. Section 40 (*k*) is specific (purchase or transfer) So far as the instrument is a changeable instrument in Tanzania.

Having explained the law applicable to both capital gains tax and stamp duty, we now propose to address the application of the law to the issue in the appeal as previously set forth.

Board: As the matter has taken too long, we shall break for a short while until 1.00 pm.

At 1.00 pm.

Dr Luoga: Your Honour, we are praying that the annual return for the year 2000 should be read together with AMEM 5 showing the shareholding status at present.

Mr Songoro: We need more time to check on these documents as we have been in contact with the registrar of companies and we were getting no document at all.

Board: The respondent to check on the document.

Submission by Dr Luoga proceeds: We now humbly wish to submit on the application of the law on the issues we pointed on.

First, I will relate to the common issues related to both appeals; the first issue is whether there were sales of any shares. The evidence adduced through documentary exhibits we have submitted shows that indeed there were share sales that took place and which enabled Placer Dome Inc to acquire a controlling interest in the Australian company East Africa Gold Mines Limited.

This fact is also acknowledged by the respondents and is therefore not in A dispute.

The second issue is which shares were sold. This issue is also answered in the documentary exhibit submitted, that the shares sold were those of the shareholders in the Australian company, East African Gold Mines Limited.

The respondent does not seem to agree with this argument. He maintains that the Australian company sold its shares to Placer Dome Inc. Your Honour, under B company law, as a general rule, a private company cannot sell its own shares in Tanzania, and in any other Commonwealth country influenced jurisdiction. In this case we are dealing with a public company as attested by annex AMEM 4. If listed, a public company can have shares floated to the general public. However in the instant case, in order to acquire a controlling interest, Placer Dome had to buy out most of the other shareholders in the Australian company. Annex AMGM C 18 shows that 100% of the shares in the Australian company had all been issued to subscribers. There were more than 20 subscribers from whom shares were bought. Annex TRA 8A shows that one of the shareholders who sold shares to Placer Dome Inc. is Anglo gold, which sold 10.3% of its equity holdings in the Australian company to Placer Dome. Annex TRA A which is sought to be relied upon by the respondent also discloses that other companies which had equity D interests in the Australian company sold shares to Placer Dome Inc. These include Good Main & Co (Canada), Mackory Bank (Australia), CDC capital partners of (United Kingdom), Anglo Gold (South Africa) and the Lion Selection Group of Australia. All these names also appear in annex AMGEM 18. This proves that the shares sold were those held by various shareholders in the Australian company.

The third issue is on the identity of the parties in the share sale transaction. The E parties were Placer Dome Inc (purchaser) and East African Gold Mines or the shareholders who sold shares to Placer Dome Inc. There was no single transaction of sale of shares but multiple transactions of share purchases by Placer Dome Inc. Since all the shares were issued, the Australian company itself had no shares for sale.

The fourth issue is where the sale of shares took place. The respondent has not F disputed that the shares were sold outside the Republic since the Australian company was incorporated in Australia under the laws of that country as attested under annex AMCM 4. The sale of shares had to take place in conformity to the laws of that country. No such shares could have been registered under the Tanzania Company Ordinance.

The fifth issue is who received consideration in relation to shares acquired by G Placer Dome Inc. It follows from the findings of the four other issues that consideration was paid by Placer Dome Inc., to the shareholders who sold their shares to Placer Dome Inc. For instance, referring to annex TRA 8, it is disclosed that Placer Dome Inc. bought the shares from share holders at a purchase price of US$ 3.02. As mentioned earlier, since all the shares had been issued, the Australian company could not have received any consideration that could lead to H a realization of capital gains.

Your Honour, the assessments raised by the respondent is presumptive assessments. They were not based on any returns filed by the appellant but through an independent interpretation of facts by the respondent and using arbitrary estimation. It is a cardinal principle in tax law that the respondent is not entitled to make guess work in raising assessments to tax. The respondent is required to

A have material on which to base this assessment, not to be capricious, not to guess
without evidence and is also required to take steps to procure materials. These are
the requirements of the Best Judgment Rule which is applicable where
presumptuous assessments are raised. The rule was clearly stated in the land mark
case of *Gunda Subbayya* v CIT [1939] 7 ITR 21.

In the instant appeal the respondent made assessments based on wrong
B presumptions. First, they made a presumption that the Australian company
sold shares which was brought to their knowledge through the newspaper
reports and which prompted the respondents to raise the assessments on the
assumption that Placer Dome Inc. was acquiring shares from other shareholders.
They also made the assumption that there was a single transaction of sale of
shares by the Australian company to Placer Dome Inc. This was a wrong,
C unjustified and arbitrary assumption, because the materials available indicated
otherwise.

Your Honour, in this respect it is very demonstrative that while the respondent
implicitly admits that the appellant did not sell any shares in the Australian
company he has refused to vacate assessment. If the documentary exhibits
submitted establish that the appellant did not sell any shares and the Australian
D company also did not sell any shares, then it follows that none of them did receive
consideration that could be subjected to a capital gains tax in anyway. It also
follows that the insistence by the respondent that the appellant should furnish
documents evidencing the sale of shares while fully being aware that neither the
appellant nor the Australian company were privy to the share sale transaction.
The persistence of such demands could only be ill based and considered as an
E abuse of powers to call for information.

Your Honour, we now wish to address the second set of issues. The first factual
issue seeks to establish the identity of assessment in the numbered assessment
issued on 31 July 2000 AMGM 8. As submitted earlier the assessment was issued
to East African Gold Mines PO Box 1422, Tarime. The Postal Box belongs to the
appellant and since there is no company by the name of East African Gold Mines
F Limited at Tarime, the assessment could not be served to any party. It is only the
respondent that can identify those assets. We offered an explanation earlier that
this could be due to a clerical error. Had that been the case, and acting diligently
the respondent should have brought to light the fact of error and vacated the
assessment as we shall point out in due course. The respondent did not act
innocently. He acted wilfully and maliciously in order to perpetuate unjustified
G demands for taxes.

The second issue arises because of the issuance of the second assessment
30F.77 which replicates everything from the previous assessment except the
name of the appellant.

Your Honour, we have to go back to the same question whether the second
assessment did displace the first assessment. There can never be two persons
H selling the same shares on the same date and realizing the same amount in capital
gains. It could have been decent, even if the respondent was ready to point out,
that the two acted jointly while that is not the case.

Again the respondents do not admit that 30F.77 was a corrective assessment.
On the one hand, this is demonstrative again of ill will and on the other hand it
demonstrates the lack of certainty by the respondents as to who is the correct
person to assess. The two assessments were left to remain in force simultaneously

as a mousetrap which may catch whoever is catchable. It is demonstrative of guesswork contrary to the Best Judgment Rule. A

The third factual issue is whether assessment 30F.77 is still in force. Again the problem is the same. Fourteen days after appellants were served to capital gains tax the respondent issued assessment No. 30F.77 bearing the same particulars as those in the assessment issued against the appellant. The only difference is in the name of the assessee. The respondent despite the objection raised by the appellant B has maintained the stance that all the three assessments remain in force.

The question is if all the shares or the majority shares in the Australian company had been bought by Placer Dome Inc from the shareholders what did the Australian company sell and what did the appellant sell? Assuming that all the assessments are valid or not valid assuming the respondent had grounds to raise the assessment he was obliged to demonstrate the grounds for raising the C assessment. In the case of the appellant being resident persons under s 13 (1) of Income Tax Act the respondent should have shown that the applicant was an owner of a financial asset owned in the United Republic and also the respondent should have materials showing that these assets owned by the appellant in Tanzania were sold. The respondent should also have shown the amount of consideration paid to the appellant and finally what was the adjusted cost based D in order to ascertain a capital gain. This obligation arises from the best judgment rule under which in absence of return filed; the respondent acted invoking powers under s 79 (3) of the of the Income Tax Act. Once that section is applied, the best judgment rule is applied.

In respect of the Australian company, again because the assessment is presumptive, he should have first established the residential status of the E company. He should also have established whether the company owns financial assets in the United Republic and also whether the company sold those financial assets, and whether it received any consideration. This was not done, contrary to the requirements of the Best Judgment Rule.

The amount denominated by the respondent as a capital gain reflects the Tanzania shillings over the amount reported to have constituted the total F consideration paid out by Placer Dome Inc, to the shareholders. Annex TRA 8B reported that Placer Dome Inc clinched the deal for a total cash consideration of US$255 million and this is exactly the figure quoted by the Regional Revenue Officer Musoma in annex 6, a complete list of figures from a newspaper report of an assessment. The respondent admits in writing that it was a newspaper figure that was used, which does not comply with the law. G

Your Honour, in order for a financial asset to be owned in Tanzania as pointed earlier it must be located in Tanzania. The property in the shares of any company is owned by the shareholders. In the instant case we have shareholders in the Australian company owning shares in that company. Then we have the Australian company owning shares in the appellant company. The question is whether at law it can be deemed that the shareholders in the Australian company are the owners H of shares held by the Australian company in the appellant.

Your Honour, the rule in *Solomon v Solomon* [1897] AC 22 (HL) poses that the shareholders are independent persons of the company. The company can own property independent from the shareholders and to that extent the respondent cannot depart from a well-established principle of law and assume that sale of shares in one company can mean a sale of shares in another company.

A Your Honour, ordinary shareholders in the company have no right whatsoever against the company except to receive a dividend if one is declared. If a dividend is not declared under the law they have no rights. They cannot participate in the day-to-day management and decisions of the company (ordinary shares). The assumption which the respondent appears to make in seeking to impose the capital gain tax has no legal legs on which to stand.

B Your Honour, may we point out that there is ample evidence that neither the appellant nor the Australian company did sell shares. There is also ample evidence that neither the two did receive consideration. There is also ample evidence that the shares were not owned in Tanzania and so are not chargeable under s 13 (1). If there is any person who received consideration that person is irrelevant to this appeal and therefore the assessments to capital gains were C wrongly issued and should be nullified with costs.

Your Honour, our submissions in respect to capital gains also address the basic issue in respect of stamp duty. If on the basis of those submissions the Board established that share sale transactions took place outside the Republic of Tanzania between Placer Dome Inc and East African Gold Mines transferring shares held in Australia from one foreign person to another foreign D person, then s 5 of the Stamp Duty Act cannot be satisfied because the instrument will not have been executed in this Republic, and secondly the instrument does not relate to a property found in Tanzania. The transaction does not relate to any matter in Tanzania. It relates to the equity changes in the Australian company.

Section 25 of the Stamp Duty Act, does not apply because the instrument E executed by foreigners in a foreign territory in respect of property held in that territory are not registrable in Tanzania and so not subject to stamp duty. We therefore pray that the assessment to stamp duty be nullified with costs. Your Honour, other prayers are as our statement of appeal in para 24 appeal No. 4 and para 24 in appeal No. 10. We humbly beg to rest our submission.

F Mr Songoro, for the respondent: Your Honour, I pray that we be given time tomorrow. I have two witnesses to proceed with in my case and after which I will make my submission.

Order: (1) Hearing on respondent's case to proceed tomorrow as prayed, at 9.00 am.

G

7 December 2004:

Mr Songoro: Your Honour the matter is coming today for hearing from our side. However, I would first like to notify the Board that the document from the registrar we had promised to go through the Registrar, we are now in the position H to state that we have no objection to the appellants replying to it.

Board: The document (annual report) admitted and marked P11.

Mr Songoro: I have two witnesses today.

(The two witnesses are examined, cross-examined and re-examined)

8 December 2004:

Mr Songoro, for the respondent: Your Honour I am ready to proceed.

Submission by Mr Songoro

Mr Songoro: The submission is in respect of appeal No. 4 of 2004 (stamp duty) and No. 10 of 2004 capital gains tax.

I would first deal with s 18 (2) (*b*) of the Tax Revenue Appeals Act. The section is about the onus of proof. It is our submission that burden of proving that the assessment of capital gains tax and assessment of sales tax were excessive or erroneous on the appellant.

We would like to refer to s 22 (5) of the Tax Revenue Appeals Act on the ways to provide evidence. It is our submission that although the appellant made submission before the Board there was no evidence at all to support the assertion made in his submission.

It is our submission that the submission of the appellant to this Board in the course of hearing may not be considered as evidence in supporting the appellant's case. I now proceed to summarize the appellant's case as the way the respondent finds it fit. The respondent agrees that the transactions which led to the respondent's demand of capital gain tax and stamp duty are contained in similar sets of facts. From the respondent's point of view the major issue in both appeals is the chargeability of the taxes themselves. Another issue which has to be determined by the Board is the relationship of appellant and East Africa Gold Mines, and the transaction of sale of shares.

The third issue which we noted is the procedure adopted by the respondent in making the assessments and the way the assessments were issued. The fourth issue is who is the taxable person in both cases. Is it the appellant, East African Gold Mines or Placer Dome? After making those submissions we submit that the two assessments (capital gains tax and stamp duty are correct, proper and are in accordance with the two laws (Income Tax Act). The respondent has produced to this Board exhibits showing that there was a transaction of sale of shares and the transaction related to the property which is situated in Tanzania. We have exhibited financial statements of 2002 and 2003, both of the appellant's company. Public notices from the appellant recruiting from the public which were very clear that the ownership of Afrika Mashariki and management is now with Placer Dome Inc. We have produced a letter from PricewaterhouseCoopers confirming sale of shares of East Africa Gold Mines. We have also produced newspapers which also state that the sale of shares has taken place and ownership of the mine and the business itself is no longer within East African Mines but has shifted to Placer Dome. The respondent has pointed specifically to TRA 8 as the basis of computing the taxes.

The other copies of newspapers TRA 8A, TRA 9, TRA 10 and TRA 11 were attached to show that the ownership details of the mining company has been published locally and internationally showing that it belongs to Placer Dome. The respondents have not seen any befitting information contained in the newspapers, financial statements of 2003 proving that Placer Dome Inc is the owner of appellant's company.

The respondent submits further that there is no law or any provision in the Income Tax Act and provision in the stamp duty which forbids the respondent to rely on the information found in the newspapers as long as it provides the true picture of the affairs. We further submit that the evidence of DW1 and DW2 was to the effect that the appellant was requested to submit details of the transaction (of sale of shares), but the respondent did not submit these details as per request. In the absence of further details from the appellant, the respondent is under an obligation, basing on information before him. It is the respondent's submission that taking into account para 9 of appeal No. 10 of 2004 that the appellant is a stranger to the transaction. The appellant had no competence to inquire into the transaction, and he had not received any documents. The appellant is *estopped* from complaining from the respondent's assessment because they do not know the transaction and they do not have the records of the transaction. The central issue here is how can a stranger or a person completely innocent on record fault the respondent who had details from a different source that the transaction was effected and consideration paid. We submit both in appeals that the appellant has no record of the transaction. He is a stranger. We submit that he cannot complain that the amount paid as consideration TRA 8B is proper or not.

After my general reservations, I now proceed to the issue of demand of capital gain tax. Your Honour, it is our submission that capital gain tax is charged under s 13 (1) and (2) of Income Tax Act. It is the respondent's submission that s 13 (1) and (2) of the Income Tax Act, imposes tax on their own without subjecting the provision on s 3 of the Income Tax Act. Similarly, it is like the repealed s 13 (6) which stood on its own.

Going to s 13 we submit that the section states "any" and so there is no distinction between resident and non-resident, "any" does not give room to any demarcation. We submit that the legal phraseology submitted on resident or non-resident is not part and parcel of s 13 of the Income Tax Act. The proviso which is in that section gives a condition of the financial asset after sale. East Africa Gold Mines sold its shares to Placer Dome Inc. The shares of East African Gold Mines (company) were transferred to Placer Dome, and the East African Gold Mines is the sole owner of the appellant. As testified by DW1 and DW2 that East Africa Gold Mines has shares in Afrika Mashariki and the shares are represented by assets available at the appellant's company. It is the respondent's submission basing on the evidence of DW1 and DW2 that East African Gold Mines has assets in Afrika Mashariki which is registered in Tanzania and has assets in Tanzania. I further submit that even relying on the annual returns and financial returns (2002 and 2003) submitted, the shares of East Africa Gold Mines are visible. It is our submission that the shares mentioned in the appellant's annual returns and financial statements of 2002 are financial assets in terms of s 13 of the Income Tax Act. The owner before the transaction was done was East African Gold Mines. We further submit that the same financial statements (shares in East Africa Gold Mines) reflected in annual returns and financial statements of 2002 are also reflected in the financial statement of 2003. It is our submission that the word "financial assets" in the Income Tax Act is not defined and so even the business and financial returns are financial assets. It is not limited to any property. Taking into account that East Africa Gold Mines was the sole owner of appellant and so the change to Placer Dome is the change of financial assessment. Since Placer Dome Inc has acquired ownership of appellant's company from East African Gold Mines, it is our submission that it is no longer the owner of the appellant's company. Since the said transaction resulted in change of ownership, the appellant cannot argue successfully that East Africa Gold Mines is the owner of the appellant company. A

You cannot sell your shares and retain ownership too. It is our submission that although the transaction took place outside Tanzania, the sale resulted in the total acquisition of shares of East African Gold Mines in Afrika Mashariki, a financial interest held in Tanzania; and the transaction attracts capital gain tax under s 13 B of the Income Tax Act.

It is our submission that East Africa Gold Mines was paid US$255 million in return for shares, and East African Gold Mines cannot receive the said money and remain the owner of the shares as submitted by the appellant. It is our submission that even if there was a single or multiple transactions, there is no limitation on s 13 of the Income Tax Act. The only relief is on s 13 (5) of the Income Tax Act. C (Dar es Salaam Stock Market Exchange).

It is our submission that the appellant's submission stated the majority of shares has been allotted and that has no legal power over them is misleading. We argue that the sale of shares of East Africa Gold Mines to Placer Dome which led to the transfer of ownership to the appellant was not done without complete knowledge of the appellant. The appellant was aware that Placer Dome Inc, D may not purchase shares of East African Gold Mines, which has the effect of transferring the ownership of the appellant company without the knowledge of the appellant. That is why we submit that in the financial statements of 2003, the transaction which brought in Placer Dome Inc, is reported.

We submit that s 13 of the of the Income Tax Act does not make any distinction between resident, non-resident, single or multiple transaction so long E as there is a sale of financial assessments owned in Tanzania. The Board should look at the transaction from Australia to the mine where Placer Dome Inc now is managing and owning the business.

We submit that the capital gains income which East Africa Gold Mines derived was derived in Tanzania. The business which East African Gold Mines has is from Tanzania. We are not told in evidence if East Africa Gold Mines had any F business in any other country.

It is our submission that computation of the taxes is proper. The respondent would like to submit on the assessment of the capital gain tax as raised by appellant. The evidence of DW1 shows there were three assessments raised but there is only one which was confirmed. The appellant is arguing that the assessments contained some errors. We submit that as pointed by DW1 that those G errors may not invalidate the assessment in view of s 87 of the Income Tax Act. If there is any mistake in the confirmed assessment, that is itself no ground for this Board to invalidate the said assessments.

We submit that with the errors pointed by the appellant the assessment is still legally proper. On the issue of service of the assessment to the appellant we submit that the assessment was properly served to the appellant. Section 52 of the H Income Tax Act is clear that for a non-resident person the assessment may be served on an agent. DW1 has testified that the appellant is a subsidiary company of East Africa Gold Mines. Even after the said transaction we are told that East Africa remained to be the holding company of the appellant. Serving of the assessment to the appellant was proper. We further submit s 135 of Income Tax Act is dealing with other notices but not notices of assessment. The serving of notices of assessments is provided by s 84 of the Income Tax Act. We submit that the service in view of s 84 of the Income Tax Act was proper.

Your Honour, I pray to shift on the issue of the stamp duty. It is clarified under s 5 (1) (*b*) of the Stamp Duty Act and the section as pointed out by DW2. Even if the transaction is done outside Tanganyika, as long as it is related to property in Tanganyika, stamp duty is payable. Since the sale of share transaction relates to property situated in Tanzania stamp duty is payable. On who is liable to pay stamp duty, it is our submission as pointed out by DW2 that it is either the purchaser or transferee (s 40 (*k*)). It is our submission that if the purchaser or transferee to pay stamp duty and so that purchaser is Placer Dome Inc. Placer Dome Inc is the owner of appellant's company, therefore I submit that it was proper for the respondent to issue demand of stamp duty to appellant. The purchaser is the one owing the appellant's company. Even the exhibits state this.

After the above submission I now submit that the assessment of the capital gain tax and stamp duty was proper. I then proceed to make a comment on the appellant's submission that the appellant's company is a separate entity from its shareholders or East Africa Gold Mines is a separate entity from its shareholders. As correctly pointed by the appellant a company is treated as a separate legal entity but what the appellant omitted to state is that there are instances in company law where the concept of separate entity may be lifted by a judicial Board like this one to see the transaction which took place between the company and shareholders. That process is known as lifting the corporate veil to see the transactions which took place between the companies. The doctrine is common in company law allowing the judicial Board like this to open all the transactions and putting them on the table without a demarcation line to see the transactions done by the shareholders or companies. This is to see the innocence of the parties (companies).

Farley ed, *Company Law* (4th edn), p. 69, states that the courts have an option not to apply the Solomon principle. On p 70 it also states that the court has on several occasions lifted the veils on fraud, group of enterprises, trusts, tort and the last one is on tax relevant to this case. It is our submission that since there is a relationship between Afrika Mashariki and East Africa Gold Mines (holding company) and Placer Dome Inc (current owner) the Board should investigate the transaction which led to the ownership of Placer Dome in the appellant's company without the appellant's assets being vested to Placer Dome basing on financial statement of 2003 and basing on the letter from PricewaterhouseCoopers.

It is our submission that in a transaction involving group of companies, subsidiary and holding companies the concept of separate entity may be disregarded to ascertain the tax issue. We submit that when there is any statutory obligation on the part of the shareholder or company the concept of separate legal entity cannot be used as a shield to obstruct a legal obligation.

It is my submission that the Board should analyze the transaction in its true commercial world from Australia to where Placer Dome now owns the business. The Board should not rely on the decision of *Solomon v Solomon* (supra) while investigating a tax matter like this one.

My last submission on this matter is on annex AMGM 13 showing that there are several share holders of East African Gold Mines. We submit that the fax message in AMGM 13 and the list of the so-called shareholders is not a concrete proof that these are shareholders. The conclusive proof of ownership of shares is the profit of share certificate as the list shown lacks proof. It does not originate from any official company either in Tanzania or Australia. We submit that annex AMGM 13 be disregarded it is just a mere correspondence and there is no credible evidence tendered here to support this document.

We submit that the two appeals be dismissed with costs and the respondent be allowed to enforce the issued assessments.

Dr Luoga, for the appellant: I am ready to submit but I will do so on 10 December 2004.

Order: Reply by Dr Luoga on 10 December 2004 at 9.00 am.

10 December 2004:

Dr Luoga, for the appellant, in reply: The respondent has made a number of points in reply. We humbly pray to raise our reply in the same sequence.

First, on the burden of proof, at the outset the counsel pointed out s 18 (2) (*b*) of the Income Tax Act, 1973, which states that the burden of proof is on the appellant in proving the assessment. The counsel also pointed out s 22 (5) of the Tax Revenue Appeals Act, the evidence for which is given orally or through affidavit. We thus submitted that the appellant had not adduced any evidence at all. We submit that the counsel did not read s 22 (5) of the Tax Revenue Appeals Act, in full. The subsection also provides that evidence may be adduced in such other manners as the Board may deem fit.

Your Honour, at the beginning of the appellant's submission we notified this Board that the appellant will not call witnesses to adduce oral evidence. The appellant will rely on annex to the statement of appeal which will be tendered as documentary exhibits. These were tendered in evidence and the respondent did not object. It is therefore incompetent to allege that no evidence was tendered. The appellant extracted evidence in the cross-examination of DW1 and DW2, which brought to light several facts for example through the examination of annex TRA 8A and TRA 8B to mention only a few.

Second, we would like to reply on the evidence adduced by the respondent. The counsel summarized the evidence adduced to include the following:

(i) That they had adduced evidence to show that shares were sold. This fact is not in dispute because even the appellant did adduce evidence that shares were sold. The appellant did make allegation that the Australian East African Gold Mines limited sold its own shares. The principle is that who alleges must prove. The respondent never adduced any evidence to show that the East African Gold Mines sold shares. To the contrary some of the documentary evidence tendered by the respondent contained information to the effect that shareholders of the Australian East African Mines Limited did sell their shares to Placer Dome Inc. There was also evidence that was initially presented to the respondent to the effect that shareholders of the Australian company sold shares and not the Australian company. In particular, annex AMGM 13 in appeal No. 10 which clearly shows that the appellant submitted a list of shares holders of the Australian East African Gold Mines Limited. The Commissioner never rejected this list and had ample time to verify the same and list any challenges to its authenticity to the appellant. In any case as mentioned in our submission in chief the names appearing in TRA 8A of the shareholders in the Australian company also appear in the list submitted to the Commissioner annex AMCM 18 in appeal No. 10. This is a collaborating effect.

(ii) The counsel submitted that they have adduced evidence that sale of shares was in respect to property held in Tanzania. No such evidence was adduced. Instead the counsel sought to draw inferences which would provide desired *nexus* between the shares sold by the vendor shareholders in the Australian company and the appellant's mining properties in Tanzania.

(iii) The counsel submitted that they have produced financial statements which show that Placer Dome Inc is the ultimate shareholding company of the appellant. Interestingly the counsel cleverly avoided bringing to the attention of the Board app 1 in annex TRA 12 which shows that the holding structure was submitted by the appellant to the respondent. The counsel emphatically argued that the mention of Placer Dome Inc as the ultimate holding company of the appellant meant that Placer Dome Inc has purchased the appellant's shares. Your Honour, we humbly submit that the practice of mentioning an ultimate holding company in financial statement has evolved from the statutory requirement that was introduced by the English Company Act 1967. In that legislature s 5 (1) required that if a company is a subsidiary company of another company the name of its ultimate holding company must be given, and if known the country of new operation. This provision is reproduced under para 66-16 on p 743 of *Palmer's Company Law* (22nd edn), vol. I. There is not a mention which evidences purchase of shares in a subsidiary company. The holding structure may be through the holding company having a controlling equity interest in a subsidiary company and that other subsidiary company having a withholding controlling interest in another subsidiary company. The law permits these corporate organizations.

In this instance we would like to address the inference which ultimately the counsel sought to use in appealing to the Honourable Board to invoke the "doctrine of lifting veil" What the counsel seeks to do is to ignore the existence of East Africa Gold Mines Limited as an independent company vested with proprietary rights of its own over the shares held by them in the appellant. It is in this context that the counsel's argument that the Board should lift the veil of incorporation in order to find the existence of a nexus between Place Dome Inc. and the equities held in the appellant.

Your Honour, with due respect had the appellant found any evidence that the existence of Australian East African Gold Mines to be a "sham" at law they would immediately exercise powers in s 27 of Income Tax Act, to challenge Placer Dome Inc that their purchase of shares from the vendor, shareholders of the Australian company constituted tax avoidance scheme.

Placer Dome Inc would therefore have been compelled to make representation challenging the description of any share purchase transaction. The Board cannot be petitioned by testimony from the Bar that there are grounds for lifting the veil of in corporation. These grounds have to come clearly from the position the respondent takes in raising assessments because the assessee has an alienable right to be held specifically on those grounds. In this case it is not even the appellant who is accused from the bar to have engaged a tax avoidance scheme. It is not

even the Australian company that has been mentioned. It is Placer Dome Inc the A
purchaser of the shares who should have been accosted, and they were not called upon to answer any such accusation. It is incompetent through submissions to make assertions which were never pursued by the respondent. To make matters worse the shareholding in the appellant company was disclosed and was never challenged and the shareholding has not changed and the respondent has never before challenged that the share holding is a "sham". DW1 and DW2 had B
opportunity to testify before the Board and explain their basis of assessment. Neither of them raised tax avoidance as one of the reasons; rather, they thought to draw inferences from their own erroneous understanding of facts.

Your Honour, the doctrine of veil of incorporation under company law is under one very stringent rule. This is called the rule of prohibition of the veil of in corporation which was developed to protect the fundamental principle in C
Solomon v Solomon (supra).

The House of Lords in rejecting of lifting of the corporate veil held that: "this should be done under very special circumstances", per Lord Justice Kerr in L S Sealy *Cases and Materials in Company Law* (7th edn), Butterworths, London, 2001.

The counsel explained that the assessment was raised because of agency. The D
Board should take note that the rule applies in very special circumstances.

Your Honour, the respondent has never adduced any evidence that the existence of the Australian company is concealing any truth. This is the company that established the mining enterprises in North Mara. In establishing the mining business they never acted under the instruction of Placer Dome Inc and had no association with Placer Dome Inc like any other multinationals around the world. E
Where lucrative business opportunities open up in any country the giant multinational companies will always seek to acquire controlling interests through corporate buyouts, and these are buyouts that occur in the developed countries. The law in Tanzania was not enacted to tax foreign corporate buyouts and cannot have such competence. We submit that there are no grounds to raise the veil of incorporation. F

The counsel has not even pointed out which veil should be raised. Is it the appellant's veil of incorporation which is already marked before this Board AMGM 5 in appeal No. 10. It is the veil of the Australian Gold mine company AMGM 13, which shows the list of shareholders as per annex AMGM 18. Should it be the veil of Placer Dome Inc? The counsel never provided any guidance or projection for raising any of the veils. It is so inappropriate to send this Board on G
a voyage of discovery after the conclusion of hearings.

Your Honour, the counsel mentioned that the respondents produced TRA 12 that confirm that the shares of the Australian East African Gold Mines Limited were sold to Placer Dome Inc and he specifically called upon DW1 to read para 1 in the said annex.

The respondent had clear information that it is East African Gold Mines that H
sold the shares. There is an apparent trend to omit information which tends to show that the respondent was making wrong decisions. In annex TRA 12 he omits reference to the fact that share holders of the Australian company are the ones who sold shares. In reference to TRA 8A they omit to read facts which state that there was a sale of shares to Placer Dome Inc annex TRA 8A and 8B, the respondent confirmed to US$25 million as very correct disclosure of consideration. Clearly

the respondent was giving out only informations which to them is useful to build up the "agency" construct.

Your Honour, we will now move to the assertion that the appellant never furnished information when directed to do so. There are four things to be noted:

(i) The respondent provided no reasonable time within which to submit any information in respect of the demand of production of sale of shares. DW1 wrote a letter to appellant, annex AMGM 7 in appeal No. 10, on 25 July 2003 which was a Friday. He demanded production of a share agreement. Assuming that there was a single share sale agreement for the purposes of the argument this was an agreement that was executed in Australia in a completely different time zone. The appellant was not a party. It might have entailed an exchange of communications: appointing Attorney to access registers, bringing the documents to Tanzania. This could take more that four working days. On 31 July 2003, hardly within four working days, DW1 had ruled that there was failure to furnish information and proceeded to raise a series of assessments.

According to the information on TRA 8, the respondent had clear information that the shareholders who were likely to have executed share sale agreements were scattered all over the world. Some of the countries mentioned include South Africa, United Kingdom, Australia, Canada etc.

This shows that the time within which DW1 expected to be furnished with the required information is manifestly, unreasonably short and indicates that there was a premeditated intent to raise an assessment at all costs.

(ii) The respondent did not only want to be furnished with information but to be furnished with information which admits facts as perceived by the respondent.

(iii) The respondent did not want to address facts, was in extreme anxiety to develop constructs which would provide a post facto nexus between the share holders of the Australian company and appellant's mining properties

(iv) The appellant that is estopped from challenging the validity of the assessment simply because the appellant has pleaded that it is a stranger to the agreements between the vendor shareholders and Placer Dome Inc.

Your Honour, the appellants are before this Board because they have been wrongly assessed. The assessments are challenged because they have been raised on the appellants. This is why only the appellants can raise the objection and can lodge the appeal. Without the need to go deeper into the law relating to the doctrine of *estoppel* the counsel did not even seek to clarify which rule of *estoppel* he was referring to. Is it the evidentially *estoppel* s 135 of evidence Act or is it the promissory *estoppel* under the law of contract? In any case, there are no grounds for invoking *estoppel* as the appellants are appealing under the law (they have right to appeal).

I will respond to the counsel's argument on "financial assets". The word "financial asset" has no statutory definition. The rule is that if there is no technical meaning then the plain meaning must be applied. The counsel attempted to move the Board to show that the word financial assets could mean the appellant's property. With due respect the ordinary usage of the word financial asset is to distinguish non financial assets from financial assets.

The encyclopedia (online), gives the meaning of financial assets. In that meaning the argument that extends to the meaning of financial assets to include the value of physical property belonging to the appellant is very far-fetched. As I have pointed out such constructions are attempted to bring into force Regional Revenue Officer made laws. The interpretation is a self-serving interpretation. This is a rule of interpretation that governs the construction of departmental practices (where a tax department develops interpretation in the course of applying a tax provision which is self favouring, that definition must be construed strictly against the tax department).

Your Honour, let me briefly respond on the validity of assessments. The assessment in respect of capital gains after examining the exhibits and evidence appears as if it was made against the East African Gold Mines and not the appellant. AMGM 10 which DW 1 referred to as the only valid outstanding assessment in its notes space is inscribed "correction of address". According to DW1 this was intended to override assessment 30F.77 issued to the appellant.

Correction of address meant that this assessment be transmitted to East Africa Gold Mines Limited. It is therefore very clear that the assessment was not raised to the appellant in a representative capacity. If that had been the case, assessment No. 30F.77 would have read "Afrika Mashariki Gold Mines Limited as agents of East Africa Gold Mine of this address".

In the own words of DW1, and the submission of the counsel, the appellant was treated as an agent. The agent cannot be referred but must be expressed. Through the direct testimonial of DW1 they intended the assessment to be served upon the East African Gold Mines Limited. Section 52 of Income Tax Act, is therefore not applicable. In this connection then the question that arose was that whether the service on the appellant was the proper service. DW1 asserted that service was affected under 84 of Income Tax Act. Section 84 is an obligation section. It imposes an obligation upon the Commissioner to cause the notice of assessment to be served on assessee. It does not provide the mode of service of such notice.

The mode of service is provided under s 135 of the Income Tax Act, which also describes in a case of corporation or a firm who is the competent person to receive any notice on such a corporation or a firm. East Africa Gold Mines Limited is a corporation under s 135 (2) notice can be sent to a principal officer of that company, director, a partner of that company and a secretary. The appellant is not any of these people.

Alternatively the respondent was required to send the notice to the last known address. Being a foreign company the only known address (assessee) East African Gold Mines is the one in the official records of the registrar of companies which the respondent had in his possession. By failing to comply with the law the respondent has never served the East African Gold Mine to date. DW1 also sought to rely upon s 87 of Income Tax Act, that errors in assessment cannot impeach the validity of an assessment.

We are not challenging that there are errors in assessment. What we are submitting is that, however defective assessment 30F.77 was it was not served upon the intended person.

The appellant had no express authority to accept any document of the East African Limited. Agency cannot be inferred by the majority shareholding it must be expressed.

Lastly, the counsel submitted that s 13 stands on its own and cannot be read with other sections. There are two important things here:

(i) The parliament of United Republic cannot impose tax on any foreign national. Taxes on non-residents are only imposed on the basis of connectivity of the source of Income. In order for a non-resident to pay tax he must earn income which arises from a source located in Tanzania. Otherwise to construe the provision the way the counsel was proposing would introduce extreme absurdity and make the law inapplicable. This is why s 13 should be read with s 3 (1) (*a* charging section).

(ii) Capital gains do not as such, constitute income. These are capital receipts which represent accretion in a value capital asset. Jurisprudentially from 1967 after the submission of the report of the royal report in Canada (carter report) capital gains were to be brought within the scope of chargeability under the income tax legislation. For countries which did not enact a separate capital gains tax legislation and which use the source concept of income as under s 3 (2) included a deeming provision and this provision is s 3 (2) (*e*). There is no way one can read s 13 without 3 (1) and 3 (2) (*e*).

In the premises we pray that both assessments be annulled and the reliefs prayed for in the statements of appeal be granted to the appellants with costs. We beg to rest our submission.

Order: (1) Judgment on 7 January 2005 at 9.00 am.

JUDGMENT

The appeals No. 4 of 2004 and No. 10 of 2004 for the purpose of this appeal have been consolidated to form one file No. 4 of 2004. In the said files the appellant Afrika Mashariki Gold Mines is duly represented by Dr Luoga, a learned counsel, and the respondent Commissioner General is represented by Mr Songoro, a learned counsel. The dispute between the parties revolves around the issue of capital gains tax and stamp duty.

To get a clear understanding, the following is the brief historical background of the matter. As submitted by Dr Luoga the appellant is a limited liability company duly registered under the Companies Act. Initially the appellant had been registered in the name of East African Gold Mines Limited but having discovered later that there is another company incorporated under the same name the appellant changed to the present name of Afrika Mashariki Gold Mines Limited.

The composition of this company by the time of the dispute had two shareholders, namely, East African Gold Mines (Australian company) holding Tshs 1,184,461 ordinary shares and secondly Mr Godfrey Hugh Stewart, holding only one ordinary share. During the year 2003, a Canadian company, known as Placer Dome Inc., went into a public takeover bid of the Australian company (East African Gold Mines Limited) and bought the majority shares in the Australian company. During the same year (2003) the respondent received information from a local newspaper to the effect that the Australian company's shares in Australia had been acquired by Placer Dome Inc. After getting wind of this piece of information both the Regional Revenue Officer at Musoma and the one at Samora, wrote letters immediately to the appellant demanding to be furnished with a contract of the sale of shares for the purposes of raising the capital gains tax under s 13 of the Income Tax Act.

As submitted by Dr Luoga the allegation by the respondent at this point was that the appellant had sold their shares. On looking from a different angle the respondent was saying that the sale of the Australian company of its shares was actually disposition of the shares in the appellant's company, hence the demand for capital gains tax on whatever gains realized therefrom in accordance with s 13 (1) of Income Tax Act, and the appellant is to pay stamp duty under s (5) of Stamp Duty Act as well as item 60.

According to Dr Luoga, the learned counsel, what actually was the position was that the Australian company had no shares to sell and did not receive any payment because it was the shareholders who sold out shares. There were more than twenty subscribers from whom shares were bought and even companies which had equity interests in the Australian company sold shares to Placer Dome Inc.

On the issue of the identity of parties in the share sale transaction it was Placer Dome Inc (purchaser) and the shareholders of East African Gold Mines who were engaged in the transaction. As the share holders were more than twenty there was no single transaction of sale of shares but multiple transactions which took place at different times.

As per appellant's evidence the shares were sold outside the Republic of Tanzania and specifically in Australia where the East Africa Gold Mines Limited had been incorporated and so the sale of shares had to take place in conformity with the Australian laws. Basing on the sale as per the historical background then it was Placer Dome Inc., which paid the consideration and as all the shares had been issued the Australian company could not have received any consideration.

Dr Luoga also touched on the issue of the best judgment requirement rule which is used where it is a matter of raising assessments on presumption. In this regard the respondent did not relate to the rule as the assessment was made basing on wrong presumptions that the Australian company sold shares and that this was under a single transaction.

Taking the above facts Dr Luoga still went further to state that even if the assessments by the respondent were valid then the respondent was to show the basis of the raised assessment. This should have gone as far as establishing that the seller was an owner of financial assets owned in the United Republic of Tanzania and these assets were sold. According to Dr Luoga on further submission he explained that the property in the shares is owned by the share holders. It follows therefore that in the Australian company the shareholders were owning shares in that company. Expounding on this point Dr Luoga quoted the rule in the famous case of *Solomon v Solomon* (supra) which does not propose that a sale of shares in one company can mean a sale of shares in another company. The shareholders are independent persons from the company.

As to the point of stamp duty, Dr Luoga basing on the historical background explained that as the transaction of sale of shares took place outside the United Republic of Tanzania between two foreign companies then s 5 of the Stamp Duty Act cannot stand as the instrument does not relate to a property found in Tanzania nor was it executed in Tanzania.

A The historical background on the other side, that is on the part of the respondent was narrated by DW1, one Herbert Kabyemela (Regional Revenue Officer of Mara Region) and DW2, Focus Mushi working as an assessor for VAT and also in the submission by Mr Songoro, a learned counsel. On their part the transaction which led to the respondent's demand of Capital Gain Tax and Stamp Duty was a transaction of sale of shares and the transaction related to property
B situated in Tanzania. According to the respondent the proof is the financial statement of 2002 and 2003 of the appellant's company, the public notices of recruitment from the public, the PricewaterhouseCoopers' letter confirming sale of shares of East Africa Gold Mines and newspaper cuttings showing that business is now with Place Dome Inc. As to the status of the sold shares the respondent through DW 1 and DW 2 state that East African Gold Mines
C Company sold its shares to Placer Dome Inc and East African Gold Mines was the sole owner of the appellant. It follows therefore that East African Gold Mines transferred shares to Placer Dome Inc. and at the same time East African Gold Mines had shares in the appellant and so has assets in Afrika Mashariki which is registered in Tanzania. That the transaction eventually ended up by change in ownership in that the ownership of the appellant has turned to Placer Dome Inc.
D As East African Gold Mines Limited was paid US$225 million in return for shares sold then capital gains tax is chargeable and was deprived in Tanzania.

On the issue of stamp duty the respondent explained through Mr Songoro, learned counsel that as the sale of shares transaction relates to property situated in Tanzania, stamp duty is payable. As the one to pay stamp duty according to law is the transferee or purchaser, then in this case Placer Dome Inc who is the owner
E of the appellant's company is the purchaser. So it was proper for the respondent to issue the demand for stamp duty to the appellant.

The respondent was in agreement with the appellant that a company is treated as a separate legal entity from its shareholders but this concept of separate entity could be looked upon by invoking the process known as lifting the corporate veil. So the respondent prayed before the Board that in order to clear the innocence of
F the parties in this issue, it should lift the veil of the companies and see what was behind the said transaction. As regards the transmission of the said assessment, it was transmitted by treating the appellant as the agent of East Africa Gold Mines Limited.

After the above summary the paramount issue that is facing this Honourable Board is which shares were sold and to whom. We have found in evidence that
G there is the appellant's return to the registrar of companies showing the share structure which in principal has not changed in this document. The shareholders are East Africa Gold Mines Limited with a number of shares 1,184,461 and Stewart A Godfrey Hugh with one share. What has changed is the list of directors as of 10 November 2003, which includes Directors from Canada originating from the Placer Dome Inc. On the same document we have found that this was never
H challenged by the respondent and this goes to give us the answer that actually there has not been any share sale transaction involving shares in Afrika Mashariki.

We have also found on record that there is a list of shareholders in the East African Gold Mines Limited. These as per the evidence on record are the ones who ultimately sold their shares to Placer Dome Inc. On this the respondents have also annexed newspaper cuttings to show that shareholders, for example,

Anglo Gold annex TRA 8 (appeal No. 8 of 2004) sold their shares to Placer A Dome. There is no evidence at all adduced to show that shares in Afrika Mashariki Gold Mines Limited were sold. The evidence before us is to the effect that the shares which were sold were those held by the shareholders of East Africa Gold Mines Limited of Australia. The position in our view is that we have two categories of shares. One is shareholder in the Australian company owning shares in that company and the second one is the Australian company owning shares in B the appellant. It is our finding then that Afrika Mashariki Limited (appellant) remained as a separate entity and what we have is Placer Dome Inc. taking up the management of Afrika Mashariki (appellant), which has nothing to do with the sale of shares in the Australian company. We have also considered on this part the evidence by DW 1 that the assessment raised was for East African Gold Mines Limited and so automatically the assessment becomes invalid as the appellant C was never a party in the sale of shares in Australia in an Australian company. On this point we totally concur with the submissions by the appellant's counsel that the shares sold are the shares of the various shareholders in the Australian company and not otherwise.

From the above finding we also come to the point of the effect of the sale of the said shares in Australia. We find the effect is that the appellant has not D acquired any shares nor have its shares been subject of sale. What the buyer has acquired over the appellant is a controlling interest or an economic interest in the appellant company although indirectly. What then is the status of the sold shares? We find on this that the shares in issue, that is the shares held by various shareholders in the East Africa Gold Mines Limited of Australia to Placer Dome Inc of Canada have never been registered in Tanzania and the respondents do not E have this piece of evidence and therefore under the Income Tax Act it cannot attract capital gains tax in Tanzania. On the same point we find that in the absence of a share sale agreement the respondent does not have any basis of demanding the capital gains tax from the appellant.

This brings us to the issue of agency. The respondent had alleged that they had issued the assessment on the appellant as an agent of the East African Gold F Mines. On this we find that as East African Gold Mines Company was the holding company; the appellant in real sense is then a subsidiary. As a result these two are separate entities and so the appellant cannot be treated as an automatic agent of East Africa Gold Mines Limited. There need to be an expressly more for the appellant to be appointed as an agent.

Coming to the fact that the appellants are also under an obligation to pay stamp G duty on this we have found in evidence that the instrument affecting the said transaction, that is the sale of shares was executed outside Tanzania and has never been registered in Tanzania. We further find that the shares as financial assets of East African Gold Mines Limited are registered in Australia and they will never be registered in Tanzania. On record we have no evidence at all of this registration in Tanzania and so the question of stamp duty cannot arise. Both the seller and H the buyer are non-residents. On record there is a question of administering the doctrine of "lifting the corporate veil" We find that there is enough evidence before us to determine the matter and so we need not to invoke the said doctrine. The evidence is so clear and does not contain any ambiguities to warrant the lifting of the corporate veil.

On record we have also found that the respondents have relied on the financial statements of the appellant of year 2002 and 2003. In these statements, the holding company is referred as "ultimate owner", and we find that this terminology should not bring any confusion. The issue before us is not on the ownership but the sale of shares in a transaction carried out outside the United Republic of Tanzania. This only goes to show the management take over of East Africa Gold Mines Limited by Placer Dome Inc in the appellant, but this is not conclusive evidence that there was a sale of shares of the appellant. It does not also mean that Place Dome Inc is a direct shareholder in the appellant. We find that the shareholding in the appellant has never changed.

In conclusion, as already found by this Honourable Board, capital gains tax is not be chargeable in this matter and the stamp duty cannot be applied as the shares sold were those of shareholders held by various share holders in the East Africa Gold Mines Limited (an Australian company). The shares themselves are financial assets held outside Tanzania and both the seller East Africa Gold Mines Limited and buyer Placer Dome Inc, are non-residents. The share sale transaction was executed outside Tanzania and has never been registered in Tanzania and will never be registered in the circumstances in the United Republic. On the basis of our conclusion we accordingly uphold the appeals with costs to the respondent.

Right of appeal explained.

Read this on 14 January 2005 in the presence of Mr Kibuta for appellant assisted by John Ignas and Mr Joseph Mwita from the appellant's office and in absence of respondent duly notified.

AIRCO (T) LIMITED T/A MWANZA GROUND HANDLING SERVICES COMPANY LTD v COMMISSIONER GENERAL

TAX REVENUE APPEALS TRIBUNAL

MWANZA

(VAT APPEAL: CASE NO 2 OF 2004)

(ORIGINATING FROM BOARD CASE NOS. 22 AND 25 OF 2003)

26 July 2004

A Shangwa J, *Chairperson*, A Makenya and N Mbisc, *Members*

Value Added Tax Act, 1997—Zero rated supplies—Whether providing facilities for handling goods and putting them into an aircraft is covered

The appellant company's appeal concerns VAT assessments for 2001 to 2003 totaling up to Tshs 93,310,381, with the company contending that both

assessments were made on zero-rated supply of services and therefore not A
valid. They were providing ground-handling services to aircraft which landed at Mwanza airport for carriage of goods, mainly fish fillet, and took off to foreign destinations.

Held:

Providing facilities or handling goods and putting them into an aircraft does
not in real sense comprise the handling of an aircraft. A distinction must be B
made between providing facilities for handling goods at an airport together with putting them into an aircraft and supplying equipment such as steps or bridges for loading and unloading an aircraft or cleaning its cabin. The former activity does not comprise the handling of an aircraft, the latter activity does so; only the latter is zero rated.

Appeal dismissed C

Cases referred to:
Attorney General v Wilts United Dairies (1922) 38 TLR 781
Russell v Scott [1948] 2 All ER 1 (HL)

Mr Kihwelo, for the appellant D
Mr Teemba, for the respondent.

19 July 2004:

Mr Kihwelo: I appear for the appellant. I am assisted by Mr Viann Komba and
Mr Ibrahimu Mustapha. E

Mr Aggrey Teemba: I appear for the respondent. I am assisted by Mr Warioba Kanire.

Order: It appears to us that the appellant's appeal is not accompanied by a copy
of the decision of the Commissioner General which gave rise to appeal to the F
Board and evidence of full payment of appropriate fees. We have therefore decided to adjourn the proceedings until tomorrow 20 July 2004 at 9.00 am. Between now and then the appellant should make efforts to make sure that a copy of the decision of the Commissioner General which gave rise to appeal to the Board and the ERV concerning payment of fees for preparation of the record of
appeal are attached before we start hearing on it. G

20 July 2004:

Quorum

Mr Kihwelo: I appear for the appellant and I am assisted by Mr Viann Komba
and Mr Ibrahim Mustapha who is the General Manager of the appellant H
company.

Mr Aggrey Teemba: I appear for the respondent. I am assisted by Mr Warioba Kanire who is a Senior Financing Officer.

Mr Kihwelo, for the appellant: My Lord and Honourable members of the Tribunal, I have already attached to the statement of appeal a copy of the decision of the Commissioner General which gave rise to appeal to the Board and a copy of ERV No. 20097912 being evidence of payment of fees for preparation of records of appeal Nos. 22 and 25 of 2003 in the Board which had been attached to the appeal. So, I pray for the hearing to start.

Tribunal: Hearing of the appeal opens:

Mr Kihwelo, for the appellant: My Lord and Honourable members of the Tribunal, the appeal before you rests on two grounds. The first ground is that the Board erred in law and in fact in failing to find that the service rendered by the appellant is zero-rated by virtue of para 4 of the First Schedule to the Value Added Tax Act, 1997 (24 of 1997). The second ground of appeal is that the Board erred in law and fact in failing to find that the services of cargo loading to a foreign-going aircraft amounts to handling foreign-going aircraft.

My Lord and Honourable members of the Tribunal, the appellant company was registered for and is actually dealing in aircraft handling at Mwanza Airport.

In its normal course of business, the appellant company handles aircraft of local as well as international destinations. During the years 2001 up to 2003, the respondent (VAT Department) issued two assessments as a VAT liability payable by the appellant company. Two assessments were issued in the year 2003. The first assessment was to the tune of Tshs 33,519,732. The second assessment was to the tune of Tshs 59,790,649. The two assessments amounted to a total of Tshs 93,310,381. I refer you to exhs AE1 (i)–(iv). These exhibits are composed of the Commissioner's decision and the relevant assessments which are attached thereto.

My Lord and Honourable members of the Tribunal, the appellant company objected to both assessments on the grounds that the services supplied by it were in respect of handling flights with international destinations which by virtue of s 9 of the Value Added Tax Act read together with para 4 of the First Schedule to the Act is zero-rated. The objection letters from the appellant company to the respondent were tendered and admitted before the Board as exhs AE3 and AE4 which are one letter dated 15 May 2003 in respect of assessment of Tshs 33,519,732 and another letter dated 6 September 2003 in respect of assessment of Tshs 59,790,649, respectively.

My Lord and Honourable members of the Tribunal, the appellant company, after receiving the assessment of Tshs 33,519,732; paid to the respondent Tshs 16,759,866 on 17 July 2003 as part of the tax in dispute as required by law. However, the respondent, knowing the existence of the law and the procedures of tax dispute demanded full payment of the amount in dispute, that is, Tshs 33,519,732.

My Lord and Honourable members of the Tribunal, on 22 July 2003 another amount of Tshs 16,759,866 was paid through the appellant's bank after the respondent's urgent notice dated 15 July 2003. The conduct of the respondent was actually meant to embarrass and frustrate the business of the appellant company. And this can be evidenced by letters which were issued, that is, exhs AE7 and AE8 in which while accepting the fact that they had received half payment of the

tax liability in dispute, they still insisted on the payment of the full amount in A
dispute contrary to the laws that govern tax disputes.

My Lord and Honourable members of the Tribunal, after demanding full payment of tax, there followed a number of correspondences relating to the disputed tax assessment but the same were fruitless. It is upon those circumstances that the appellant company filed an appeal before the Board. That is appeal No. 22 of 2003 in respect of the first assessment of Tshs 33,519,732. It B
is pertinent to point out that before this appeal could be entertained and determined by the Board, the respondent issued the second assessment of Tshs 59,790,649 by a letter dated 2nd September 2003 which I have already referred to as exh AE2 (i)–(iv). Again, this assessment was objected to by the appellant company as being zero-rated supplies covered by s 9 read together with para 4 of the First Schedule to the Value Added Tax Act. I would also like to refer to C
exhs AE11 and AE12. These were correspondences with respect to objections to the second assessment issued by the respondent to the appellant's tax consultant in reply thereof.

My Lord and Honourable members of the Tribunal, having failed to reconcile this issue of the second assessment between the appellant company and the respondent, the appellant company decided to file an appeal before the Board, D
that is appeal No. 25 of 2003 in respect of Tshs 59,790,649. As it may be noticed in the proceedings of the Board, the two appeals were consolidated at the first hearing. Since the appeal failed before the Board, the appellant company decided to appeal to this Honourable Tribunal.

My Lord and Honourable members of the Tribunal, as I pointed out earlier, the service rendered by the appellant company falls under s 9 (1) of the Value Added E
Tax Act read together with para 4 of the First Schedule to the Value Added Tax Act, if the supply is of a description specified in the First Schedule to this Act. Para 4 of the First Schedule to the Act provides for the supply of services which comprise the handling, packing, pilotage, salvage or towage of any foreign-going ship or aircraft while in mainland Tanzania. The provision of s 9 (1) together with para 4 of the First Schedule to the Act makes the provision of services of ground F
handling of foreign-going aircraft a zero-rated item and this was not disputed even by counsel for the respondent before the Board. The only and only contention before the Tribunal is that the services rendered by the appellant falls within the ambit of the above-named provision and not otherwise. Unlike the way the members of the Board sought to interpret the provision at hand, that is, s 9 (1) read together with para 4 of the First Schedule to the Act, this provision does not G
qualify or put qualification or make qualification as to how and who should enjoy the services, but rather it is all about handling of foreign going aircraft which is mainly and only the activity which the appellant company was registered for as clearly depicted in the name of the company itself which is Mwanza Ground Handling Service Company Limited.

My Lord and Honourable members of the Tribunal, the appellant company H
was registered as a ground handling company. It is licensed as such. This company has been accredited and certified by the International Air Transport Association Ground Handling Council. Section 9 (1) read together with para 4 of the First Schedule to the Value Added Tax Act are quite simple and unambiguous as they refer to supplies that are related to handling foreign-going aircraft. The provision in question does not confine to a specific category of group of persons

or people but rather it merely refers to foreign-going aircrafts. The judgment and opinions of members in arriving at their decision basing on para 3 of the First Schedule to Value Added Tax Act was a total misconception and untenable. Paragraph 3 of the First Schedule to the Value Added Tax Act refers to the supplies which comprise the transport or any ancillary transport of loading, unloading, wharfage, shore handling, storage, warehousing and handling supplies in connection with goods exported from the United Republic of Tanzania or goods in transit. Applying the provisions of para 3 in this scenario of the appellant is a great mischief since even by resorting to the simple rules of statutory interpretation and more specifically the *ejusdem generis* rule, the line of business of the appellant is not confined to para 3 but rather that which is stipulated in para 4 as it specifically relates to handling of outgoing aircrafts. I wish to refer to art 138 of the Constitution of the United Republic of Tanzania as amended from time to time which unambiguously stipulates that no tax should be levied without clear authority of parliament. The conduct of the respondent to levy tax on an item which is zero-rated, was totally unconstitutional and it cannot be justified. In the case of *Attorney General v Wilts United Dairies* (1922) 38 TLR 781, the court held that tax should not be levied without clear authority of parliament. In the case of *Russell v Scott* [1948] 2 All ER 1 (HL), Lord Simons was quoted as saying on p 5:

> "It may thus be taken as a maxim of tax law, not to be overstressed and not to be forgotten either that the subject is not to be taxed unless the words of the taxing statutes unambiguously impose the tax on him".

My Lord and Honourable members of the Tribunal, it is my humble submission that the services rendered by the appellant company falls under para 4 of the First Schedule other than the purported para 3 which does not mention anything relating to handling of foreign-going aircraft. Had it been that the legislature meant to treat the services which were supplied by the appellant under para 3 of the First Schedule, the same would have been expressly provided for as it was done for shore handling which is covered under para 3. My Lord and Honourable members of the Tribunal, I wish to ask Mr Ibrahim Mustapha to continue from here.

Mr Ibrahim Mustapha, for the appellant: My Lord and Honourable members of the Tribunal, the appellant company's activities are chocking of the aircraft, positioning of passenger steps, provision of ground power, cleaning of the aircraft cabin and toilet services, road control, passenger and baggage handling, provision of equipment for handling of unit load devices and air starting of aircraft.

My Lord and Honourable members of the Tribunal, during the years 2001, 2002, and 2003, we did handle various types of foreign going aircrafts. These are Llyushin 76, Antonov 12, DC8 and Boeing 707. The first two are Russian. The rest are American. All are cargo aircraft. Other types of foreign-going aircrafts that we did handle during the same period are passenger types of aircrafts. These are Precision Air, Eagle Air and Air Tanzania Charter Air (South Africa). That is all.

My Lord and Honourable members of the Tribunal, I wish to ask Mr Kihwelo to proceed with our submissions.

Mr Kihwelo, for the appellant: My Lord and Honourable members of the Tribunal, I would like now to address the Tribunal on our second ground of appeal which is whether the service of cargo loading to a foreign-going aircraft amounts to handling foreign-going aircraft.

My Lord and Honourable members of the Tribunal, on our second ground of appeal, as I pointed out earlier the appellant company was registered for ground handling. It was licensed for such handling. Above all, it was contracted with the Tanzania Airport Authority to undertake ground-handling activities at Mwanza Airport. The main contention in respect of the second ground of appeal and which actually arose in the proceedings of the Board was the context of ground handling services. It is a cardinal principle of law that lack of precision of some words and of phrases used in tax make it necessary to define them by either practice or precedent to enable whoever is applying or construing those tax statutes to decide various tax issues. In that respect this has made us to refer to the international Air Transport Association Standard Ground Handling Agreement to which the appellant company is the accredited member of its council in order to get a precise meaning or scope of ground handling services. For that matter, I refer the Tribunal to annex A of the said agreement which gives various definitions. Under para 6 which concerns RAMP it is indicated loading and unloading. Looking at the range of services, which falls under ground handling services, it will be noticed that loading and unloading is merely one item that falls under the category of RAMP.

My Lord and Honourable members of the Tribunal, by any stretch of imagination loading and unloading cannot be isolated from other ground handling services as seen in the International Air Transport Association Standard Ground Handling Agreement so as to qualify under para 3 of the Value Added Tax Act instead of para 4 of the First Schedule to the Act. Treating the services of the appellant under para 3 instead of para 4 of the First Schedule to the Act as amended by the Finance Act, 1999 and 2000 instead of para 4 would be unconstitutional and would lead to injustice to the appellant company. In totality, the services rendered by the appellant amount to ground handling as such zero-rated, and in no way can the same be severed from one another when offered to the foreign going aircraft. At this juncture, it is pertinent to point out that the spirit of the law was and still is to attract or encourage exports and air traffic so as to enhance increased foreign exchange, foreign direct investments and revenue at large. And applying this law to the contrary as the respondent sought so to do would not lead to the intended spirit of the law. Having said that, I humbly pray that the Honourable Tribunal be pleased to reverse the decision of the Board with costs.

Respondent's submission opens:

Mr Aggrey Teemba, for the respondent: My Lord and Honourable members of the Tribunal, we are submitting that the appellant never offered any services to any foreign-bound aircraft during 2001 to 2003. The taxes raised were specifically mentioned as based on tax invoices raised against specific local companies based in Mwanza. These are not airline companies. At no time did the respondent raise tax against airliners. Exhibit RE 2 in the Board is a sample. It contains a sample of tax invoices issued by the appellant against several local companies based in Mwanza. These are Tanzania Fish Processors Ltd, Tanperch Ltd, Mwanza Fish Industries among others. That was a sample and it was not objected to. The respondent has never raised taxes in respect of foreign-bound aircrafts and the tax invoices are clearly indicated. It is the appellant raising invoices against local companies. Looking at one of the tax invoices which we submitted as sample of several invoices issued by the appellant, it shows the appellant demanding payment of US$6,650 as subtotal and they added VAT of US$1,330, which brings the total amount to US$7,980. Why did we demand VAT to be paid? We did so because as indicated in the several tax invoices, the appellant collected VAT on each of the tax invoices, and this is the amount which was due to the respondent and it was duly demanded.

My Lord and Honourable members of the Tribunal, we have legal authority to make such a demand. This authority has to be found under s 57of the Value Added Tax Act, which provides as follows:

> "Any amount shown on an invoice, a receipt, or similar document as VAT chargeable on a supply of goods or services, shall be recoverable as VAT due from the person issuing the invoice, regardless as whether:
>
> (*a*) The invoice is a tax invoice as prescribed in the Act,
> (*b*) Tax is chargeable in respect of the supply to which the invoice relates; or
> (*c*) The person issuing the invoice is a taxable person".

The above-quoted provision covers the situation in this case. This is the position in law. The issue whether or not the appellant is covered by para 4 of the First Schedule to the Act is irrelevant in this case. This is because from the record there is no evidence of any deal with any foreign-bound aircraft. Once we submit as we do that the appellant does not fall under para 4 of the First Schedule to the Value Added Tax Act, it is my humble submission that it is unnecessary to go to arguments as to what amounts to cargo handling as they never dealt with any foreign bound aircraft. So, it is immaterial to go to definitions provided by the International Air Transport Association. The appellant has never raised invoice against any foreign-bound aircraft. Once it is accepted that the appellant has never raised invoice against such aircraft, it becomes unnecessary for me to make any submission on whether the services rendered are zero-rated or not. I therefore pray the Tribunal to dismiss this appeal with costs.

Order: We adjourn the proceedings for hearing the rejoinder tomorrow 21 July 2004 at 9.00 am.

21 July 2004:

Tribunal: Rejoinder opens

Mr Kihwelo, for the appellant: My Lord and Honourable members of the Tribunal, I would like to rejoin the appellant's submissions as follows:

Mr Aggrey Teemba did point out that the appellant company never offered any service to any foreign-going aircraft during the period in question. This assertion is ridiculous since there is ample evidence which clearly points out that the A appellant company did offer such service during the period at issue and that is why this matter did not arise during the proceedings in the Board. The only thing that the counsel for the respondent disputed before the Board was that such service did not amount to ground handling as envisaged in para 4 of the First Schedule to the Value Added Tax Act. I would like to refer to exhs AE9, AE10, AE11, AE14 as well as exh RE2, which clearly indicate and or point out *inter* B *alia*, the handling of any foreign-going aircraft while in mainland Tanzania and that the same does not make qualification as to who enjoys the service and or who owns the aircraft provided the service is of handling a foreign-going aircraft, it should be zero-rated. That is the end of my rejoinder and I pray that the services that were provided by the appellant company be treated as ground handling of foreign-going aircraft by virtue of para 4 of the First Schedule to the Value Added C Tax Act as such zero-rated.

Order: Opinion by Honourable members of the Tribunal to be heard on 23 July 2004. Judgment on 26 July 2004 at 2.00 pm.

JUDGMENT D

A Shangwa J:

This is an appeal against the decision of the Tax Revenue Appeals Board dated 25 March 2004 in the tax appeal Nos. 22 and 25 of 2003, respectively, wherein VAT assessments raised by the Tanzania Revenue Authority against the appellant Air Co (T) t/a Mwanza Ground Handling Service Co Ltd were confirmed by the E Board. In tax appeal No. 22 of 2003, the tax in dispute was Tshs 33,519,732; and in tax appeal No. 25 of 2003, the tax in dispute was Tshs 59,790,649. Both sums totaled Tshs 93,310,381.

The appellant company is of the view that both assessments were made on zero-rated supply of services and therefore not valid. Two grounds of appeals were raised against the decision of the Tax Revenue Appeal Board which F confirmed these assessments. The first one is that the Board erred in law and fact in failing to find that the service rendered by the appellant company is zero-rated by virtue of s 9 (1) of the Value Added Tax Act read together with para 4 of the First Schedule to this Act. The second one is that the Board erred in law and fact in failing to find that the services of cargo loading to a foreign-going aircraft amount to handling foreign-going aircraft. G

The appellant company states that between 2001 and 2003, Tanzania Revenue Authority assessed it to VAT which totaled Tshs 93,310,381 on ground handling services rendered to aircraft which landed at Mwanza Airport for carriage of goods mainly fish fillet, and took off to foreign destinations. These foreign-going aircrafts were mainly Russian and American cargo aircrafts named as Llyushin 76, Antonov 12, DC 8 and Boeing 707. H

Learned counsel for the appellant company Mr Kihwelo submitted that the services which were provided by his client were in respect of handling flights with International destinations. He argued that under s 9 (1) of the Value Added Tax Act read together with para 4 of the First Schedule to the same Act such services are zero-rated. He pointed out that loading and unloading of an aircraft

A is one of the items which fall under ground handling services and that it should not be isolated from other ground handling services shown in the International Air Transport Association Standard Ground Handling Agreement of 1993 exh AE 13 to which the appellant company is an accredited member of the Association's Council. He further submitted that the conduct of the respondent to levy tax on an item which is zero-rated was totally unconstitutional.

B The respondent denied to have assessed and charged VAT against the appellant company in respect of its supply of service which comprised the handling of any foreign-going aircraft which landed at Mwanza airport between 2001 and 2003.

Learned counsel for the respondent Mr Aggrey Teemba submitted that the Value Added Tax which was assessed and charged against the appellant company was based on invoices issued by it against several local companies dealing with C fish fillet processing at Mwanza which include Tanzania Fish Processors Ltd, Tanperch Ltd, and Mwanza Fish Industries. He said that as those invoices were not issued to airliners, it was not necessary for him to make any submission on whether the services rendered by the appellant company are zero-rated or not.

Due to the fact that the Tribunal has been called upon to determine as to whether the services which were rendered by the appellant company are zero-D rated or not, we have decided to address ourselves intensively to this issue. First, we wish to express our concern from the outset that when we went through the entire record of the lower appellant authority in consolidated tax appeal Nos. 22 and 25 of 2003, we did not find any evidence in support of the appellant company's claim that between 2001 and 2003, Tanzania Revenue Authority assessed and charged it VAT on ground handling services rendered to Russian and E American cargo aircrafts which landed at Mwanza Airport for carriage of fresh fish or fish fillet exported to overseas markets by Fish Processing Companies and Industries based in Mwanza. In particular, we have not seen any evidence on record to show that between those years Tanzania Revenue Authority assessed and charged VAT against the appellant company in respect of services which comprised the handling of any foreign going aircraft.

F Secondly, we wish to state that there is no doubt in our minds that the appellant company did supply equipment for loading those aircrafts and provided facilities for handling fresh fish and fish fillet belonging to local companies based in Mwanza, and put such cargo into those aircrafts for carriage overseas. However, we are of the considered view that providing facilities or handling goods and putting them into an aircraft does not in real sense comprise the handling of an G aircraft. A distinction must be made between providing facilities for handling goods at an airport together with putting them into an aircraft and supplying equipment such as steps or bridges for loading and unloading an aircraft or cleaning its cabin. The former activity does not comprise the handling of an aircraft. The latter activity does so. These two different activities should not be misinterpreted or even misjudged to be one and the same.

H The record of the lower Appellate authority shows that the appellant company issued invoices to local companies dealing with fish processing in Mwanza for exportation upon which Tanzania Revenue Authority assessed and charged it with VAT.

We have examined seven copies of these invoices which were tendered as a sample and marked as Exh. RE2 during the hearing in the lower appellate authority. Three of them are headed "invoices". These were issued to Mwanza Fish Industries on various dates during the month of November 2001. They do not show that VAT rate of 20% was charged by the appellant company in respect of the services it supplied to the said industries. Four of them are headed "Tax Invoices". These were issued to Tanzania Fish Processors Ltd and Tanperch Ltd on various dates during the month of May 2002. They show that VAT rate of 20% was charged by the appellant company in respect of the services it supplied to the said companies.

If the services rendered by the appellant company upon which these invoices were issued did comprise the handling of foreign-going aircrafts as argued on its behalf by Mr Kihwelo and Mr Viann Komba, why did the appellant company demand payment of these invoices from the local companies which did not own those aircrafts? In actual fact, there is no evidence on record to show that the local companies to whom these invoices were issued were locally based agents of foreign companies which owned those aircrafts.

Another snag is that these invoices do not show the particular type of service or work which was rendered or done by the appellant company to those local companies to whom they were issued. What is particularized thereon are the types of foreign-going aircrafts and their registration numbers. This sort of preparing invoices for services rendered is unacceptable in commercial law as it is bound to mislead tax assessors and consultants.

Much as these invoices might have been made to appear for having been issued in respect of handling the foreign-going aircrafts which are listed thereon, the truth is that they were not issued in respect of that particular type of service. As the appellant company does not deny to having rendered service to local companies of providing facilities for handling their fish fillet and putting them into those aircrafts for export, we conclude that those invoices were issued for such a supply of service and not otherwise. As that particular type of supply did not comprise the handling of foreign-going aircrafts in which the said goods were loaded, it cannot be said to be zero-rated by virtue of s 9 (1) of the Value Added Tax Act read together with para 4 of the First Schedule to the same Act.

We find therefore that between 2001 and 2003, the appellant company was properly assessed to VAT in both assessments which totalled Tshs 93,310,381. The respondent's conduct of levying this amount on non-zero rated supplies is not unconstitutional. Therefore, the two grounds of appeal have failed. The appellant company should therefore remit Tshs 59,790,649 which is due to Tanzania Revenue Authority as assessed in the second assessment. This amount should be paid without any delay.

Whereas we thank the appellant company in advance for the contribution it is further expected to make in the development of this nation by paying taxes on due dates out of its business, we dismiss this appeal and order that each party should bear its own costs.

Delivered at Mwanza this 26 July 2004, in the presence of the appellant company's General Manager, Mr Ibrahim Mustapha, and Mr SS Switi for Mr Aggrey Teemba, for the respondent.

BRITISH AIRWAYS v COMMISSIONER GENERAL

TAX REVENUE APPEALS BOARD

DAR ES SALAAM

(VAT TAX APPEAL: CASE NO 3 OF 2004)

20 January 2005

BR Mutungi, *Vice-Chairperson,* I Dullushi and J Karashani, *Members*

Appeals—Procedure for appeals—Mandatory requirements in filing an appeal—Tax Revenue Appeals Act, 2000 and Tax Revenue Appeals Board Rules, 2001

In an appeal filed before the Board there was no evidence that the respondent was served with the Notice of Intention to Appeal under rule 4 (5) of the Tax Appeals Board Rules, nor evidence of payment of fees under rules 7 and 8.

Held:

Failure to serve the respondent with the written Notice of Intention to Appeal within 30 days of the notice of assessment, and failure to attach payment receipts to appeal documents renders the appeal incompetent since these requirements are mandatory.

Appeal struck out.

Mr Busigara, for the appellant
Mr Shigela, for the respondent

17 January 2005:

Asha Nassoro, for the respondent: The counsel handling this case is away on a safari. I pray for an adjournment till tomorrow so that I attend the matter.

Busigara, for the appellant: I have no objection

Order: Matter adjourned till tomorrow.

18 January 2005 at 9.00 am

18 January 2005:

Preliminary objection opens

Mr Shigela, for the respondent: Your Honour, we wish to raise a preliminary objection in respect of rule 4, 7 and 8 of the Tax Revenue Appeals Board Rules, 2001. It is our submission that the appellant failed to comply with the provisions of rule 4, 7 and 8. Starting with rule 4 the provisions clearly provide that any person who wishes to appeal to the Board shall issue to the Board a written notice of intension to appeal. The appellant filed his appeal on 15 April 2004; however,

there is no evidence which show that the appellant complied with the provisions A
of this rule. The notice of intention to appeal is to be filed with the Board within 30 days from the date of service of notice of assessment was not made as per provisions of this rule neither was it annexed to the statement of appeal.

According to rule 7 of the Tax Revenue Appeals Board Rules, the appellant was required by rule 7 (2) (*f*) to file his appeal with evidence of payment of appropriate fees. Nothing in the statement of appeal shows that the appellant B
complied with this rule.

Probably the appellant did not comply with the provisions of rule 8 (1) which provides for a requirement while instituting to the Board an appeal, fees should be paid. There is no evidence at all to show that the appropriate fee was paid as per law. In the context of this it is my submission that the appeal lodged by appellant is bad in law for failure to comply with the Tax Appeals Board Rules C
2001. To that effect, the appeal is not competent before the Board and so I pray the appeal so filed by appellant be struck off with costs to the appellant.

Reply by Mr Busigara for the appellant:

Your Honour, I pray for a short adjournment to arrange my documents. D

Board: Prayer granted and the matter will proceed at 10.00 am

Quorum (as before at 10.00 am)

Mr Busigara, for the appellant: I pray to proceed as I have my documents s 16 (2) E
of the Tax Appeals Act is to be referred.

I pray to tender the letter dated 31 March 2004 for the first objection of rule 4. This shows our notice for intention of appeal was filed, as regards to the payment of fees. I have copies for showing that we paid our fees; one is for Tshs 50,000 and the other for Tshs 5,000.

In dealing with this case we faced technical problems as we used s 14 but then F
we used the procedure in normal appeals, as this matter is not covered in s 14, for example, s 14 (*e*). In this case we were talking of cancellation as it is not a normal appeal matter.

Mr Shigela, for the respondent, in reply: Your Honour, the appellant has tendered a letter showing a notice of intention to appeal served to the respondent, this letter does G
not sufficiently show that the notice to appeal was duly served on the respondent as per rule 4 of the Tax Revenue Appeals Board Rules. The letter is subject to manipulation. There is no record showing that it was served to the respondent. The appellant should have shown that it had been dispatched to us since rule 4 (5) imposes a mandatory obligation. "It must be served" which I state was not done.

As regards payment of fees it is a mandatory stipulation of 7 (2), which H
requires that the appellant when lodging an appeal should attach a document showing payment of fees.

Your Honour, the wording is "shall". When you look at the list of annexures or appendices for evidence of payment of fees, the evidence is not there.

As regards the submission on s 14 of the Tax Revenue Appeals Act it was not part of our objection. This is a normal appeal which is to be attended by the available provisions of the law. There is no lacuna as far as this appeal is concerned. I pray the appeal before the Board is incompetent and bad in law for failure of the appellant to comply with rule 4 (5) and rule 7 (2). It is my submission that the appeal be struck out with cost.

Order: (1) Ruling on 20 January 2005 at 9.00 am.

RULING

The ruling is in regard to two parties British Airways appellant represented by Mr Busigara (tax consultant) and the respondent the Commissioner General represented by Mr Shigela (legal counsel).

The respondent in this matter has raised a preliminary objection before the determination of the appeal to the effect that in pursuing his appeal the appellant had not complied with the provisions of rule 4, 7 and 8 of the Tax Appeals Board Rules. To be specific the respondent through his counsel was referring to rule 4 (5) and rule 7 (2) (*f*) of the rules.

In reference to rule 4 (5) he submitted that any person who wishes to appeal to the Board shall issue to the Board a written Notice of Intention to Appeal within 30 days of the notice of assessment made to him and the said notice shall be duly served on the respondent. On this point the learned counsel stated that there is no evidence whatsoever to show that the notice of intention to appeal was served on the respondents nor is there any annexure to the statement of appeal to the same effect. The service is a mandatory procedure on the part of the appellant.

As far as rule 7 (2) (*f*) is concerned Mr Shigela, legal counsel explained that this rule imposes a mandatory requirement to the effect that while filing his appeal the appellant was supposed to file his appeal with evidence of payment of appropriate fees. If one takes the statement of appeal nothing is annexed to evidence the payment of fees which also extends to rule 8 of the same rules.

Reacting to the above submission Mr Busigara submitted before the Board copies of a letter to the Board showing his Notice of Intention to appeal and the notice itself. As to the issue of payment of fees he tendered copies of receipts showing the payments. He then brought up an issue of there being no provision governing this kind of appeal.

In reply Mr Shigela, learned counsel still submitted further that the letter to the Board and the written Notice of Intention to appeal do not mean anything if they were not served upon the respondent as envisaged by rule 4 (5) of the Tax Revenue Appeals Board Rules.

As far the payment of fees is concerned the learned counsel still insisted that these should have been annexed or formed appendices to the statement on lodging the appeal failure to do so makes the appeal incompetent before the Board and should be struck out with costs. As to the issue of which provision should apply in this appeal, he dismissed it as it was a new issue introduced by the appellant.

In deliberating on the preliminary objection we revisited the provisions cited that is rule 4 (5) rule 7 (2) (*f*) and rule 8 we are in agreement with the legal counsel for the respondent that these provisions, to be specific rule 4 (5) and rule 7 (2) (*f*) impose a mandatory obligation on the part of the appellant. The word used "shall" connotes a mandatory obligation.

To ascertain ourselves of the above obligation we have gone through the documents before us and we find that on lodging his appeal the appellant had only brought to the Board Form TRB 1 the Notice of Intention to appeal itself and a letter tendered before us during his submission before the Board which was dated 31 March 2004 addressed to the Secretary of the Board. We have also copies of receipts of payment. On scrutinizing these documents we find they were never served on the respondent (the TRB 1) as required by the law nor were they attached (receipts) to the appeal documents as mandatorily required by the law.

Before our decision we have strongly considered the general view that courts are not there to punish parties for the mistakes they make, consequently the Board is not also there to punish the parties as to the mistakes they make but we have also carefully considered the fact that the rules of procedure are there to be followed. We find that by enacting the rules of procedure it is purposely intended to curb any mischief and to prevent ad hoc litigations and so the parties are legally bound by these rules.

With the above in our minds we find that the appellant miserably failed to comply with the mandatory obligations found in rule 4 (5) and rule 7 (2) (*f*) of the Tax Revenue Appeals Board Rules.

This brings us to our decision that as a result of this the appeal before us is incompetent before the Board as it is bad in law and we accordingly strike it out with costs to the appellant. It follows therefore that the preliminary objection is accordingly upheld.

As to which law is applicable to this appeal we find that this was not part and parcel of the preliminary objection and hence there being no need for going into this matter.

Read this 20 January 2005 in presence of Mr Felician Busigara, Teddy Hylton and Fatuma Harris for the appellant and Mr Shigela, legal counsel for respondent.

CAR AND TRUCKS DISTRIBUTORS LTD v COMMISSIONER GENERAL

TAX REVENUE APPEALS BOARD

DAR ES SALAAM

(VAT TAX APPLICATION: NO. 3 OF 2004)

12 April 2005

RKB Meela, *Chairperson*, F Mteteleka and D Mwaibula, *Members*

Appeal—Limitations and Extension of time—Whether notice issued by respondent in 2004 against an objection of 2002 was valid—Tax Revenue Appeals Act, 2000

A *Appeals—Deposits as condition for appeal—Whether partial deposit can warrant determination of an objection—Tax Revenue Appeals Act, 2000, s 16 (5) and (6)*

This was an application for extension of time within which to give a Notice of Appeal as well as for waiver of the requirement to make deposit with the
B Commissioner General as required under s 16 (5) and (6) of Tax Revenue Appeals Act, 2000. The applicant invited the Board to rule on whether notice issued by the respondent in the year 2004 against an objection that arose in the year 2002 was valid.

Held:

(1) If, for any reason, the Commissioner General has not determined the
C applicant's notice of objection filed, then the applicant cannot come to the Board under an application filed under s 16 (4) of the Tax Revenue Appeals Act.

(2) The fact that the applicant company had deposited a sum of Tshs 25,000,000 with the respondent, a sum intended for the partial discharge of the applicant's tax liability, the respondent is advised to issue a decision upon the appellant's filed notices of objection on the VAT and Stamp Duty assessment
D as quickly as practicable.

Application dismissed.

Case referred to:
Afrika Mashariki Gold Mines Ltd v Commissioner General [2003] 1 TTLR 1 (TRAB).

E

Dr Ringo, for the applicant.
Mr Kidaya, for the respondent.

1 November 2004:

F Chairperson: Are there any preliminary matters before we start the hearing, learned gentlemen?

Dr Ringo, for the applicant: The applicant has paid to the Commissioner General Tshs 25 million on 31 May 2004 as payment of a lesser sum and the Commissioner General has agreed, and subject to Mr Kidaya making representations thereof, has
G allowed the applicant to file its objections under s 12 (3) of the Tax Revenue Appeals Act, 2000.

Therefore, subject to Mr Kidaya's representations, the applicant considers the request for Order No. 2 as withdrawn as well as Order No. 3.

In the light of the submissions, only the request for Order One subsists in this application. That is all we submit for the preliminaries, Your Honour.

H

Mr Kidaya, for the respondent: Your Honour, the law allows the respondent Commissioner General to allow a lesser sum to suffice the amount assessed to be deposited with the respondent. Since the applicant has not even shown before this Board any receipt to that effect, I will have to crosscheck with the respondent to ascertain the position. If proved that the applicant has paid the said Tshs 25 million to the Commissioner General, then I will have no objection to make.

That is all, Your Honour.

Dr Ringo, for the appellant: Your Honour, as far as the main application is concerned, we have had discussions with the respondent and both parties are of the opinion that the matter can be settled out of this Board. Therefore, subject to the express consent of the counsel for the respondent, we pray for the issuing of two orders:

1. That the applicant files a receipt evidencing the payment of Tshs 25 million to the respondent.
2. An adjournment for three months for both parties to settle the matter out of the Board.

In the event that an amicable settlement is not reached, we pray for the matter to be heard before this Board.

That's all, Your Honour.

RULING

Dr Ringo in his very brief submissions has intimated to this Board that upon filing this application in this Board, the parties' positions have changed as the applicant company has paid Tshs 25 million, which the respondent, the Commissioner General, accepted as being a lesser sum for the purpose of making a deposit in order for the applicant's notice of objection to be admitted.

Since Dr Ringo has to file a receipt acknowledging the receipt of the said Tshs 25 million, which also Mr Kidaya, the respondent's counsel has to verify, then Dr Ringo prayed for an adjournment. It is further submitted that there is a possibility that the parties may settle the matter at issue out of this Board if they are granted a three month adjournment. If no settlement is reached then, the Board should allow the application to proceed for hearing.

We the Board members are of the considered opinion that the Board usually should not unnecessarily refuse to grant an adjournment prayed as in this present circumstance, since such procedure is envisaged under rule 15 (1) of the Tax Revenue Appeals Board Rules, that in hearing appeals or applications the Board should encourage actively, parties to disputes, cases or applications before the Board to determine their disputes through mediation, conciliation and arbitration by facilitating such procedures.

Accordingly, the applicant's counsel is allowed to file the receipt for the payment of Tshs 25 million paid to the respondent, and the adjournment sought for by the applicant's counsel is granted, with a variation that the applicant's counsel can file a written notice to this Board whenever the parties will have effected any settlement out of the Board so that the Board can accordingly appraise the progress of the said anticipated settlement.

Board: The matter is to be mentioned on 28 January 2005.

28 January 2005:

Chairperson: This matter is coming for a mention today so that the parties can appraise the Board about the current status of the application as per the prayer of the parties when applying for the last adjournment.

Dr Ringo, for the appellant: May it please the Board. The Board ruled, among other things that the applicant file a receipt evidencing payment of Tshs 25 million as a lesser sum per s 16 (3) of the Tax Revenue Appeals Act. Secondly, the Board granted an adjournment for three months to allow settlement out of the Board by the parties, and the filing of a written notice whenever such settlement is reached or there is a failure to settle.

Your Honours, the Board is hereby apprised that. First, the receipt has been filed. Secondly, no settlement out of the Board has been reached, and by consent of both parties, the matter is returned to the Board for adjudication. We therefore pray for a hearing date to be set.

I rest my submission, Your Honours.

Mr Tito, for the respondent: Your Honour, I have nothing more to say save all that has been said by my learned brother, Dr Ringo that the parties have failed to settle out of the Board and pray for a hearing date.

Board: As the parties have failed to settle out of the Board, a hearing date will be scheduled and the parties would be duly informed by the Secretary to the Board through a written notice for hearing in the very near future since we have issued the cause list for the month of February, 2005.

7 March 2005:

Board ruling:

We are in receipt of the respondent's letter dated 4 March 2005 to the effect that due to technicalities involved in the issuing of the tax decision giving rise to the anticipated appeal, he is withdrawing the said decision pursuant to rule 19 of the Tax Revenue Appeals Rules, 2001. Such a withdrawal means that the present application concerning VAT assessment has been arrested, since the offending decision subject of the anticipated appeal is no longer in existence.

Accordingly, as far as the application on the limb of the VAT assessment is concerned, the same is withdrawn, and we would proceed to hear the application on the demand for stamp duty and penalties as filed.

The hearing of the application is to proceed on 9th and 10 March 2005, as prayed for by the applicants counsel.

9 March 2005:

Chairperson: Are there any preliminaries before we start the actual hearing of the application?

Dr Ringo, for the appellant: Yes, Your Honours. The first preliminary is that because the respondent has withdrawn the assessment as regarding VAT, and in the light of the Ruling of this Board made on 7 March 2005, we would only make submissions as regards the assessment of stamp duty and the penalties thereof. We will not call any witness. And by consent between the parties, the matters will be made by oral submissions.

That is all Your Honours.

Mr Kidaya, for the respondent: Your Honour, I have none to make. A

Applicant's submissions in chief

Dr Ringo, for the appellant: Your Honours, the applicant made an application for five orders to be issued and is withdrawing two of the sought-for orders. The reasons for the withdrawal of orders Nos. 2 and 3 in the application as regards B waiver are that the respondent has agreed and accepted the payment of a lesser sum of Tshs 25 million for which we have filed a receipt in this Board as required under s 16 (5) and (6) of the Tax Revenue Appeals Act.

Therefore, the only order now applied for in this Board is the extension of time to give the notice of appeal and for costs of this application.

The applicant prays for extension of time within which to give the notice of C appeal for the following reasons. Under s 16 (2) (*b*) of the Tax Revenue Appeals Act, 2000 (15 of 2000), no appeal can be heard before this Board unless the notice of appeal is filed within 45 days from the day the respondent serves notice as per the provision of s 12 (4) of the same Act. It is submitted that as regards the withdrawal of the VAT assessment, the respondent had given notice, but as regards stamp duty, the applicant has received no notice from the respondent. Therefore, D as regards stamp duty, the applicant does not have time, running against it due to the failure by the respondent to give notice to the applicant on stamp duty.

As the objection raised by the applicant was made on 15 November 2002 and no notice from the respondent to date, the law deems that the respondent has accepted the position of the applicant as regards stamp duty and penalties thereon per s 13 (3) of the Tax Revenue Appeals Act. E

The respondent attempted belatedly to issue a notice dated 12 March 2004. We pray that this Board makes a ruling on this matter accordingly.

The second and final reason as regards s 16 (6) (*a*) and (*b*) of Act No. 15/2000. There are fundamental questions of law and fact that require adjudication by this Board, these are:

F

(a) Whether the notice issued by the respondent in 2004 against an objection rose in the year 2002 in valid in law.
(b) Whether landed properties and motor vehicles transferred to the purchaser over an ongoing concern are transfer *inter vivos* and transferable by a memorandum of agreement for sale, hence stamp duty at conveyance rates being chargeable. G

It is our submission that this Board correctly ruled in the case of *Afrika Mashariki Gold Mines Ltd v Commissioner General* [2003] 1 TTLR 1 (TRAB), unreported, that where there are uncertainties as to matters of both law and fact, an application should be entertained.

Under s 16 (6) (*b*) of the Tax Revenue Appeals Act, if the applicant was H obliged to pay the combined amount of VAT and stamp duty, it would have caused an undue hardship to the applicant, and would have forced it to sell property far below its market value or placed it under liquidation.

On the above grounds, we pray for the issue of the respectful orders and allow us to file the notice and the statement of appeal, and we also pray for costs. Much obliged, Your Honours.

Respondent's submissions

Mr Kidaya, for the respondent: Your Honours, the applicant is praying for an extension of time to file a notice of appeal out of time. Going through the submissions made by the applicant's learned counsel, he has not shown anywhere in his submissions as to why he is praying for an extension of time. In other words, he has not answered the question as to why he has failed to file the notice to appeal within time.

The applicant's counsel has raised an issue that the respondent has not responded to his Notice of Objection in respect of stamp duty, raised sometime in 2002. It is within our records that the respondent has responded to the Notice of Objection as per his letter ref. no. CVAT/VAT/10.10716 dated 11 November 2002. In this letter the respondent informed the applicant that his decision would be communicated to the applicant after scrutinizing all the relevant evidence pertaining to the disputed assessment. That letter covers the objection to both, VAT and stamp duty.

The work of scrutinizing the relevant evidence was so difficult, so it took quite a considerable time. The respondent communicated again with the applicant in respect of both objections as per letter ref. no. CVAT/VAT/10/1174/87 dated 12 March 2004, whereby the respondent clarified on the objection of VAT and stamp duty.

It is our submission that the respondent has fulfilled all the requirements under the Tax Revenue Appeals Act. It is thus our prayer that the application be dismissed with costs. I beg to submit.

Dr Ringo, for the appellant, in reply: On the first ground raised by the respondent that the applicant has not shown reasons for not filing the application within time, it is submitted that the assessment as regards VAT was the matter between the parties that had limitation of time running against it, as the respondent had issued a notice as required under s 12 (4) of the Tax Revenue Appeals Act. As that matter has been withdrawn, the issue as regards limitation of time to file the Notice of Appeal does not arise. Therefore, the applicant is not obliged to state reasons as to why he did not file notice to appeal within time.

In our earlier submission we stated that as regards stamp duty, no notice has been given and therefore no time runs against the applicant. Had it not been for the counter affidavit of the respondent, the applicant could have withdrawn this application.

On the second issue raised by the respondent that its letter dated 11 November 2002, was a notice responding to the applicant's objection, we submit that the response was with regard to VAT assessment only in response to the applicant's letter of objection with ref. no.VCS/RM1/LO. 64/CARO 5C dated 5 November 2002, which is annex PR 3 in the affidavit.

Therefore, the submission by the respondent does not relate to Stamp Duty as the objection to stamp duty by the applicant against a separate assessment was made to the respondent by letter ref. no. VCS/RM 1/LO 65/CAR 07C dated 15 November 2002, which is after the letter by the Commissioner. To date no notice has been issued by the respondent as regards stamp duty.

However, in March 2004, the respondent made attempts to combine stamp duty and VAT amounts and penalties thereof.

Therefore, we pray that the application be entertained. We submit respectfully. A

Board: We now come to the end of the hearing of the application. Board Members will deliberate on the proceedings and thereafter the ruling will be issued next week on Tuesday 15 March 2005 at 2.30 pm.

Board: In the course of the Board Members' deliberations, they noted that the B
Board does not have in its records two documentary exhibits referred to especially by the respondent's counsel, Mr Kidaya. The first one is a letter with ref. no. CVAT/VAT/10.10716 dated 11 November 2002. Since Mr Kidaya claims that this letter covers the notice of objection on both VAT and stamp duty, a fact which is refuted by Dr Ringo, counsel for the applicant, that the said letter does
not cover stamp duty. And precisely for that argument, the Board desires to see C
the letter to scrutinize its contents and interpret the same.

We also call upon the respondent's counsel to supply this Board with the respondent letter with ref. no. CVAT/VAT/10/11724/87 of 12 March 2004.

The two letters are important since they will allow this Board to rule on the disputed content as to whether they each cover the two separate notices of
objection variously written and filed or the first one covers only the respondent D
response regarding the notice of objection by the applicant covering only the VAT assessment.

Accordingly, the Ruling is adjourned to a convenient date to allow the respondent's counsel to file the said two letters and the Board to scrutinize them.

The two letters are to be filed as soon as possible by the respondent's counsel.
The ruling will be on a date to be notified to the parties by the Secretary to the E
Board.

RULING

The applicant, Messrs Car and Trucks Distributors Ltd, filed this application
under s 16 (4) of the Tax Revenue Appeals Act, and rule 9 of the Tax Revenue F
Appeals Board Rules, 2001, applying for the following orders to be issued by this Board, upon hearing the parties:

1. For an extension of time within which to give the Notice of Appeal;
2. For a waiver of the requirement to make a deposit with the Commissioner
General as required under s 16 (5) and (6) of Tax Revenue Appeals Act; and G
in the alternative and without prejudice;
3. For directing the respondent to issue a waiver of the requirement to make a deposit as required under s 16 (5) and (6) of the Tax Revenue Appeals Act;
4. For costs of this application to be provided for; and
5. Any other and further orders or directions, which this Honourable Board may
deem just and equitable to grant. H

This application is supported by the affidavit of Mr Shabir Abji. The respondent in this application, the Commissioner General of the Tanzania Revenue Authority, filed a counter affidavit sworn by its officer, one Ms. Rehema K Shao, the Acting Regional Revenue Officer of the Value Added Tax department at Sykes street.

A Initially, this application was scheduled for hearing on 1 November 2004, when Dr Ringo appeared for the applicant and Mr N Kidaya, appeared for the respondent Commissioner General. Dr Ringo moved this Board to grant the parties an adjournment of three months within which the parties could initiate a settlement out of this Board. Mr Kidaya for the respondent was not opposed to the prayer for adjournment and possible inter-parties settlement out of the Board.
B For that reason, this Board granted the prayed for adjournment under rule 15 (10) of the Tax Revenue Appeals Board Rules, which provides that in hearing appeals or applications, the Board should encourage actively the parties to settle their disputes through mediation, conciliation and or arbitration by facilitating such procedures.

On the 28 January 2005, this application was scheduled for a mention, whence
C Dr Ringo for the applicant, informed this Board that the parties had failed to settle their disputes out of the Board and had mutually agreed to come back for adjudication. This Board scheduled the application for a hearing on 7 March 2005, and on that same date, before the Board was submitted a letter with ref. no. CVAT/VAT/10/11724/117 dated 4 March 2005. This letter informed this Board that the Commissioner General had withdrawn the VAT assessment totalling to
D Tshs 247,993,220 pursuant to rule 19 of the Tax Revenue Appeals Board Rules. The Board duly accepted the withdrawal of the VAT decision and accordingly endorsed the withdrawal, and called upon the parties to proceed with the second limb of the application which emanates from dispute based on stamp duty assessed on the applicant by the respondent.

Dr Ringo for the applicant opened his submissions in chief by informing this
E Board that taking into consideration the foregone events, the applicant is now praying this Honourable Board for an order granting extension of time to the applicant to give notice of appeal and costs of this application to be provided. Dr Ringo submitted further that the applicant was praying for an extension of time within which to give notice of appeal for the following reasons. In the first reason, it was submitted that under s 16 (2) (*b*) of the Tax Revenue Appeals Act,
F no appeal can be heard before this Board unless the notice of appeal is filed within 45 days from the date the respondent serves notice under s 12 (4) of this same Act. Now as regards the withdrawn VAT assessment, the respondent had given notice to the applicant, of which the applicant admitted its receipt, while denying having received any notice as regards the respondent's decision on the Stamp duty.

G Dr Ringo submitted that the applicant filed its notice of objection against the Stamp Duty assessment on 15 November 2002, and no notice from the respondent had been received up to the day this application was heard on 9 March 2005. For that reason, the law deems it that the respondent accepted to amend the Stamp Duty assessment in accordance with the applicant's notice of objection as per the provisions of the now repealed s 13 (3) of the Tax Revenue Appeals Act
H Thus this Board should rule on the fact that the respondent had belatedly attempted to issue a notice to the applicant on 12 March 2004.

It was further argued by Dr Ringo, as a second ground supporting this application, that as regards s 16 (6) (*a*) and (*b*) of the Tax Revenue Appeals Act, there are fundamental questions of law and fact that require this Board's adjudication, which are:

(i) Whether the notice issued by the respondent in the year 2004 against an objection rose in the year 2002 is valid;

(ii) Whether landed properties and motor vehicles transferred to purchaser over an ongoing concern are transfer *inter vivos* and transferable by a memorandum of agreement for sale, hence stamp duty at conveyance rate being chargeable.

Dr Ringo submitted that where there are uncertainties as to matters of both law and fact, an application such as the present one should be entertained. And that has correctly been ruled so by this Board in the case of *Afrika Mashariki Ltd v Commissioner General* (supra).

In closing his submissions in-chief, Dr Ringo, counsel for the applicant, submitted that if the applicant was obliged to pay the combined amount assessed for Stamp Duty and VAT, that would have caused undue hardship, for the same would have obliged it to sell property below its market value or even place the applicant company under liquidation. And that this is what is ameliorated by the provisions of s 16 (6) (*b*) of the Tax Revenue Appeals Act, which allows the respondent to waive the depositing of half of the assessed tax as a condition precedent in accessing the Board to prefer an appeal against a decision of the Commissioner General's refusal to amend tax assessments which is objected to by a taxpayer.

Accordingly, Dr Ringo, upon these foregoing submissions, prays this Board to issue the applied-for orders—that is allow the appellant to file a notice of appeal and a statement of appeal.

On the other hand, Mr Kidaya, learned counsel for the respondent tax authority, submitted that the applicant was praying for an extension of time to file notice of appeal out of time, but Dr Ringo, learned counsel for the applicant, had not in his submissions in-chief, precisely informed this Board the reasons why the applicant company failed to file its notice to appeal within time. Mr Kidaya went on to submit that the allegation by the applicant's counsel, Dr Ringo, that the respondent never responded to the applicant's notice of objection raised in 2002 as not being true, for records of the respondent show the same to have been responded to vide a letter with ref. no. CVAT/VAT/10.10716 dated 11 November 2002. That letter was to the effect that the respondent would have responded to the VAT and Stamp Duty objections in due course upon the respondent reviewing all relevant evidence. Then later the respondent communicated with the appellant with a letter dated 12 March 2004 vide a letter ref. no. CVAT/VAT/10/11724/87. Mr Kidaya concluded by submitting that in all respects, the respondent had complied with all the relevant provisions of the Tax Revenue Appeals Act, and for that reason, the application should be dismissed by this Board with costs.

In response, Dr Ringo, advocate for the applicant making a rejoinder, submitted that, as regards the VAT assessment, the parties had time limit running, but as the decision giving rise to the would be appeal had been withdrawn by the respondent, then the applicant was no longer required to state reasons why they had failed to file their respectful appeal in time.

Moreover as regards stamp duty notice of objection, Dr Ringo submitted that they still held the same view that the respondent had not issued any notice

A regarding the applicant company's notices of objection and for that reason there was no time limit running against the applicant. The applicant's counsel also submitted that the respondent's letter dated 11 November 2002 was only a response covering the applicant's VAT notice of objection, referring to the applicant's letter with ref. no. VCS/RM1/L064/CARO5 C dated 15 November 2002. This letter was written later after writing the notice of objection concerning
B the VAT assessment. Dr Ringo accordingly concluded that to date the respondent Commissioner General has not responded to the applicant's notice of objection on the stamp duty assessment.

As stated earlier, this application is a result of the decisions made by the respondent on VAT and stamp duty assessments and as the respondent has withdrawn the VAT decision, the application on that limb also abates, and we
C remain with the orders prayed for in respect of stamp duty.

The applicant's counsel, Dr Ringo, has argued that the respondent, the Commissioner General, has not responded to the applicant's notice of objection filed on 15 November 2002, and for that reason, the applicant cannot run out of time in filing its notice of appeal before this Board. If really that is the case, then it means that the applicant cannot be said to be late to file a notice of appeal
D before this Board. Time starts to run out of a would be appellant where he has been served with a decision of the respondent regarding a notice of objection from the date of service of such notice as per the provisions of s 16 (1), read together with s 13 (4), both of the Tax Revenue Appeals Act, and also subs (2) (*a*) of s 16 of the same Act, which provides that the Board shall not entertain an appeal under this section unless the appellant had previously issued a notice of
E appeal in writing to the Commissioner General within 30 days upon being served with a notice under subs (4) of s 13 of the Tax Revenue Appeals Act.

Therefore, if for any reason the Commissioner General has not determined the applicant's notice of objection filed on 15 November 2002, then the applicant cannot come to this Board under an application filed under s 16 (4) of the Tax Revenue Appeals Act, since the respondent Commissioner General has not
F notified the applicant of a decision made on the filed notice of objection. We find this application to have no merit as the same is not tenable under the provisions of the law as filed. This application is dismissed in its entirety.

However, given the circumstances of the facts leading to the filing of this application, and the fact that the applicant company has deposited a sum of Tshs 25,000,000 with the respondent, a sum intended for the partial discharge of
G the applicant's tax liability, the respondent is advised by this Board to reciprocate by issuing its decisions upon the appellant's filed notices of objection on the VAT and Stamp Duty assessments as quickly as practicable, to allow the applicant's company to execute its business accordingly with a settled frame of mind.

Each party is to bear its own costs.

The ruling is delivered to the parties' representatives, Mrs S Gupta holding
H brief for Dr Ringo for the applicant, and Mr Kidaya, advocate for the respondent. The ruling is delivered this 12 April 2005.

CELTEL TANZANIA LTD v COMMISSIONER GENERAL

TAX REVENUE APPEALS BOARD

DAR ES SALAAM

(VAT TAX APPEAL: CASE NO 10 OF 2004)

8 April 2005

BR Mutungi, *Vice-Chairperson,* J Karashani and I Dallushi, *Members*

Value Added Tax—Value Added Tax on export of services—Roaming Service—Assessment of inward roaming services and output VAT—Value Added Tax Act, 1997

The dispute between the appellant and respondent is over two main issues. First, the appellant is contending that the respondent's notice of assessment on inward roaming services for Tshs 755,000,284 is erroneous and contrary to the law having included Tshs 349,655,922.49 assessed on inward roaming services which were up to 30th June, 2003 zero-rated. Secondly, the respondent's notice of assessment for output VAT in the amount of Tshs 463,210,926 is erroneous as the Commissioner refused to exercise his discretion not to asses the appellant for output tax on interconnection services supplied to the appellant by other service providers; the appellant having paid to the other service providers input tax of Tshs 667,687,500.

Held:

(1) The roaming service provided by the appellant does not fall in the ambit of export of service and automatically does not meet the requirements of s 9 of the Value Added Tax Act, 1997 read together with the First Schedule, Part 1 of the Act;

(2) The Foreign Service provider is only a go between for the foreign subscriber to get his services in Tanzania and pays the appellant after having received payment from the foreign subscribers.

Appeal dismissed

Case referred to:

Iron & Steelwares Ltd v CW Martyr & Co (1956) 23 EACA 175
O'Brien v Associated Fire Alarms Ltd [1968] 1 WLR 1916
Osenton (Charles) & Co v Johnston [1942] AC 130

Dr Nguluma, for the appellant
Mr Teemba, for the respondent

A **7 February 2005:**

Preliminary objection opens

Mr Teemba, for the respondent: The objection is based on s 12 (6) and 16 (5) both
of the Tax Revenue Appeals Act, 2000 (15 of 2000). They are both related to the
B mandatory provision of depositing money before coming to the Board. This has
not been complied with so. In failing to comply with these mandatory provisions
we pray that the appeal is incompetent and we pray that it be struck out.

The second ground of our preliminary objection is based on the appellant's failure
to attach among others a copy of notice of objection submitted to the respondent
rule 7 (2) (*b*) of the Tax Revenue Appeals Board Rules, 2001. In this appeal this
C record was not attached. Another failure is rule 7 (2) (*d*), is to attach a statement
to refuse to admit a notice of objection. This appeal relates to the respondent's
refusal to admit a notice of objection. I submit that this was not annexed.

There is no evidence of payment of appropriate fees on filing this appeal
7 (2) (*f*) of the rules. It is strengthened by rule 8 (1) of the rules. To the best of my
knowledge the fees were not paid at the time of filling this appeal.

D In total these failures above lead us to only one conclusion: that the appeal is
incompetent in total and should be struck out and this is our prayer.

I beg to submit.

Dr Nguluma, for the appellant: Your Honour, we would wish to submit as follows:

E First on the preliminary objection based on 12 (6) and 16 (5) of the Tax Revenue
Appeals Act. Regarding non-payment of assessment tax or part thereof has no
merit. The appellant duly paid part of the assessed tax in terms of s 12 (2) of the
Act. In the present case the whole of the tax assessed was in dispute and so in
terms of s 12 (2) the appellant paid in fact half of the assessed tax. The appellant
believed that the respondent would be the first to know that it was paid. We have
F evidence of the payment. On 27 February 2004 the appellant wrote to the
Commissioner regarding the demand to tax subject to this appeal and paid 100
million (deposit against the liability). On 23 April 2004 the appellant again wrote
to the respondent advising the respondent that they were not in agreement with
assessed tax but in good faith they were willing to deposit 50% of the assessed tax.

The total assessed tax was Tshs 784,136,363 of which ½ would be Tshs
G 392,068,182 and after this they made reference to the 100 million already paid.

The appellant made the payment in two installments as follows: on 30 April
2004 he made a payment of Tshs 161,378,788. This was remitted directly by
electronic transfer to the Bank of Tanzania and again on 28 May 2004 the
appellant made a third payment of Tshs 130,689,994.

Your Honour, we request that we be allowed to show the documents now, as
H we did not know the details of the preliminary objection. We could not file the
documents before in anticipation of the preliminary objection.

We submit that s 12 (6) is not applicable in this dispute as the respondent
admitted the notice of objection and considered the same in terms of s 13 of the
Act and wrote to the appellant confirming the determination. In other words we
are appealing against the assessment, not refusing to admit a notice of objection
of assessment. The notice was admitted and attended to.

As regards rule 7 (2) (*b*), (*d*) and (*f*) and rule 8 of the Tax Revenue Appeals A
Board Rules we submit that:

(1) Rule 7 (2) (*d*) and (*f*) are not applicable for purposes of this appeal as in the case of 12 (6) of the Act. The appeal does not relate to refusal of respondent to admit the notice of objection.
(2) Rule 7 (2) (*f*) and 8 have been satisfied as the appellant duly paid the fees B
when instituting the appeal. The evidence of payment is contained in the Board's file and the copy is with us. On 6 June 2004 just before the appeal was lodged a fees of Tshs 5,000 was paid and again a fee on statement of appeal was paid on 5 July 2004 before documents were presented to the Board. We plead that the payment was made by appellant and they lodged an appeal before securing the assistance of the lawyer and so they could not C
attach the receipt as it was the hand of the lay man who did this. Your Honour, the fact that the copy has not been made available to the respondent would prejudice the respondent in any way by failure to give them a copy. I submit that as we did not save the notice as required, the mission has not occasioned any fate or miscarriage of justice on the respondent.

D

On the point of objection in regard to failure to attach notice of objection we would wish to admit that the appellant inadvertently failed to attach such a copy. The referred omission on rule 7 (2) (*b*) is not a fatal omission as the respondents have a copy of notice of objection of the assessment without which this appeal would not be necessary. It is only the Board that will be missing a copy in issue.

The respondent is not prejudiced in any way by the omission. We plead that at E
the time of filling the appeal the appellant were not represented by any legal firm and they appealed on their own and it is due to their ignorance of the requirement, we pray that we tender the document at this juncture. The wording of rule 7 (3) is permissive much as it appears to be compulsory by the use of the word "shall". By reading the sections this is why I say so. The words that proceed shall … import an element of flexibility that each case should be looked into its F
circumstances rule 7 (3) shows this. The interpretation of rule 7 (3) shows that an additional document is of rule 7 (1) and 7 (2) and the Board may order submission of documents omitted by the parties. This is why 7 (3) was enacted by the legislature as they anticipated that same documents could be missing and so for the sake of justice these would be called upon to the benefit of the parties.

Your Honour, we submit that the Board be pleased to order that the documents G
inadvertently omitted be submitted to the Board with a copy to the Commissioner General. We have the copies with us; it is just a matter of photocopying. All the fees were paid and all the documents to be attached were in place by the time the appeal was lodged. I would like to refer you to the case of *Iron & Steelwares Ltd v CW Martyr & Co* (1956) 23 EACA 175 It states "procedural rules are there to serve as the lord maidens of justice, not to defeat it". H

In other words the procedural rules are not to defeat the purpose of the law that had been enacted. We have a firm opinion that the Tax Revenue Appeals Board Rules are there to guide the parties on substantive issues before the Board and how they have to be determined. In the present appeal the substantive issues are centred on liability of VAT. The respondent should not be allowed to hide behind

A the rules and avoid determination of the real issues of the appeal. We submit that
our submissions be entertained and preliminary objection be dismissed.

Mr Teemba, for the respondent, in reply: Your Hounor, as you might
appreciate my colleague has admitted failure of all the provisions that I have
pointed out. He cannot take rules of procedure for granted. These documents he
wants the Board to see now were supposed to accompany those of appeal. He
B cannot be heard that the appeal was filled by a person who is not an advocate.
I know the person who filled this appeal. He is a competent, experienced tax
consultant. He knows and ought to know all the rules. He did not start to appear
before this Board today or yesterday. To put this matter forward but about a week
or two weeks ago the Board threw out another appeal with less serious omissions
than this one. He is only purporting to do this today. The Board must not be
C ambushed by the parties, what the appellant has done is ambush the Board and
respondent today. Since, I have clearly cited the non-compliance of the Tax
Revenue Appeals Act and Tax Revenue Appeals Board Rules. I submit that it is
incompetent before the Board and it should be struck out.

I humbly submit.

D Order: (1) Ruling on 9 February 2005 at 11.00 am.
(2) Deliberations on 8 February 2005.

RULING

This ruling is based on a preliminary objection raised by Mr Teemba, learned
E counsel for the respondent, namely the Commissioner General. The preliminary
objection itself is based on points of law that the appeal is incompetent for failure
to comply with the provisions of ss 12 (6) and 16 (6) of the Tax Revenue Appeals
Act as well as rule 7 (2) (*b*), (*d*), (*f*) and Rule 8 of the Tax Revenue Appeals Board
Rules.

In urging the preliminary objection Mr Teemba learned counsel explained that
F ss 12 (6) and 16 (5) relate to the mandatory provision of depositing a sum of
money before coming to the Board and in this appeal the appellant has failed to
comply with this requirement and so the appeal is incompetent before the Board.

He further argued that the appellant has failed to attach necessary document as
per rule 7 (2) (*b*) and 7 (2) (*d*) of the Tax Revenue Appeals Board Rules. These
being the notice of objection submitted to the respondent and a statement of
G refusal to admit a notice of objection.

Mr Teemba also referred to rule 7 (2) (*f*) and rule 8 which relates to the evidence
of payment of appropriate fees. In this appeal according to Mr Teemba the
appellant had not attached this kind of evidence.

In conclusion Mr Teemba submitted that with these failures, the appeal is
incompetent and should be struck out.

H On the other hand the appellant Celtel Tanzania Limited duly represented by
Dr Nguluma learned counsel reacted to the preliminary objection raised as
follows:

First and foremost, the preliminary objection based on s 12 (6) and 16 (5) of the
Tax Revenue Appeals Act as to payment of assessed tax or part thereof does not

hold water. On this Dr Nguluma stated that the appellant actually paid half of the assessed tax as deposit. On 27 February 2004 they deposited Tshs 100 million on 30 April 2004 they deposited Tshs 161,378,788 and on 28 May 2004 they deposited Tshs 130,689,394. And to these they have documentary evidence but the respondent was in a better position to know of the payments as the payments were made directly to his office.

Dr Nguluma also submitted that they did not contest s 12 (6) as it is not applicable in this appeal. To elaborate on this point Dr Nguluma stated that their notice of objection as to the assessment was admitted by the respondent and actually has been determined and so the appeal is not in relation to refusal to admit a notice of objection as per s 12 (6) of the Tax Revenue Appeals Act.

As far as rule 7 (2) (*d*) is concerned Dr Nguluma submitted that this was not applicable as the appeal is not in relation to the respondent's refusal to admit the notice of objection.

As for rule 7 (2) (*f*) and rule 8, these were adhered to as the appellant before lodging his appeal paid the necessary fees and the receipts are contained in the Board's file, and a copy is with the appellant. The said receipts were not attached due to the fact that by then the appellant had not engaged the services of a competent lawyer but this would not in any way prejudice the respondent by failure to give them a copy or does not in anyway cause a miscarriage of justice.

The omission of rule 7 (2) (*b*) according to Dr Nguluma is not fatal to the appeal as the respondent has a copy of the notice of objection to the Assessment without which the appeal would never have come to the Board. Dr Nguluma on this point once again emphasized the fact that the appellant was ignorant as to the requirement of attachment of the said notice on lodging the appeal.

Dr Nguluma turned to rule 7 (3) as being permissive and importing an element of flexibility as to the circumstances of each case. That rule 7 (3) cures a situation whereby a party omits to attach any document in rule 7 (1) or (2) and so the Board can order the submission of the same. Dr Nguluma further explained that this is so as the legislature anticipated such a situation and as it has happened in the appeal the appellant should be allowed by the Honourable Board to photocopy the omitted documents and serve them to the respondent.

Dr Nguluma pleaded with the Board in his submission that rules of procedure should not be used to defeat justice and to this he quoted the case of *Iron & Steelwares Ltd v CW Martyr & Co* (supra).

He stated that the rules are there to guide parties on substantive issues of which in this appeal centred on liability of VAT and so the preliminary objection should be dismissed.

In reply to the above contentions Mr Teemba, learned counsel for the respondent still insisted that rules of procedure should not be taken for granted and as it was apparent that there were procedural omission by the appellant, this means that the appeal is incompetent before the Board and ignorance of the procedure is no defence at all.

In considering the preliminary objection we had to first consider s 12 (6) of Tax Revenue Appeals Act and rule 7 (2) (*d*) of the Tax Revenue Appeals Board Rules as these were strongly dismissed by the appellant's counsel as being irrelevant. We have carefully gone through the said provisions and we find that they are not relevant in this matter as they are concerned with the refusal by the Commissioner to admit a notice of objection. In the present appeal the

Commissioner did admit the notice of objection and in fact went ahead to determine the said objection.

The other provision that we have gone through is s 16 (5) of the Tax Revenue Appeals Act, which provides a procedure of depositing part thereof the assessed tax or the assed tax itself. On this, as properly put by the appellant's counsel the respondent was in a better position to know that the appellant had deposited half of the assessed tax as it was directly paid to him. It follows therefore that as even the respondent did not refute the same during his submission in the reply we are of the finding that what was necessary as per the law s 16 (5) was only to deposit, which we declare was done by the appellant and so any objection basing on s 16 (5) has no merits at all.

After the above we had to consider the omissions created by the appellant so far as rule 7 (2) (*b*) and (*f*) are concerned. We find that it is crystal clear that the appellant did not attach a copy of notice of objection submitted to the Commissioner and also did not attach the evidence of payment of appropriate fees. The appellant's counsel admitted to this failure but on the pretext of the fact that the appellant had not deplored the services of a lawyer. To this we find no defence at all as it is a known maxim that ignorance of law is no defence at all.

The appellant has introduced rule 7 (3) of the Tax Revenue Appeals Board Rules of which we find that it does not offer him any remedy at all as it is talking of additional documents not found under rule 7 (1) and 7 (2) which can be ordered by the Board to be attached or produced.

As argued by Dr Nguluma we had to see what would be the effect of one failing to adhere to the laid down rules of procedure. We find that the paramount effect should be that the opposite party should not be injured or there should not be any miscarriage of justice on the part of the opposite party and each case should be considered on its merits.

In the present appeal the failure is on the attachment of a copy of a notice of objection to an assessment submitted to the Commissioner General by the appellant. It will not have to take a genius to know that by whatever means the respondent has the copy of the said notice of objection as this is the core of the present appeal. On the same reasoning failure to attach the same will in no way cause any injury or occasion miscarriage of justice on the appellant. As for the attachment of the evidence of payment of appropriate fees we find that this too is obvious that there was no way the appellant could have pursued his appeal without payment of appropriate fees. We find that the spirit behind this requirement was to ensure that the appellant pays all the appropriate fees before the Board which in our opinion was duly done by the appellant. We do not see how the failure to attach the said evidence would injure the respondent or cause him to suffer any damage or injustice.

It follows therefore that it is our settled decision that as there was no injury or miscarriage of justice occasioned by the above failure of the appellant to comply with rule 7 (2) (*b*) and 7 (*f*) read together with rule 8 of the Tax Revenue Appeals Board Rules the preliminary objection is also dismissed and the appeal to proceed on merits. We further order that the omitted documents be photocopied and supplied to the Board and respondent immediately.

Each party to bear own costs.

Right of appeal explained.

Read this 9 February 2005 in the presence of Dr Nguluma for the appellant and Mr Teemba for the respondent. A

Order: (1) Submissions in writing, by the appellant on 18 February 2005
(2) Reply by respondent on 11 March 2005
(3) Reply by appellant 18 March 2005
(4) Judgment on 1 April 2005 B
(5) Deliberation on 25 March 2005

Appellant's written submissions

May it please you Madame Chairperson and Honourable Members:

C

Orders sought:

The appellant is seeking for your consideration of facts of the appeal before you and for orders that:

1.1 The respondent's Notice of Assessment on inward roaming services, for Tshs 755,000,284.00 is erroneous and contrary to the law having included Tshs 349,655,922.49 assessed on inward roaming services which were up to 30 June 2003 zero-rated. D

1.2 The respondent's Notice of assessment for output VAT in the amount of Tshs 463,210.926.00 is erroneous as the Commissioner refused to exercise his discretion not to assess the appellant for output tax on interconnect services supplied to the appellant by other service providers, the appellant having paid to the other service providers input tax of Tshs 667,687,505.00 contrary to the rules of natural justice. E

2.0 Introduction

F

Honourable Madame Chairperson and Members, this appeal concerns a dispute over assessment for Additional Value Added Tax Due (Form VAT 312) dated 27 February 2004 issued to the appellant by the respondent. A copy of the assessment document is included as Document No. 1 herein and the assessment. The total assessment is in the sum of Tshs 784,136,356.00.

G

- The tax is assessed on the basis that VAT was not accounted for by the appellant on certain taxable sales in the period from January to December 2002. The alleged discrepancy was disclosed by officers from the respondent's Large Taxpayers' Department in comparing the revenue declared by the appellant in the audited accounts, with the revenue declared on the VAT returns for the same period. H
- The respondent's officers made no attempt to investigate the reasons for the discrepancy or to establish whether the discrepancy did in fact represent undeclared taxable sales, but instead issued a letter on 20 January 2004 demanding payment of this amount (together with amounts of other taxes allegedly underpaid), as per document 2 herein.

- The formal assessment on VAT (as required by s 43 of the Value Added Tax Act) was eventually issued as described at para 2.0 above.
- Subsequent meetings and negotiations took place between the appellant and respondent but no agreement was reached in the matter. In the circumstances a notice of objection was lodged by the appellant on 30th March. A latter confirming the assessment in the accordance with s 12 (4) of the Tax Revenue Appeals, Act. 2004 was sent to the appellant by the Commissioner Large Taxpayers Department on 21 May 2004, as shown in document No. 3 attached herein.

Honorable Chairperson and members, the appellant contends that no additional VAT is due on the roaming income and considers that on the interconnected charges, the Commissioner should have exercised his discretion and withdrawn the assessment in the interest of natural justice. Our explanation for both these matters is given below:

3.0 Roaming service

With regard to them 1.1 above, that is, whether the assessment of VAT on roaming services rendered prior to 30 June 2003 is correct the appellant would wish to submit as follows:

3.1 The appellant's contention on roaming services

Honourable Chairperson and members, with regard to the assessment of VAT on roaming services we strongly contend that the respondent erred in law in assessing the appellant for VAT on roaming services for the amount of Tshs 349,655,922.49 as the services rendered related to export of services which prior to 30 June 2003 VAT was zero-rated.

3.2 It should be noted that roaming services are structured as follows:

- Roaming services are supplies by the appellant to foreign mobile phone service providers to enable their subscribers to use their phones in Tanzania through the Celtel network. This income has been regarded as zero-rated. Roaming Income in the period assessed was Tshs 1,748,279,612 (VAT) assessed at 20% Tshs 349,655,922.49.
- The appellant offers the services to the service provider abroad through a legal contract (see example attached as document No. 3 herein).
- The supply definition for VAT purposes should be taken into account. Can we argue that the person we issue an invoice to is the user/consumer of service? In our opinion the foreign services provider is the consumer and user of service whom the appellant invoices. There is no link between the individual who makes calls or receives calls. Similarly, the individual person roaming does not know the appellant nor does the appellant know him or his presence in Tanzania.
- When a foreign mobile subscriber with roaming facilities comes into Tanzania before he makes a call a signal is sent to his home network to seek authentification. The authentification signal is transferred to the

terminating on the subscribers which are routed and authenticated by this home network. Therefore, authority is granted by the foreign operator, if the access status of the subscriber can only be changed by the home network with which Celtel has an agreement. For instance whereas the home network can cancel his access on Celtel network, the individual person using roaming services cannot. A

- Everyday call records are collected in bulk for each service provider and are submitted in bulk to the foreign network. The files details do not distinguish subscribers but only relate to the service provider abroad. B
- We thus can argue that although the mobile subscriber received or made calls whilst in Tanzania the service was consumed by the service provider situate abroad.

C

3.3 The appellant strongly considers these services as exported and it is highly unpractical and unusual for any person/authority to assume otherwise. At the time in question, the export of any service was zero-rated under para 1 of the First Schedule to the Value Added Tax Act, which granted zero rating to:

(1) Exportation of goods and services from the United Republic of Tanzania. D

Provide evidence of exportation is produced to the satisfaction of the Commissioner.

Notes:

E

For the purpose of this schedule, goods or services are treated as exported from the United Republic of Tanzania if (a) In the case of services, the services are supplied for use or consumption outside the United Republic of Tanzania as evidenced by documentary proof acceptable to the Commissioner.

F

3.4 Honourable Chairperson and members, the appellant contends that since these roaming services were "used and consumed" outside Tanzania. The appellant has contracted with the foreign network to provide the services, and the foreign network pays the appellant for these services. We reiterate that there is no relationship, either contractual or financial, between the appellant and the foreign subscriber in Tanzania. Indeed, it is unlikely that G the foreign subscriber is aware, or cares, that it is the appellant's network which allows him to use his mobile phone in Tanzania. As the contractual and financial relationship is between the appellant and the foreign service provider, it is that foreign service provider who is using and consuming the services provided by the appellant. As the foreign services provider has no establishment in Tanzania, the services must be used and consumed H in the country where he is domiciled. The services must therefore be exported, and subject to satisfactory documentation of the transactions, be zero-rated.

3.5 We would also draw your attention to the regulations agreed in Melbourne in 1988, which supplements the International Telecommunications Convention (known as the Melbourne Treaty) to which the Government of

A the United Republic of Tanzania is a signatory. This states at subpara 6.1.3 of art 6 that:

"Where in accordance with the national law of a country, a fiscal tax is levied on collection charges for international telecommunications services, this tax shall normally be collected only in respect of international services billed to
B customers in that country, unless other arrangements are made to meet special circumstances".

3.6 The charges for inbound roaming made by the appellant are not billed to customers in Tanzania, but to providers in other countries. We submit that this being the case, our argument that the charges should not bear VAT
C (through the mechanism of para 1 of the First Schedule) is given the correct interpretation of Law. A copy of the relevant part of the Melbourne Treaty is included as Document 4 herein.

4.0 Interconnect charges

D With regard to item No. 1.2, this is whether the respondent is justified in refusing to exercise his discretion not to assess the appellant for output tax on inter connect services, the appellant having paid to the other services providers input tax in excess of the output tax assessed.

4.1 Appellant's contention on interconnect charges
E According to the respondent VAT has not been accounted for on charges made by the appellant for "Interconnect" services provided to other Tanzania Mobile phone networks to enable their subscribers to communicate with the appellant's subscribers. Interconnect Income in the period assessed was Tshs 2,316,054,630 (VAT at 20% Tshs 463,210,929).

F
- The appellant does not dispute that the discrepancy exists, and after considerable investigation, attributes it to two aspects of their operations, and that the assessed VAT is not payable.

4.2 It is important for the respondent to appreciate the fact that:

G
- Interconnect is the fee paid by one operator to another for "inter-connecting" with each other's network. Interconnection fee compensates the receiving operator for accepting carrying and successfully terminating these calls onto their network. The absence of such arrangement would mean either calling from one network to another would not be possible or users would alternatively have to pay a charge
H to receive incoming calls.
- Interconnection charges refer to what mobile and fixed line telephone operators charge to each other for carrying calls into their respective networks and transmitting them onto customers to facilitate communication.
- Without interconnection when the customer makes a call to another Mobile customer, the latter charges some amount of money (Interconnect)

for receiving and successfully terminating that call into its network. What Mobile charges Celtel to effect the communication operation is the interconnection charge/tariff while the same will appear in Mobile books as interconnection revenue for termination calls from another operator. A

- Every operator, that is interconnect has both interconnection charges and interconnection revenue. Interconnection charges for the calls made terminating on other operators and interconnection revenue being the fee levied for calls originating on other networks but terminated on the host network. B

4.3 Honorable Vice Chairperson and members, Interconnect charges are made between all the Telecommunication services providers in Tanzania. As both suppliers and recipients of the services for a long time after the introduction of VAT the liability of these services was uncertain, leading to considerable doubt and confusion on the part of both the TRA and the companies in question. Although it was eventually established and accepted that the charges were taxable, the actual modalities of charging and accounting for the services supplied and received by each company remained problematic. This situation has led, in the appellant's case to the failure to properly account tax either on the charges made, or those incurred. The appellant has calculated that the output tax due on the interconnect services supplied to other providers was Tshs 463,210,926.00. However, the input tax claimable on the interconnect services supplied to the appellant by the other providers is not less that Tshs 667,682,505. C D

E

- In correspondence and in meetings with the TRA the appellant has pointed out this imbalance and asked that input tax credit be allowed. The response from the TRA has been that the claim for input tax is time barred under s 16 (5) of the Value Added Tax Act, which limits deduction to no more than one year after the date of invoice.
- We submit that in the interest of natural justice the unclaimed input tax should be set against the output tax. If VAT on the interconnect charges had been properly dealt with, the appellant, as a net recipient of such services, would have been in credit by Tshs 204,471,579 and the TRA because of the nature of the tax, would have been in a revenue neutral position as all the output tax charged by the providers would be balanced by the input tax deducted by the recipients. F G
- However, if the TRA's current position is maintained, it benefits from a "windfall" of up to than Tshs 1,130,893,431 being the total of the input tax on which deduction is denied and the output tax now assessed. It is recognized that the TRA is a revenue collecting department, but we would suggest that is against natural justice that a tax authority, is allowed to benefit on such a scale from the entirely innocent errors and omissions of a tax payer, and also in a way which files in the face of the intention of the tax in question. VAT is not intended to be a burden on the fully taxable business, but should be a matter of throughput and cash flow only. H

A 4.4 We would draw the attention of the Board to s 43 (1) of the Value Added Tax Act which states that:

> "43. (1) Where, in the opinion of the Commissioner, taxable person has failed to pay any of the tax payable by him by reason of–
>
> ...
>
> B (b) his failure to make, or delay in making, any return required under this Act or the incorrectness or indecency of any returns, the Commissioner may assess the tax due and any interest payable on that tax both of which shall be due for payment within one month of the date of the assessment, unless a longer period is allowed by the C Commissioner or elsewhere in this Act."

4.5 This section by the use of the phrase "... may assess ..." as to "... shall assess..." gives the Commissioner discretion to assess or not, presumably depending on the circumstances. Although this point was specifically raised in the notice of objection there is no suggestion in the correspondence from the TRA that the use of the Commissioner' discretionary powers has been D considered. We submit that the circumstances here are precisely the type in which the Commissioner should use that discretion, in the interests of equity, reasonableness and natural justice.

5.0 Honourable Vice Chairperson and members, we reiterate our submission that:

(1) The respondents Notice of Assessment on inward roaming services, for E Tshs 755,000,284.00 is erroneous and contrary to the law having included Tshs 349,655,922.49 assessed pm inward roaming services which are zero least up to 30 June 2003.

a. The respondent's Notice of assessment for output VAT in the amount of Tshs 463,210,926.00 is erroneous as the Commissioner refused to exercise his discretion not to assess the appellant for F output tax on interconnect services supplied to the appellant by other service providers, the appellant having paid to the other service providers input tax of Tshs 667,687,505.00 contrary to the rules of natural justice.

In the premise we pray that the appeal be allowed with costs.

G

Respondent's written submission in reply:

The Appeal concerns a dispute over an assessment for additional VAT due (Form VAT 312) dated 27 February 2004. The assessment is in the sum of Tshs 784,136,363 due to discrepancy noted when comparing the Revenue declared by H the appellant in the audited accounts with revenue declared in the VAT returns for the period January to December, 2002.

The appellant's contention:

The appellant does not dispute that the discrepancy exists. Those taxpayers attribute this discrepancy into two aspects.

(1) Roaming services and
(2) Interconnection charges

Roaming services:

The appellant is contending that these services are supplied to foreign mobile phone service providers to enable their subscriber to use their phones in Tanzania through the Celtel network.

Interconnection charges:

The appellant has calculated that the output tax due on the interconnect services supplied to other providers was Tshs 463,210,926. However, the input tax claimable on the interconnect services supplied to the appellant by other providers is not less than Tshs 667,682,505. The appellant in meetings with the TRA officials asked that input tax credit be allowed. The response from the TRA officials was that claim for input tax is time barred under s 16 (5) of the Value Added Tax Act.

The TRA's stance on the contention of the appellant:

Roaming services:

(1) The TRA maintains that there is discrepancy when comparing the revenue declared by the appellant in the audited accounts with revenue declared in the VAT returns for the period January to December 2002.
(2) Roaming services providers while in Tanzania: The foreign mobile phone service providers have contracts with Celtel to enable their subscribers to use Celtel network. This service is not zero-rated, as it does not meet requirements of s 9 of Value Added Tax Act read with First Schedule para 1 to the same.
(3) Revenue from interconnection services provided to other Tanzania mobile phone networks to enable their subscribers to communicate with the appellant's subscribers is liable to VAT.
(4) As explained above inbound roaming service is subject to VAT at standard rate of 20%. The Value Added Tax Act does not give the Commissioner discretion to abandon or remit tax.

Defense on further explanations given by the appellant:

Roaming services:

(1) Inbound roaming services are liable to VAT at the standard rate of 20%. Paragraph 1 of the First Schedule to the Value Added Tax Act, explains categorically as to what constitutes (is regarded as) export:

Exportation of goods and services from the United Republic of Tanzania provided evidence of exportation is produced to the satisfaction of the Commissioner.

A (2) These services were used and consumed in the United Republic of Tanzania. The foreign provider requires services of the appellant so as to enable their subscribers to communicate while in Tanzania. The foreign provider does not require the appellant services or facilities to service their subscribers in countries where they operate. Therefore the appellant's services are effectively used when subscribers of foreign networks are physically in
B Tanzania. Hence the issue of export does not arise.

(3) Melbourne Agreement 1988:
This applies only when a fiscal tax is imposed on collection charges for International Telecommunication Services. This is not what is being contested. The issue is VAT on the Telecommunication Services and not VAT in collection charges so this is not relevant.

C (4) Effective use takes place where a recipient actually consumes services irrespective of the commercial arrangements, payments or beneficial interest.

Additional explanations:

(1) The location of the recipient of service does not determine export of
D services. It is place of use or consumption, which matters. A person can be outside Tanzania but use the services supplied by a Tanzanian provider in Tanzania. Such services will not be regarded as having been exported to a country where the recipient belongs and therefore zero-rated.

(2) It is indisputable that the foreign network owners/providers are the
E recipients of the services provided by the appellant. It is also indisputable that these foreign providers do not have residence in Tanzania. However, having no residence in Tanzania does not mean that these providers cannot use and enjoy services supplied by a Tanzanian provider in Tanzania.

(3) The services supplied by the appellant to foreign providers cannot be
F deemed to have been exported if the place where they are effectively used by the recipient is in Tanzania.

(4) The TRA maintains that inward roaming services are subject to VAT at the standard rate. The basis for charging VAT on inward roaming at standard rate is that the facility of the network (that is place of supply) is in the United Republic of Tanzania at the time of supply and the
G service is consumed in the United Republic of Tanzania. Although the contractual and financial relationship is between the local provider and the Foreign Service provider the consumer as already explained above is in the United Republic of Tanzania. As the third party can pay for the transaction entered into between two parties, modality of payment should not be an issue in this case.

H

Interconnection charges:

(1) It is not correct to contend that the taxability of Interconnection charges had been uncertain for a long time after the introduction of VAT. The taxability of Interconnection charges was very clear right from the

beginning that they are taxable at the standard rate. It was the service providers who were for their own reasons not accepting the TRA's advice. However, even if the uncertainty is assumed to have prevailed (as alleged by Celtel) we submit that it will apply to Celtel because by the time Celtel went into business the liability status on inter connection charges had already been resolved, that is, the alleged uncertainty had already been cleared.

(2) As regard to failure to claim input tax amounting to more than Tshs 667,682,505 for the reason of being time barred, we submit that the TRA is not to blame because it has not in any way contributed to the failure to claim the tax. Section 16 (5) is very clear with regard to the time limit for the documents used in claiming input tax.

(3) As pointed above s 16 (5) states that "input tax may not be deducted or credited after a period of one year from the date of the relevant tax invoice …"

(4) As explained above there is no provision in the Value Added Tax Act which gives the Commissioner such powers to allow the taxable person to claim input tax after expiration of time set under s 16 (5).

(5) Section 43 of the VAT Act gives the Commissioner discretions to assess or not to assess. This section does not give the Commissioner discretion to abandon or remit tax assessed.

(6) Petition or prayer for discretional reconsideration cannot be presented in the form of appeal as the appellant has done, and doing so entails questioning the use and application of discretional powers of the Commissioner drawn from the law.

The respondent prays for the dismissal of the appeal with costs.

Appellant's rejoinder to the submissions of the respondent:

May it please you Honourable Madame Chairperson and members, these submissions are made in response to the respondent's submissions dated 11 March 2005.

Honourable Madame Vice Chairperson and members, it is apparent from the appellant's submissions dated 18 February 2005, and the respondent's submissions hereinabove referred that the here are two basic issues before you on which the parties hold different opinions, that is.

1. Roaming services—whether the roaming services assessed for VAT were used and consumed in Tanzania.
2. Whether the Commissioner's discretional powers were exercised in a proper and lawful way in accordance with the presumed intentions of the legislature that provide such powers.

It is our submission that the respondent's submissions are totally wrong on both issues and that the TRA's position is held without due regard to the technical aspect of roaming services and the uncertainty in the taxability of interconnection charges with the introduction of VAT which caused the delay in the claim for input tax credit by the appellant.

Madame Chairperson and Honourable members let us now look at the respondent's submissions and the contentions regarding the two pertinent issues:

1. Roaming services:

It is our humble submission that the TRA's approach to the construction of the term "roaming services" is totally wrong, and it is the failure to construe the true mechanics of roaming service that has led the TRA to treat such a service "as locally consumed" while it is not. The TRA's submission (p 2) merely asserts that the roaming service is not zero-rated as it does not meet requirement of s 9 of the Value Added Tax Act read with para 1 of the First Schedule of the Act. No explanation is given as to why it does not meet the set requirement and what requirement that is.

Section 9 of the Value Added Tax Act provides that a supply of goods or services is zero rated by virtue of this subsection. Where a taxable person supplies goods or services and the supply is zero rated no VAT shall be charged on the supply, but it shall in all other respects be treated as taxable supply. The First Schedule to the Act provides under "zero rated supplies":

> '1. Exportation of goods and services from the United Republic of Tanzania provided evidence of exportation is produced to the satisfaction of the Commissioner.'

1.1 It is our humble submission that the Commissioner has not appreciated what roaming services entail as demonstrated in the TRA's submissions. The failure on the part of the Commissioner to interpret and understand what roaming services entail should not be used to punish the appellant. The Commissioner must have good reason to show why he is not satisfied that roaming service is an export of services.

1.2 It is further not correct to observe that "it is the place of use or consumption which matters". This is where the respondent puts the facts upside down and thus misapplies the law to the unfair detriment of the appellant. The fact is a person outside Tanzania who uses the services supplied by a Tanzanian provider while he/she is abroad cannot be said to have facilitated export of service to the foreign country. This is a very simplistic way of looking at the whole concept of roaming service. The fact, is when a service provider (like the applicant) connects a customer to its network, the said customer enjoys connection wherever he is in Tanzania or elsewhere in the world. The said customer will always enjoy the connection enabled in Tanzania and for all practical purposes receive those services in Tanzania where the equipment or connection service is installed. Where the customer travels abroad, he still enjoys the network in Tanzania. The local provider (such as the applicant) does not go with the customer to a destination abroad nor does he move the equipment or connection service to the destination abroad. Indeed, wherever the customer goes, whether to the UK, South Africa or USA, none of the local provider's business. At the end of the day the local provider will charge the customer in Tanzania for the network service basis of the time and distance covered, notwithstanding where he made calls.

1.3 The fact that a local customer used his Tanzanian network to speak while in A
London does not at all mean the provider or the customer has consumed the network service in London, hence export service by the local provider. It is pertinent here to remember that the network services are still provided in Tanzania and not London as it was ever moved to London. It is only the customer who has moved and decides to use the network service made available to him in Tanzania. However, since the network service provided in B
Tanzania is not customized for automatic use in London the Tanzania provider enters into an arrangement with a UK provider to provide network authentication signal so that the Tanzanian network can be accessible while the Tanzanian customer is in the UK. This kind of connection is not export of merchandise or other goods where a Tanzanian producer exports to; let us say London, where there is physical export of goods. It is also not like the C
case where a professional provides a professional opinion to a London-based enterprise. The latter is a clear export of service.

1.4 The TRA's position may be likened to the situation where a person rents a television set in Tanzania and travels with it to London. If whilst in London he cannot have access to some Television Channels in the world but the Tanzanian owner has made arrangements such that the customer can secure D
a cable in London that would enable him secure access to such other television channels, the use television equipment rented from Tanzania cannot be said to be an export of goods or service.

1.5 Thus the respondent's argument that it is place of use or consumption which matters is erroneous as he fails to comprehend the dynamics of roaming service. E

1.6 The respondent is equally wrong when he assumes that the services supplied by the appellant to foreign providers cannot be deemed to have been export of service as the place where they are effectively used by the recipient is in Tanzania. The respondent is wrong for the following reason. A foreign customer of a foreign provider who uses a cell phone facility via a Tanzania provider's network whilst in Tanzania cannot be said to have been supplied F
with any roaming services by the Tanzanian provider. The fact is a foreign customer of, let us say, a provider known as "Londonphone" who comes to Tanzania and secures the use of his Londonphone network to speak to UK or Australia via Celtel, effectively not supplied by Celtel the interconnection to speak to UK or Australia. The foreign customer is effectively interconnected by the foreign-based Londonphone. Celtel would never know such a foreign G
customer nor has even his name or identity in its network. Indeed there could be at any particular time a number of such foreign persons in Tanzania who enjoy roaming services to speak to a number of countries but Celtel will never know them, track them down, or bill them for they are not connected.

1.7 A Londonphone customer can only secure access to roaming service whilst in Tanzania if he is interconnected in his country of origin. He has no link at H
all with Celtel, and Celtel will never have the legal right to bill him for communicating through its network.

1.8 Indeed it is important to elaborate here the mechanics of the service. What happens is that Londonphone makes arrangements with Celtel for Celtel to provide authentication signal so that the Londonphone connection to its

> A customer is activated in Tanzania. Celtel will then bill Londonphone for the authentication signal service. The individual foreign customer will remain Londonphone's customer notwithstanding the fact that an authentication signal is secured while in Tanzania and it will be billed in London being enlisted and connected in London. In essence, the service is supplied to the foreign customer by its provider Londonphone and not Celtel. In other words
> B Celtel cannot be a foreign visitor to roaming service where the foreigner is not a local subscriber. It also goes that the recipient (that is, the foreign customer) is not supplied the roaming service by Celtel because the interconnection is effected in London not Tanzania. It is obvious; however, that the purchase by the foreign provider of the Celtel, signal to enable its foreign customer to communicate abroad whilst in Tanzania is an import of
> C a service from Celtel, a Tanzanian company. In effect the purchase service is not used by the foreign provider in Tanzania. It is used in London where the foreign customer is connected and enlisted as a customer. Londonphone does not move its network to Tanzania to enable its customer to roam or communicate whilst in Tanzania. It merely purchases the signal to enable its customer to communicate whilst in Tanzania. Thus the use of the Celtel
> D signal by Londonphone is certainly an import of service on the part of Londonphone and an export of service on the part of Celtel.

Honourable Madame Vice-chairperson and members, the TRA's contentions on the issue of roaming service are erroneous as demonstrated in the explanation above of how the service works. Their understanding of where the service is
E consumed is upside down hence their assumption that the services were consumed in Tanzania while they were not. The TRA's position would appear to be that since the foreign customer communicated with the outside world whilst in Tanzania then they consumed the roaming in roaming service in Tanzania. This is where the TRA's view of roaming service becomes totally wrong.

The fact is the service in the case of roaming service is the provisions of
F network connection giving access to the foreign mobile subscriber to communicate locally and internationally. Making a phone call in Tanzania is not itself use or consumption of the service in Tanzania because the service is elsewhere abroad. Its use or consumption remains the country where the service is made available for use not in Tanzania where the foreign provider of the service merely secures authentication signal to use the foreign network.

G We submit that the roaming services assessed for VAT were neither used nor consumed in Tanzania. The purchase of the authentication signal was an import of service for the foreign provider and an export of service on the part of Celtel hence the service was zero-rated in terms of s 9 of the Value Added Tax Act and Schedule 1 to the Act.

H 2. With regard to whether the exercise of the Commissioner's discretionary powers was done in proper and lawful way in accordance with the presumed intentions of the legislature that provides for such powers

2.1 Honourable Madame Vice-chairperson and members, counsel to the respondent has submitted that the TRA is not to blame because it has not in any way contributed to the failure by the appellant from claiming the tax. Essentially, the respondent does not dispute that it collected tax over and above the deserved tax to the Authority as per our submissions made on 18 February 2005. It merely asserts that the Authority is not to blame for the delay in claiming the input tax.

2.2 We humbly submit that the intention behind tax legislation is to ensure payment and also timely payment of tax dues. Nevertheless, the TRA has the administrative responsibility to ensure that all due taxes are collected. It is not, however, the intention of the statute to empower the TRA to grab or retain amount of money collected as tax even where such taxes are not due or there is a legal basis to credit the taxpayer for the excess tax collected. The TRA is not intended to forfeit amounts collected as tax where the law clearly allows a taxpayer to claim credit on the amount overpaid. The issue here is why should the TRA unfairly enrich itself at the expense of overpaid taxes hiding behind a technicality of its enabling statue and refuse to exercise a statutory discretion without justifiable cause.

2.3 Honourable Madame Vice-chairperson and Members the respondent's counsel admits that s 16 (5) gives the Commissioner discretionary powers to allow the taxable person to claim input tax after expiration of time set under s 16 (5). The claimant applied and appealed to the Commissioner to allow it to claim input tax after expiration of time set but the Commissioner refused (we enclose herewith an evidence to that effect as documents 5–9).

Contrary to what is alleged in para 5 of the respondent's submissions the Commissioner was not asked to abandon or remit tax assessed but to allow the appellant claim input tax. We humbly submit that the Commissioner's powers are quasi judicial and not absolute. Such powers have to be exercised reasonably and fairly. Each case ought to be considered on its merit.

2.4 Honourable Madame Vice Chairperson and members, s 16 (5) is not absolute as it gives the Commissioner the discretion to deduct or credit input tax after a period of one year. The language of the section being permissive the Commissioner may or may not allow deduction or crediting of input tax after a period of one year.

According to *Blacks Law Dictionary* (7th edn) West Group St Paul, Minn, 1999 the word means:

"is permitted to" … termed the "permissive" or "discretionary" sense

The word shall on the other hand mean "has a duty to".

2.5 It is our humble submission that if the legislature intended that the Commissioner should not allow deductions or crediting of input tax after a period of one year the word "shall" would have been used and not "may".

Section16 (5), therefore, gives the Commissioner discretionary powers to allow or not to allow crediting of input tax claimed after a period of one year from the date of relevant tax invoice. Such discretionary powers must be exercised upon the objective facts.

2.6 The nature and process of the referred discretionary powers is such that the Commissioner had to consider the grounds advanced by the appellant for the delay in seeking crediting of input tax particularly when it had remitted input tax in the amount of Tshs 667,682,505 and the output tax due on the interconnect services was Tshs 463210,026.00. It is apparent that by disallowing the appellant the deserved credit from the Tshs 667,682,505 the Commissioner would virtually collect VAT more than twice the deserved amounts from the same taxpayer. Even if the Commissioner allowed the deduction the TRA would have collected Tshs 204,471,579 beyond what the appellant was legally bound to pay, that is:

Tshs 667,682,505 = input tax
Tshs 463,210,926 = output tax
___
Tshs 204,471,579 = excess tax amounts

2.7 Honourable Vice-chairperson and members, the appellant in its application to the Commissioner for input tax credit the appellant held several meetings with the respondent and exchanged written communications explaining the reason for the delay in claiming credit in particular uncertainty of the law at the material time and also complicated audit exercise which was still on going on various aspects of taxes payable including

— VAT
— Withholding tax on consultancy/management fees; and
— Withholding tax on rental income.

We enclose just a sample of documents evidencing the discussions before the tax assessment in dispute was made and after documents 5–8). It is therefore not correct for the counsel to the respondent to allege that "The taxability of Interconnection charges was very clear right from the beginning that is even before Celtel came to business".

2.8 It is also not true that it was the service providers who were for their own reasons not accepting the TRA's advice. The documents above clearly show that the appellant had been negotiating with the TRA in good faith and it never refused to accept TRA's opinion. It would appear clear from the TRA's submissions that once it makes an opinion then it takes that opinion as the law and every taxpayer has to accept it as the proper advice or the law. This is not a healthy trend in view of the fact that smooth interaction between the taxpayer and the administrator is crucial. It is also not healthy for the TRA to habour the view that its advice is always right.

2.9 Honourable Vice-chairperson and Members, as detailed in our submission in terms of s 43 of the Value Added Tax Act the Commissioner has the discretion to revise his assessment of tax if there are good grounds to move him/her so to do.

The fact is, uncertainty on the taxability of interconnection charges was not resolved before the matter before the Board came into being. The law is still evolving. That is why on 1 July 2003 the Value Added Tax Act was amended by the Finance Act, 2003 (15 of 2003) and a number of amendments to the sections of the statute made including what is entailed in "export of services". A

2.10 In its submission at p 7 the appellant has made it clear that:

'The VAT liability of interconnect charges was for a long time uncertain leading to considerable doubt and confusion on the part of the TRA and the providers (appellant inclusive). Similarly that the actual modalities of charging and accounting for services supplied and received by each company remained problematic, a situation which led the appellant to fail to properly account for tax either on the charges made or those incurred'. These were the reasons given to the Commissioner requesting him to allow crediting of input tax over output tax the appellant having discovered rather late (and late for the reasons already given) that he had a large credit in its favour. The Commissioner declined or refused to take into consideration the reasons given for the delay in filing documents claiming input tax credit. Instead the Commissioner interpreted the provisions of s 16 (5) that the request to credit input was time barred. It is clear from the respondent's submissions that the Commissioner considered the ground that the appellant's claim was time barred rather than the grounds why the appellant failed to claim input tax within time. In other words the Commissioner failed to take account of relevant considerations, thus he acted unreasonably. B C D

2.11 In accordance with Wade and Forsyth *Administrative Law*, (7th edn), 1994 pp 405–406 the celebrated jurist on administrative law observes that failure to take account of some consideration which is necessarily relevant, similarly taking irrelevant considerations is an erroneous, assumption of discretion and violates the rules of natural justice which nullifies the decision made by the authority having discretionary powers. E

2.12 Honourable Madame Vice-chairperson and Members, the argument in para 6 of the respondent's submissions that a petition or prayer for discretional reconsideration cannot be presented in the form of appeal as the appellant did is totally erroneous. What the appellant is seeking is for the Board to overrule the Commissioner's refusal to exercise his discretionary power to allow the appellants' claim for credit of input tax. F

It is our humble submission that the Tax Revenue Appeals Act and the Tax Revenue Appeals Boards Rules do not limit the scope of appeals against the Commissioner decision in the exercise of his powers within the law. Further it has long been the practice of appellant Tribunals elsewhere in the world to allow appeals where a decision is vitiated by unreasonableness, self misdirection, irrelevant considerations or some other legal error particularly, where the decision appealed against produces "manifest injustice"or it is "plainly wrong" (*O'Brien v Associated Fire Alarms Ltd* [1968] 1 WLR 1916. The appellate Tribunal may, where evidence is entirely documentary, exercise the discretion that would otherwise be exercised by the discretionary authority (*Osenton (Charles) & Co v Johnston* [1942] AC. 130. The above authorities are drawn from common law jurisdiction and they are highly persuasive to the Honourable Tax Appeal Board. G H

2.13 According to Wade and Forsyth (op cit) at p 953, appellate jurisdiction is statutory as such there is no restriction on the jurisdiction of an appellate Tribunal. That is, if the appellate Tribunal sees that on other grounds the decision of the discretionary authority will result in injustice it has both the power and the duty to remedy it. An appellate Tribunal keeps its options open and in practice it is likely, on its own discretion, to allow an appeal when it thinks that a substantial mistake has been made.

Honourable Chairperson and members, we reiterate our prayers in that:

(a) The respondent's notice of assessment for output VAT in the amount of Tshs 463,210,926.00 is erroneous as the Commissioner refused to exercise his discretion not to assess the appellant for output tax on interconnect services supplied to the appellant by other service providers, the appellant having paid to the other service providers input tax of Tshs 667,687,505.00, contrary to the rules of natural justice, it is entitled to input tax credit.

(b) The respondents Notice of assessment on inward roaming services, for Tshs 755,000,284.00 is erroneous and contrary to the law having included Tshs 349,655,922.49 assessed on inward roaming services which are zero-rated up to 30 June 2003.

2.15 The appellant stands to suffer irreparable loss by paying the TRA more than double the deserved VAT on interconnection charges. Similarly the appellant is being forced to pay VAT on roaming services which were in the years assessed qualified as "export of services" hence zero-rated. We humbly submit that your Honourable Board be pleased to order that:

(1) The VAT assessed on roaming services is erroneous as the services were at the material time zero-rated; and

(2) The appellant is entitled to claim input tax after expiration of the time set under s 16 (5) as the grounds given for the delay in claiming input tax were strong enough to warrant consideration by the Commissioner.

In the premise we pray that the appeal be allowed with costs.

JUDGMENT

In this appeal the appellant Celtel Tanzania Limited is represented by Dr Nguluma, learned counsel and the respondent the Commissioner General is duly represented by Mr Teemba, legal counsel.

The dispute before this esteemed Board as between the two parties is over two main issues.

The first being that the respondent's notice of assessment on inward roaming services, for Tshs 755,000,284.00 is erroneous and contrary to the law having included Tshs 349,655,922.49 assessed on inward roaming services which were up to 30 June 2003 zero-rated.

Secondly, the respondent's notice of assessment for output VAT in the amount of Tshs 463,210,926.00 is erroneous as the Commissioner refused to exercise his discretion not to assess the appellant for output tax on interconnection services supplied to the appellant by other service providers. The appellant having paid to the other service provides input tax of Tshs 667,687,505.00, contrary to the rules of natural justice.

For one to understand the mechanism of the roaming services hence the appreciation of the dispute, the appellant through the written submission by Dr Nguluma explained that the London phone makes arrangements with Celtel for Celtel to provide authentication signal so that the London phone connection to its customer is activated in Tanzania. Celtel will then bill London phone for the authentication signal service.

From the above it is clear then the individual foreign customer will remain London phone's customers regardless the fact that an authentication signal is secured while in Tanzania and it will accordingly be billed in London as it is connected in London and so the supplier in this case is supplied to the foreign customer by its provider Londonphone and not Celtel.

From the same reasoning then, it follows that the purchase by the foreign provider of Celtel signal to enable its foreign customer to communicate abroad while in Tanzania is an import of service from Celtel by London phone but an export of service on the part of Celtel. In furtherance to the clarification Dr Nguluma submitted that to be precise the roaming service is the provision of "network", connection giving access to the foreign mobile subscriber to communicate locally and internationally. The use or consumption remaining in the country, where the service is made available for use not in Tanzania where the foreign provider of the service merely secures authentication signal to use the foreign network.

In conclusion from Dr Nguluma's written submission the roaming service assessed for VAT were neither used nor consumed in Tanzania as the service was zero-rated in terms of s 9 of the Value Added Tax Act and Schedule 1 of the Act.

On the second issue as regards the exercise of the Commissioner's discretionary powers Dr Nguluma, learned counsel submitted that as much as he admits that s 16 (5) (1) gives the Commissioner discretionary power to allow a taxable person to claim input tax after expiration of time set under 16 (5) but these powers should be exercised reasonably and fairly and based upon the objective facts. Dr Nguluma, learned counsel in this matter found as fact that the Commissioner despite the explanations advanced to him by the appellant went ahead to consider the ground that the appellant's claim was time barred rather than the grounds as to why the appellant failed to claim input tax within time. In reference to Wade and Forsyth (op cit) Dr Nguluma submitted that "failure to take into account some consideration which is necessarily relevant, similarly taking irrelevant considerations is an erroneous, assumption of discretion and violates the rules of natural justice which nullifies the decision made by the authority having discretionary powers". Dr Mguluma went further to submit that where an Appellate Tribunal finds that a substantial mistake has been made which could lead to injustice being done then it can allow an appeal and this Board is vested with such powers in dealing with its appeals.

On the other hand Mr Teemba in his reply on behalf of the respondent submitted in writing to the effect that what is to the understanding of the respondent is that "Roaming services" are supplied to foreign subscribers belonging to foreign phone services providers while in Tanzania under a contract

A and in this case with Celtel. In order to use Celtel network and so cannot be termed as zero-rated as suggested by the appellant. What the foreign provider was doing was to use the services of the appellant so as to enable their subscribers to communicate while in Tanzania.

As the appellant had relied on the Melbourne Agreement of 1988 Mr Teemba, learned counsel submitted that this Agreement had no relevance in this issue as it
B relates to fiscal tax imposed on collection charges for international Telecommunication Services but not on the issue at hand which is VAT on the Telecommunication services.

According to Mr Teemba the material issue is the place of use or consumption of the service and in this matter it is in the United Republic of Tanzania.

As for the question of the Commissioner's discretion to assess or not to assess,
C Mr Teemba submitted that these cannot be subject to an appeal as this would be tantamount to questioning his discretionary powers. Be it as it may the respondent had nothing to do with the delay as he was not party to the failure of the appellant to claim tax. More so the liability status on inter-connection charges had been resolved by the time Celtel was coming into being.

In conclusion, Mr Teemba found no merits in this appeal and prayed for this
D Honourable Board to dismiss the same.

In order for this Honourable Board to proceed to its decision we had first and foremost to agree upon what actually is a roaming service. It is our settled opinion after going through the well-argued submissions before us that it is a service provided by Celtel (appellant) to foreign subscribers while such subscribers are in Tanzania. We are also of a common opinion that such service is provided by
E Celtel after a contract has been concluded between Celtel itself and the foreign service provider whereby subscribers of the foreign services provide access to the Celtel network signals while in Tanzania, in return for this service Celtel gets its payment for the roaming service from the foreign service provider. With the above in mind the pinching question would then be who is the consumer of Celtel's roaming service? From the submissions before us we get two different
F answers. The appellant submits the consumer to be the Foreign Service provider whilst the respondent submits that it is the foreign subscriber. We had expected to be availed the contract between the appellant and the foreign service provider but this was not done and so we had to consider the facts before us to arrive to the answer.

In our view in the arrangement between the foreign service provider and
G appellant we find that what actually the foreign service provider was doing was to facilitate to activate the roaming service when the foreign subscriber uses the service while in Tanzania. It is our further opinion that in order to use the service while in Tanzania the foreign subscriber is a very important element in order to complete the cycle otherwise the arrangement between the foreign provider and Celtel will be of no effect at all. The position of the foreign service provider in our
H finding is only a go between for the foreign subscriber to get his services in Tanzania and pays Celtel after having received payment from the foreign subscribers. We further find that the Usage or consumption of service by the foreign subscribers is not conditioned by the commercial agreements which in our view are only private arrangements to facilitate trade and financial transactions.

It thus goes without saying that we concur with the respondent's argument that the roaming service provided by Celtel (appellant) does not fall in the ambit of export of service and automatically does not meet the requirements of s 9 of the Value Added Tax Act read together with para 1 of the First Schedule of the Value Added Tax Act.

As to the question of the discretionary powers conferred on the respondent the appellant was mainly concerned with s 16 (5) of the Value Added Tax Act. This section confers discretionary powers to the respondent to allow the appellant to claim credits after the expiration of the time limit. On this issue we find that the respondent does not have to give reasons, as the basis should be time barred on the same understanding, we find no basis of stating that the discretionary powers conferred on the respondent were unlawful and improper.

All in all it is our settled decision that the appeal before us lacks merits and is accordingly dismissed with costs.

Right of Appeal explained.

Read this day of 8 April 2005 in presence of Mr Teemba for the respondent and Robert Mills for the appellant.

DHL TANZANIA LTD v COMMISSIONER GENERAL

TAX REVENUE APPEALS BOARD

DAR ES SALAAM

(VAT TAX APPEAL: CASE NO. 11 OF 2004)

25 May 2005

BR Mutungi, *Vice-Chairperson,* F Mteteleka and D Mwaibula, *Members*

Assessment—Assessment under Value Added Tax Act—Limitation of time for making assessment—Value Added Tax Act, s 43

This appeal concerned VAT assessment made under s 43 of the Value Added Tax Act to the tune of Tshs 132,785,065 which was alleged to have been not accounted for by the appellant on international carriage of parcel in the period from 1 July 1999 to 6 December 1999. The first ground of appeal was that the assessment issued on 5 March 2004 was time barred, and the second (in the alternative) was that even if the assessment was to be accepted as valid, the tax charged from 1 July 1999 should not have been chargeable because the change in the Value Added Tax Act had no legal force until the stated date of publication of the Finance Act, 1999 which was on 22 October 1999.

Held:

(1) The wording first had reason to believe found in s 43 (4) of the Value Added Tax Act are of great significance as they project when the counting of time should start.

A (2) The time when the respondent first had reason to believe that the return was correct or inadequate was after the audit was done, therefore, the period of limitation starts running from that date.

Appeal dismissed.

Cases referred to:

B *Gunda Shubaya v CIT* (1939) 7 ITR 20

Kliman v Winkworth (1933) 17 TC 569

Nassor Athuman Gogo and Jessy William Lugiana and Others v The Board of Trustees of the Parastatal Pensions Fund and Another (Misc Civil Cause 76/03), unreported

C *Mr Alex Balomi*, for the appellant.

Mr Shigela, for the respondent.

14 March 2005:

Mr Shigela, for the respondent: Your Honour, in this appeal the respondent raised D a preliminary point of objection and I pray to withdraw the preliminary objection as it has been overtaken by events.

I propose we proceed with hearing of the appeal. I would also like to point out that in hearing this appeal the appeal has two aspects. First, for the refusal of the respondent, to waive the deposit of half of the tax assessed. The second aspect is in respect of the appeal on assessment of additional added tax. My point here is E if it pleases the Board we can proceed with the second aspect and disregard to first aspect out as it has been taken up by events and proceeding will only be an academic exercise as the respondent had already determined the assessment to its finality. The issue of deposit the amount is a pre-condition for the respondent to determine the assessment, by determining the assessment the respondent has already waived. On 24 May 2004 he determined the objection to its finality. We F should do well on the second aspect of the appeal.

Mr Alex Balomi, for the appellant: We subscribe on the counsel's submission in view of abandoning the first limb of appeal and this is what we wanted to submit before.

Mr Mteteleka: I concur

G

Mr Mwaibula: I concur

BR Mutungi: This should be the proper way to proceed.

Board: In view of the submission of the respondent's counsel the preliminary H objection is marked withdrawn and it is also ordered that the appeal is to proceed based on the second limb of the appellant's appeal as prayed.

Mr Alex Balomi, for the appellant: As we had prepared to proceed on the preliminary objection until when it was withdrawn by the respondent we therefore pray that the substantive preparation and submission on the second part, proceeds tomorrow so that we have the necessary documents we are intending to relied on.

Mr Shigela, for the respondent: I have no objection A

Board: The matter is hereby adjourned to tomorrow morning at 9.00 am.

15 March 2005:

Mr Alex Balomi, for the appellant: The substantive appeal itself appears to be B
supported with extensive arguments which involve points of law. We humbly pray that with leave of this Honourable Board in the interest of justice and the consistence we proceed to dispose off the appeal by way of written submissions and in actual fact we are prepared to file the submission before the midday today for the respondent to reply.

Mr Shigela, for the respondent: Your Honour, I have no objection to the prayer C
by the appellant.

Mr DA Mwaibula: I have no objection

Mr FD Mteteleka: No objection D

Honourable BR Mutungi: No objection

Board: There being no objection to the above prayer we fix the matter as follows:

(1) Submission by appellant on 15 March 2005. E
(2) Reply by the respondent by 24 March 2005.
(3) Reply if any by 7 April 2005.
(4) Deliberations by 14 April 2005.
(5) Judgment by 21 April 2005 at 9:00 am

Appellant's written submission in support of the appeal F

(Pursuant to the Board's Order dated 4 March 2005 by Mrs Mutungi, Vice-chairperson)

Honourable Vice-chairperson and members of the Tax Revenue Appeals Board, the appellant in support of its appeal wishes to submit as follows:

This is an appeal against the assessment by the respondent for VAT made G
under the provision of s 43 of the Value Added Tax Act, 1997 (24 of 1997) as amended which as such assessed the additional tax payable by the appellant in connection with the allegation that the sum of Tshs 32,785,065 was not accounted for by the appellant on international carriage of parcels and courier services in the period from 1 July 1999 to 6 December 1999.

On 1 April 2004 the appellant lodged a notice of objection to the respondent H
in accordance with s 12 (1) of the Tax Revenue Appeals Act, 2000 (15 of 2000) objecting the assessment hence this appeal on two main grounds namely:

Firstly, the assessment which was issued on 5 March 2004 is invalid because it is time barred.

A Secondly, in the alternative, even if the assessment was accepted to be a valid document/assessment, we consider that no tax was chargeable from 1 July 1999 because the change in the Value Added Tax Act had no legal force until, at the earliest, the stated dated of publication of the Finance Act, 1999 which was on 22 October 1999.

We proposed two main issues to be adopted and determined

B

1. Whether or not the assessment issued on 5 March 2004 was time barred.
2. Whether or not the appellant was liable to pay Value Added Tax (VAT) on international carriage of parcels and courier services in the period from 1 July 1999 to 6 December 1999.

C Honourable Vice-chairperson and members of the Board in reply to the grounds and issues stated above we wish to submit as follows:

First ground of appeal and first issue are combined and are all answered in affirmative that the issued assessment was time barred.

Honourable Vice-chairperson and members of the Board, para 4.3 in the D Statement of Facts and Reasons of the appellant in support of the appeal refers to s 43 of the Value Added Tax Act which gives power to the Commissioner for Value Added Tax to assess a taxpayer for VAT which has for whatever reason been underpaid. The Commissioner has no power to assess or demand tax from a registered person other than under this section of the Act, which as such allows assessment if returns are missing, or if they have been submitted are faulty.

E However, there is no mechanism for a taxpayer to pay or account for tax other than through the VAT return. In this case then, any assessment to recover the tax alleged to be unpaid must therefore be raised on the basis that the VAT return from 1 July 1999 to 6 December 1999 were incorrect because they did not include the VAT, which is in dispute.

It is further supported under para 4.4 of the Statement of Facts of the appellant F by making reference to s 43 (4) which provides that:

> '... an assessment based on the incorrectness or inadequacy of return shall be void and of no effect if it is not made within one year after the Commissioner first had reason to believe it was incorrect or inadequate'.

We further submit that, in the respondent's letter dated 28 January 2000 (see G TRA 3) addressed to the appellant was acknowledged by the Commissioner for VAT expressly saying that the appellant had not charged VAT from 1 July 1999 to 6 December 1999. That being the case, we humbly submit that in the eyes of s 43 (4) of Value Added Tax Act, the VAT department had one year from that date to issue an assessment on 5 March 2004 which is more than one year. This being the case the assessment by the respondent is time barred.

H Furthermore, the VAT department failed to raise any assessment. Therefore even if VAT was chargeable with effect from 1 July 1999 still the assessment (in dispute) raised by the Large Taxpayers Department (respondent) is out of time, invalid, and has no legal force in the light of the above-cited section.

In addition to that, the respondent's letter dated 5 March 2004 (See document 1 attached to the statement of facts and reasons in support of the appeal) which accompanied the disputed assessment; as such the letter does not disclose any previous claim or stand by the respondent to evidence that had been made an assessment issued. Therefore, the letter is vague and does not disclose the material aspect in dispute.

Further reference to the respondent's letter dated 3 April 2003 (see TRA 4) under para 4.7 it indicates that the respondent was aware that no assessment had been issued up to 3 April 2003 after a silence of three years. Contrary to the law cited above, the actual assessment in dispute was issued on 5 March 2004 (see the attachment to the statement of appeal) which makes a period of delay by the respondent to be almost four years and therefore was inordinately out of time.

Honourable Vice-chairperson and members of the Board, tax advisers of the appellant (PricewaterhouseCoopers) replied to the respondent's above letter of 3 April 2004 on 29 April 2003 (see para 4.9 statement of facts and reasons in support of Appeal) clearly setting out the arguments as submitted above. However, the respondent chose not to reply to tax adviser of the appellant until 5 March 2004 which made only a very cursory attempt to answer any of the material points raised by the tax adviser of the appellant. The letter of the respondent in late reply instructed the appellant to settle the liability as per the attached demand letter mentioned (the assessment Form VAT 312).

On the strength of the above, we therefore submit that the assessment in dispute and by making reference to s 43 (4) the assessment is hopelessly out of time, invalid and has no legal force.

In reference to the respondent's reply to Statement of Facts and reasons in support of the appeal, upon reading para 17 of the reply by the respondent, we contend that there was no good cause which prevented the audit exercise to be performed by the respondent within a prescribed period of one year as required by law so as to establish the existence of incorrectness or inadequacy of the appellant's return. The section should plainly be interpreted that time span to make assessment is one year and therefore the respondent ought to have conducted the audit and subsequently communicate the findings including assessment, if any, within one year as clearly required by the s 43 (4) of the Value Added Tax Act.

I addition to that, we submit that the general rule is that tax statutes must be strictly construed. Strict construction means basically two things:

First, it means the use of the plain meaning approach. That is one merely to look at what is clearly said. This rule requires that the courts must have regard to the exact words used in a taxing statute and not suppose any general principle underlying them and remaining unexpressed. As Rowlatt, J observed in *Kliman v Winkworth* (1933) 17 TC 569 at p 572:

> '… in taxation you have to look simply at what is clearly said. There is no room for any intendment; there is no equity about tax; there is no presumption as to tax; you read nothing in; you imply nothing, but you look fairly at what is said clearly and that is tax.'

Second, it also means the use of the contra-referendum rule that is regard is to be had to all the word used without making any addition to them. Where there is ambiguity the taxing statute should be construed in favour of the taxpayer.

Regarding para 16 which is read together with para 17 of the respondent's reply, we further contend that the enabling provision require the Commissioner to make assessment within one year even though he had all the reasons to believe that the returns were incorrect or inadequate. To sorting out of the problem of incorrectness or inadequacy by the Commissioner ought to have been done within one year. That is to say, the Commissioner ought to have invoked the audit exercise within one year and not later on. The annexed audit report relied on as annex TRA 4 by the respondent does not help him since the assessment had already been time barred.

The answer to the second issue as to whether or not the appellant was liable pay VAT on international carriage of parcels and courier services in the period from 1 July 1999 to 6 December 1999 is that the appellant was not liable to pay VAT from the above period for the following paras 5, 5.1, 5.2 and 5.3 of the Statement of Facts and reasons in support of the appeal by the appellant.

In further support of the above paras, we submit that in alternative, even if the assessment was within time, still we maintain that no tax was chargeable from 1 July 1999 because the law was not in force and therefore the appellant was acting lawfully in accordance with the law which was in existence by then which termed the appellant's services as zero-rated.

Further regard should be made on the effect of the Provisional Collection of Taxes and Duties Act (Cap 515) on the Finance Bill 1999, and regarding the retrospective VAT payment demanded by the respondent. We further submit that, prior to 22 October 1999, when the Finance Act 1999 was published, courier services companies were VAT zero-rated for their international services. There are two amendments of ss 1 and 3 of the First Schedule to the Value Added Tax Act which gave zero-rated status to, *inter alia*, international courier services.

On 6 August 1999 an order dated 11 June 1999 and signed by the Minister for Finance was published thereby bringing the Finance Bill, 1999 signed earlier on 11 June 1999 into effect provisionally. Clause 10 of Order No. 233 entitled Provisional Collection (Finance Act, 1999) Order, 1999 reads as follows:

> '10. With effect from the 1st day of July, 1999, value added tax payable under the Value Added Tax Act, 1997 shall be paid in the manner provided by the provisions of the Act as is sought to be amended in Part X1 of the Finance Bill, 1999 as if the Bill had been passed into law in lieu of the law as is now provided'.

Part XI of the Finance Bill, 1999, a copy of which is annexed as annex TRA 2 introduced amendments to the Value Added Tax Act but did not change the zero-rate status of international courier services.

Under the provisions of s 64 of the Constitution of the United Republic of Tanzania, 1977, legislative powers vest in parliament and the usual procedure of passing an Act involves publishing a Bill in the official *Gazette* at least 21 days before the National Assembly convenes to consider the Bill. The Bill is passed if the required majority of Members of Parliament vote in favour and becomes law when it is assented to by the president and published or on any other date cited in the Act or any other written law as the commencement date. Section 10 (2) of the Interpretation of Laws and General Clauses Act, 1972 (Cap 1) states:

> '(2) … Every Act shall come into operation the date of its publication in the *Gazette* or, if it is provided either in such Act or any other written law that it shall come into operations on some other date, on that date'.

Why the Finance Bill is different from other Bills A

Except for Finance Bill, which becomes effective provisionally on the date the Provisional Collection (Finance Act) Order is published and definitively when the Finance Act is published all other Bills may not be implemented however provisionally until the National Assembly has published them in the Gazette. Normally the Order is published on the same date. The Finance Bill, 1999 was B
signed by the Minister for Finance on 10 June 1999 but the Order became effective after being published in the Gazette on 6 August 1999.

The provisional effect of the Finance Bill before it is passed by the National Assembly and assented to by the president and published in the *Gazette* is possible through the provisions of the Provisional Collection of Taxes and Duties Act which empowers the president to effect the Finance Bill before it is C
published, typically by publishing the Finance Bill in the *Gazette* in October or in some cases later than October. Section 2 of the Provisional Collection of Taxes and Duties Act, which provides this specially procedure, reads as follows:

> "2. (1) If the President at any time approves of the introduction into the National Assembly of a Bill whereby, if such Bill be passed into law, any tax or duty, or rate of tax or duty, or any allowance in respect of such tax or duty, D
> would be imposed or created, or whereby any such tax, duty rate or allowance would be varied or removed, he may, subject to the provisions of this Act and not withstanding the provisions of any other written law, make an order that there shall be charged, levied and collected the tax or duty which would become payable if such Bill were passed into law in lieu of the tax or duty (if any) which would otherwise be payable or, as the case may be that there shall E
> cease to be charged, levied and collected any tax or duty which would cease to be payable if such bill were passed into law".

An amendment to the Provisional Collection of Taxes and Duties Act through Act 12 of 1972 authorized the Minister for Finance to move an amendment to a Finance Act by notice published in the *Gazette*. F

When passed and assented to by the President and published in the *Gazette* unlike other Bills which become effective as from the date of publication in the *Gazette*, the Finance Bill becomes an Act on the date of its publication and as it was provisionally made effective prior to that date, it becomes effective definitively retrospectively on the date the Bill become provisionally effective which in this case was 6 August 1999 and not 1 July 1999. G

If there are changes effected on the finance bill by parliament, those changes may not become effective retrospectively since they were not provisionally effective in the first place. The Finance Act, imposed VAT on international courier services by omitting them from the zero-rated list. Prior to 22 October 1999 the above services were zero-rated and in accordance with the law not to charge VAT on the said services; customers would have within their legal rights to refuse to H
pay since the services were still zero-rated.

Any changes effected in the Finance Bill presented to the National Assembly had to be through the Ministry of Finance raising another Order to amend the original Finance Bill. It can be established that the Finance Bill, 1999 was not amended by another Order being made before it was presented to the National

Assembly. Therefore, the changes in the Finance Act, 1999 could only be effective from the date of publication of the Act itself namely 22 October 1999.

To make the changes to the Finance Bill enacted on 22 October 1999 effective as from 1 July 1999 would be to legislate retrospectively. Neither the Constitution of the United Republic of Tanzania, 1977 nor the Interpretation of Laws and General Clauses Act, nor any other law empowers parliament to backdate a law. Our parliament is not supreme, the law is. Parliament is obliged to abide by the constitution and by the laws it passes. Any changes to the law have to be brought about in accordance with the provisions of s 10 (2) of Interpretation of Laws and General Clauses Act of the laws in the manner therein set out which allows a current not retrospective notification of the new law to the public.

We have examined the provisions of s 10 (2) of the Interpretation of Laws and General Clauses Act, 1972 and concluded that the phrase in the said s 10 (2) "every Act shall come into operation in the *Gazette*....", appearing in that subsection means that the earliest date for an Act to be operational is the date it is published in the gazette and not before except for a Finance Act which becomes backdated to the date of publication of the Order affecting the finance Bill. This is because, in our opinion, the people to whom the law is applicable are deemed to know of the existence of the law on the date it is published in the *Gazette* which is the instrument for officially notifying the public of the commencement of the operation of a new law by which their conduct is to be regulated. Otherwise how could anyone could be expected to act in accordance with a law that was not in existence at the time of the act or omission to which a retrospective law applies?

In our opinion the second phrase in s 10 (2) which reads:

> '...or, if it is provided either in such Act or any other written law that it shall come into operation on some other date, on that date' means any other dates subsequent to and not prior to the date of its publication.

On the basis of the foregoing hereunder is our humble submission that:

(a) That the Parliament in Tanzania is subordinate to the constitution, and is bound by the laws it legislates.

(b) That the Finance Bill, 1999 did not remove the zero-rated status of international courier services and the said Bill was never amended by another Order before it was presented to the National Assembly.

(c) That the Finance Bill was signed by the Minster for Finance on 11 June 1999 but became effective on 6 August 1999 when the Provisional Collection Order No. 233 was published; the Finance Act, 1999 could only be backdated to 6 August 1999 and that only with respect to provisions thereof, similar to the Finance Bill, 1999 and not with international courier services which were zero-rated in the Finance Bill. The relevant provisions of the Finance Act, 1999 became operational on 22 October 1999, the date appearing on the Act as its date of publication.

(d) In the case of appellant up to until 22 October 1999 it was merely complying with the law by not charging VAT on its International courier services for which it may not legally be penalized. If appellant was penalized and made to pay VAT as demanded, it would be contrary to the provisions of s 13 (6) (*c*) of the constitution of the United Republic of Tanzania, 1977.

(e) That the retrospective application of the changes made by Finance Act, 1999 to the Finance Bill, 1999 is contrary to the provisions of s 10 (2) of the Interpretation of Laws and General Clauses Act and the above-mentioned provisions of the Constitution. A

(f) The parliament has no power to legislate retrospectively and change the character of past lawful acts or omissions to unlawful acts or omissions.

B

In summing up, we wish to submit that all the paras 7, 8, 9, 11, 15, 18, 19, 20 and 22 of the reply by the respondent save where admitted by the respondent all the above paras are disputed. Also we submit that at all the material times there was no ignorance of law as such but the law in issue was not operational as generally required by law and general guidelines in construing tax statutes. We therefore pray that the appeal be allowed as prayed. C

Dated at Dar es Salaam this 15 March 2005.

Respondent's submission

Honourable Vice-chairperson and members of the Board I have read and understood well the written submission by the appellant on the dispute before the Honourable Board. D

The arguments, by the appellant's counsel in essence articulate on two points that:

1. The assessment which was issued on 5 March 2004 is invalid because it is time barred. E
2. Even if the assessment was accepted to be a valid document of assessment, no tax was chargeable from 1 July 1999, because the change in the Value Added Tax Act had no legal force until at earliest the stated date of publication of the Finance Act, 1999 which was on 22 October 1999.

F

Honourable Vice-chairperson and members of the Board, before making our reply submission to the two points raised by the appellant's counsel, we would like to draw the attention of the Honourable Board to a brief back ground of the dispute at hand.

Honourable Vice-chairperson and members of the Board the matter at hand arose from an amendment effected in the First Schedule to the Value Added Tax Act by the Finance Act of 1999 which was passed into law on 6 August 1999 and assented to by the president on 20 October 1999. The amendment affected transport and ancillary services relating to exportation of goods from Mainland Tanzania, in this case international courier services, which were zero-rated prior to the Finance Bill, 1999 under the First Schedule to the Value Added Tax Act, were then made taxable. G H

The appellant on 3 December 1999 had an audience with the then Commissioner for Value Added Tax where the subject matter of discussion was the issue of amendment to the Value Added Tax Act made by the Finance Act of 1999 (letter dated 7 December 1999 from the appellant is attached marked TRA 1). The appellant was advised to charge and collect VAT on international courier services. Subsequent to that, there were several correspondences between the appellant and the Commissioner for VAT (as per attached letters marked collectively TRA 2). In all such correspondences, the Commissioner for VAT essentially insisted the appellant to comply with the requirement of the law and nothing else. After a period of almost three years, sometimes between January and February 2003, the Commissioner, through his officers from the Large Taxpayer Department conducted an audit on the appellant's accounts. On 3 April 2003, the trader was informed by the respondent Commissioner Inter alia the VAT liability of Tshs 132,785,067 established as a result of the audit performed by the respondent's officers (as per annex TRA 4 to the respondent's reply to statement of facts and reasons in support of the appeal). The appellant having failed to comply with the notice issued on 3 April 2003, the respondent Commissioner on 5 March 2004 made another demand notice for requiring the appellant to make payment within 30 days of the said demand note or assessment. It is from such an assessment or demand notice the appellant filed notice of objection on 14 April 2004 (as per annex 2 to the appellant's Statement of Facts) to the respondent Commissioner. On 24 May 2004 the respondent Commissioner confirmed the assessment, hence the appellant was aggrieved and filed the appeal at hand.

Honourable Vice-chairperson and members of the Board, in reply to the first point raised by the counsel for the appellant, that the assessment which was issued on 5 March 2004 is invalid because it is time barred, we wish to draw the attention of the Honourable board to the plain meaning of s 43 (4) of the Value Added Tax Act referred to by the learned counsel for the appellant, which provides:

> '(4) notwithstanding the foregoing provisions of this section, an assessment based on incorrectness or inadequacy of a return shall be void and be of no effect if it is not made within one year after the Commissioner first had reason to believe it was incorrect or inadequate.'

The respondent Commissioner could be said to have first had reason to believe that VAT returns submitted by the appellant, for the period from 1 July 1999 to 6 December 1999, were incorrect or inadequate, right after an audit was performed by his officers from the Large Taxpayer Department, between January and February, 2003, out come of which was brought to the attention of the appellant by a Notice dated 3 April 2003.

It is strongly submitted here that on 3 April 2003, after the audit was performed and completed by the respondent Commissioner that is when the respondent became aware and had reasons to believe that the VAT returns submitted by the appellant were incorrect or inadequate. In the words of Dr Luoga F D Makinyika in his book entitled *A Sourcebook of Income Tax in Tanzania*, DUP (1996) Ltd (2000) at p 183 states that:

> 'The assessment is made after such returns have been subjected to audit involving the examination of accounts and other documents to determine the reliability of the return. The process may also involve a visit to a tax payer's premises where it is considered necessary and such other things as may be necessary to verify the truthfulness of the statement contained therein'.

This stand is as well sanctified by the case of *Gunda Shubaya v CIT* (1939) 7 ITR 20 at pp 22–24 where it was stated that the Commissioner must have material on which to base his assessment, must not be capricious and is not entitled to make

a guess without evidence in that he must himself take steps to produce material A
for the purpose if it is not already in his possession. The Commissioner in this case has power to call witnesses and can make his own enquiries.

In the context of the above authority, the respondent had no sufficient data and or information to make him believe that the returns submitted were incorrect or inadequate until when he had all the material evidence after conducting an audit on the appellant's books of account. B

Subsequent to the performed audit, the respondent issue and assessment or demand not on 5 March 2004 within the period of one year, where in this case the latest date for issuance of assessment was 2 April 2004 as per requirement of the provisions of s 43 (4) of the Value Added Tax Act. In the circumstance the assessment issued by the respondent is not void neither was it time barred.

Honourable Vice-chairperson and members of the Board, the appellant C
counsel that the respondent's letter dated 5 March 2004, which accompanied the disputed assessment, does not disclose any previous claim or stand by the respondent to evidence that had been made an assessment issued argues it. It is clearly established above that, on 3 April 2003 a notice was caused by the respondent to the appellant requiring him to settle the liability otherwise assessment and demand note could be issued. This is what was referred to as the D
previous stand, the later dated 5 March 2004 was in compliance to this previous stand and nothing else, and hence the later is not vague as claimed by the learned counsel for the appellant.

In other words, such a letter by the respondent cannot be taken to refer to the correspondences between the appellant and the Commissioner for VAT as such correspondences could not amount to an assessment within the meaning of E
assessment which refer to amount fixed for payment. However, it can be further noted here that the issue of assessment is not a dispute in this appeal before the Honourable Board. What is disputed is the issue of whether the assessment issued on 5 March 2004 is time barred.

It is further argued by the appellant counsel that, there was no good cause which prevented the audit exercise to be performed by the respondent within a F
prescribed period of one year as required by the law, so as to establish existence of incorrectness or inadequacy of the appellant's return. This is totally not true and the counsel for the appellant intends to mislead and confuse the Honourable Board. The law does not provide for an audit to be made within a year but it clearly provides for an assessment to be made within a year since the Commissioner first had reason to believe that returns submitted were incorrect or G
inadequate. The statutory period limitation for an audit to be performed on the business of a particular taxpayer is five years and that is why the provisions of s 25 (2) of the Value Added Tax Act provides for a maximum period of five years and or such longer period which the Commissioner may require for a taxpayer to keep records. The section is hereby reproduced as follows:

H

> '(2) a taxable person shall keep the records required under subs (1) for a period of five years or such longer period which the Commissioner may require in writing, in a particular case.'

In that context, an audit as differentiated from an assessment can be within a period of five years and not restricted to one-year period. The counsel for the respondent has misconceived and tries to mislead and drive astray the Honourable Board as far as the limitation period to an assessment is concerned. Since the respondent Commissioner performed an audit between January and February 2003 and the subject matter of the dispute arose in 1999 about three years then the performed audit was made within the statutory five years period. Ignoring this fact means the provisions of s 25 (2) cited supra has no legal force, effect and is meaningless, hence defeating the purpose of this law. In order for the Commissioner to believe that there is a liability, there must be evidence to his satisfaction which can only be made by performing an audit in the manner he did to the appellant and nothing else, the case of *Gunda Shubaya v CIT* (supra) and the words of Dr Luoga cited supra clearly clarifies on this matter.

The general rule that tax statutes must be strictly construed as submitted by the counsel for the appellant, totally subscribed to our submission in the sense that, the respondent used the plain meaning approach and looked at what is clearly said in the Act. The words "the Commissioner first had reason to believe it was incorrect or inadequate" have been strictly construed to their plain meaning. It cannot be said that through the correspondences between the respondent and the appellant made between 3 December 1999 and December 2002 or by mere submission of VAT returns in the period the respondent had reasons to believe that returns submitted were incorrect; it was until an audit was performed and completed, is when the respondent is said to first have reasons to believe within the meaning of the law. The respondent could not just act on mere words by the appellant and issue an assessment; doing so is unjustifiable, dangerous and embarrassing to the Commissioner in case such an assessment is objected for in the same way as the appellant did. Fairly, looking at what is said clearly by the act, and using plain meaning of the law, it is not presumed but it is true that the respondent was not supposed to act on assumption and mere words by the appellant that he did not charge VAT on courier services during the period, but rather to act on the fact which was established by an audit conducted by a team of officers, from the Larger Taxpayer Department and findings thereafter made available to the appellant by a notice made on 5 March 2003 which in itself, leave alone the notice of assessment dated 3 April 2004, sufficiently amounted to an assessment recognized under the law.

In view of our above reply submission of the first point of argument by the counsel for the appellant ought to be disregarded by the Honourable Board, as the assessment was made within time prescribed under the provisions of s 43 (4) of the Value Added Tax Act hence is valid and has legal force in the light of the above cited section.

Honourable Vice-chairperson and members of the Board it is argued by the counsel for the appellant on the second issue that the appellant was not liable to pay VAT in the period from 1 July 1999 to 6 December 1999 because the law was not in force, and therefore the appellant was acting lawfully in accordance with the law which was in existence by then, which termed the appellant's service as zero-rated.

Honourable vice chairperson and members of the Board, the Finance Bill 1999 before it was passed into law by parliament was printed on 10 June 1999 and published in the *Gazette*, No. 23, Volume 80 dated 11 June 1999. The implementation of the said Bill before its being passed into law was with effect from 1 July 1999 by virtue of the provisional collection order GN No. 233 cited by the counsel for the appellant in their submission and reproduced hereunder: A

> '10. With effect from the 1st day of July, 1999, value added tax payable under the Value Added Tax Act, 1997 shall be paid in the manner provided by the provisions of the Act as is sought to be amended in Part X1 of the Finance Bill, 1999 as if the Bill had been passed into law in lieu of the law as is now provided'. B

Before the Finance Bill 1999 was passed into law, the amendment sought in Part XI of the Bill did as well include international courier services by way of schedule of amendments (a copy of which is annex TRA 2 to our reply to the statement of appeal by the appellant) made by the Minister for Finance under standing order 70 (3), (a copy of which is attached marked TRA 3) which provides and I quote: C

> '70 (3) Iwapo katika hatua hii Waziri anataka kufanya mabadiliko katika Muswada huo kutokana ama na ombi liliofanywa kwa mujibu wa kanuni ya 69 au na sababu nyingine yoyote, basi atamjulisha mwandishi Mkuu wa sheria ili atayarishe na Katibu atamugawia kila Mbunge, ama: (a) nakala ya muswada uliochapishwa upya, inayoonyesha wazi yale mabadiliko yanayokusudiwa kufanywa; au (b) Nakala ya orodha ya mabadilko yanayokusudiwa kufanywa. D
>
> Endapo orodha ya mabadiliko hayo itayarishwa, basi yanaweza kuambatishwa kwenye orodha ya shughuli.'

In essence such schedule of amendment forms part of the parent Bill as they are made before the Bill is passed into law. However, there are two alternatives for making, such schedule of amendment as shown under (a) and (b) above, either by reprinting the bill including the amendment or to make separate copy of the schedule of amendment as it was in the case at hand. E

Prior to the amendment para 3 of the First Schedule to the Value Added Tax Act stated that: F

> 'The supply which comprises of the transport of or any service ancillary to transport of or loading, unloading, wharfage, shore handling, storage, warehousing and handling, supplied in connection with goods in transit through the United Republic of Tanzania, whether such services are supplied directly or through an agent to a person who is not a resident of the United Republic of Tanzania.' G

A copy of the above-cited law is annexed herewith marked TRA 4.

Whereas the amendment sought in Part XI as contained in the schedule of amendment to the Finance Bill, 1999 and which was passed into law and subsequently appeared in the Finance Act, 1999 deleted the underlined words goods exported from the United Republic of Tanzania and it read as follows: H

> 'The supply which comprise the transport of or any ancillary transport service of or loading, wharf age, shore handling, storage, warehousing supplied in connection with goods in transit through the United Republic of Tanzania whether such services are supplied directly or through an agent to a person who is not a resident of the United Republic of Tanzania'.

A Honourable Vice-chairperson and members of the Board, the amendment effected in part XI contained in the schedule of amendment to the Finance Bill, 1999 cited above, are part and parcel of the Finance Bill, 1999 and had an effect of making taxable the supply which comprised the transport of any ancillary transport service of or loading, wharfage, shore handling, storage, warehousing supplied in connection with goods exported from the United Republic of Tanzania. In the B circumstance the appellant's International courier service business was made taxable, and with effect from 1 July 1999 by virtue of GN No. 233 cl 10 cited above, was supposed to charge and collect VAT on International courier services. In this case, it is absurd and it does not sound before the clear position of the law, for the appellant to argue that Part XI of the Finance Bill, 1999 introduced amendment to the Value Added Tax Act, but did not change the zero-rate of C International courier services. The position of the law is clear from doubt, that the amendment made International courier services taxable and the appellant was obliged to comply to the law, to charge and collect VAT with effect from 1 July 1999.

Honourable Vice-chairperson and members of the Board, the legislation of the Finance Act, 1999 clearly was in compliance with the law of the land, that is, D the constitution, it can be seen here, that the Finance Bill, 1999 was printed on 11 June 1999, gazetted on 11 June 1999, passed in the National Assembly on 6 August 1999 and where the Finance Act, 1999 was assented on 20 October 1999 and printed on 22 October 1999 its applicability became effective from 1 July 1999 by virtue of the Provisional Collection (Finance Act, 1999) Order No. 233. In this case the provision of s 64 of the Constitution of the United Republic of E Tanzania 1977 was complied with, where the bill was published in the *Gazette* at least 21 days before the National Assembly convened to consider the bill and satisfied other requirements thereafter as demonstrated above.

Honourable Vice-chairperson and members of the Board, neither art 64 of the Constitution of the United Republic of Tanzania nor s 10 (2) of the Interpretation of Laws and General Clauses Act prohibits or restrict the operational date set by F GN No. 233 Provisional Collection (Finance Act, 1999) Order (supra).

The Constitution under art 64 as argued by the counsel for the appellant makes commencement of a Bill to be after it has undergone other processes, when it is assented to by the president and published on any other date cited in the Act, or any other written law.

The Finance Act, 1999 under Part XI p 305 clearly shows the amendment G effected in the Value Added Tax Act where s 32 of the Finance Act, 1999 provides that:

> '32. This part shall be read as one with the Value added Tax Act, 1997 and shall be deemed to have come into operation on the first day of July, 1999'.

The above-cited section of the Finance Act, 1999 provides commencement date H in the same way as per requirement of the article in the constitution cited by the counsel for the appellant in their submission in chief, the words or any other written law fully gives support to the operational date as provided by the provisional collection (Finance Act 1999) Order No. 233 as this amount to any other written law. Hence the submission by the learned counsel for the appellant sufficiently subscribes to our view as demonstrated above.

Honourable Vice-chairperson and members of the Board, it is further noted A
from the submission by the counsel for the appellant at p 5 para 3 that the
appellant essence subscribe and support the retrospective operational effect of the
Finance Bill by virtue of the Provisional Collection of Tax and Duties Act, s 2 (1)
provides for a special procedure as quoted by the counsel for the appellant and
I reproduce the same as hereunder for easy reference: B

> '2 (1) if the president at any time approves of the introduction into the National
> Assembly of a bill whereby, if such bill be passed into law, any tax or duty,
> would be imposed or created, or whereby any such tax, duty rate or allowance
> would be varied or removed, he may subject to the provisions of this Act and
> notwithstanding the provisions of any other written law, make an order that
> shall be charged, levied and collected the tax or duty which would become C
> payable if the bill were passed into law in lieu of the tax or duty (if any) which
> would otherwise be payable, or as the case may be, that there shall cease to be
> charged, levied and collected any tax or duty which would cease to be payable
> if the bill were passed into law'.

The above-quoted section of the Provisional Collection of Tax and Duties Act
clearly substantiates the retrospective effect of the Finance Bill, as differentiated D
from other bills. In such circumstances the Finance Bill, 1999 and its schedule
of amendment made on 21 July 1999 which are part and parcel of the bill had
legally retrospective effect from 1 July 1999. Unless the appellant wants to
challenge the constitutionality of the Provisional Collection of Tax and Duties
Act and the Provisional Collection (Finance Act, 1999) Order No. 233 however
the Honourable Board is not the proper forum for that therefore the current E
position of the law is as submitted unless overruled by a competed court of law
for such matter.

Furthermore, it should be understood here that the legislation procedure as far
as schedule of amendments are concerned, the Minister for Finance moves the
schedule of amendment into parliament under the powers vested into him under
Standing Order 70 (3) cited supra and such schedule of amendment become part F
and parcel of the parent Bill. Long in the history of the parliament, schedules of
amendment have never been gazetted separately from the parent Bill; this is not
in the spirit of the law as far as enactment process is concerned. It is therefore
submitted here that, the Minister under the powers vested into him by Standing
Order 70 (3) properly moved the schedule of amendment into the parliament that
became part and parcel of the Bill and hence need for gazetting the same could G
not arise as it was part and parcel of the Bill, which later was passed into law.

In view of our above reply submission, it is evident that the parliament in
enacting the Finance Act, 1999 properly complied with the provisions of the
Constitution of the United Republic of Tanzania.

The Finance Bill, 1999 by the schedule of amendments made by the Minister
under Standing Order 70 (3) on 21 July 1999, did remove the zero-rate status of H
international courier services. The Finance Bill became effective on 1 July 1999,
by virtue of the Provisional Collection (Finance Act, 1999) Order No. 233,
which of course as a tax statue should as well be construed strictly and that only
plain meaning of the word should be assigned to by looking merely at what is
clearly said.

Honourable Vice-chairperson and members of the Board, the appellant cannot be heard saying that he was complying with the law until the 22 October 1999, when the Act was published, by not charging VAT on international courier services. It is clear here that even after the said publishing date on which the appellant claims to have become aware of the existence of the law, that he did not forthwith start charging VAT until 6 December 1999. This shows that he deliberately declined to comply with the requirement of the law. Further that the respondent was not legally duty bound to inform the appellant on the existence of the changes and if was done it was not in compliance with any law, and if the appellant was not aware of the existence of such a law, then ignorance of law afford him no excuse. The appellant was obliged to charge and collect VAT right from the 1 July 1999 as clearly submitted above. The amount of VAT demanded by the respondent from the appellant is justifiable under the law and lawfully made, hence did not contravene the provisions of art 13 (6) (*c*) and that of s 10 (2) of the Interpretation of Laws and General Clauses Act. The provisions giving effect to the collection of tax was made under the authority of same Constitution of the United Republic of Tanzania, where special procedure is only given to the Finance Bill as differentiated from any other bills.

Furthermore, the appellant's argument that the retrospective application of the changes made by the Finance Act, 1999 to the Finance Bill, 1999 is contrary to the provisions of s 10 (2) of the Interpretation of Laws and General Clauses Act and the provisions of the constitution. Reference to the constitutions means that the appellant questions the constitutionality of that law and raising such an argument at this stage renders the Honourable Board incompetent to determine such an issue; hence the Board should pay no attention to the argument and disregard it as it is not the proper forum for that matter.

Honourable Vice-chairperson and members of the Board, in view of our above reply submission, it is well established here that, first, the assessment which was issued on 5 March 2004 is valid and was made within the statutory period of one year since the Commissioner first had to believe that returns submitted were incorrect or inadequate. Secondly, the changes effected in the Value Added Tax Act as from 1 July 1999 had legal force as they were properly backed by an enactment of the parliament that is the Provisional Collection of Tax and Duties Act and GN 233 of 1999. In these circumstances, the appeal has no merit at all and it is our prayers that the Honourable Board be pleased to dismiss the entire appeal with costs.

Appellant's written rejoinder

(Pursuant to the Board's Order dated 14 March 2005 by Mrs Mutungi, Vice-chairperson)

Honourable Vice-chairperson and members of the Tax Revenue Appeals Board, these are the submissions in joining issues and support of the appeal to the Tax Revenue Appeals Board based on the main grounds disclosed in the Statement of Facts and Reasons of the appellant.

Honourable Vice-chairperson and members of the Tax Revenue Appeals Board, we have carefully read the submissions by the respondent opposing the submissions by the appellant and we would like to join the issues and finally submit as follows:

Honourable Vice-chairperson and members of the Tax Revenue Appeals Board, our thrust on our rejoinder is extensively covered under our main submissions I which all the three vital grounds for appeal are argued.

It is important however, therefore to note that the submissions by the respondent is misconceived; in the outset that the relied on several correspondences between the appellant and the respondent had no legal force until on 6 August 1999 when an order dated 11 June 1999 signed by the Minister of Finance was published in the *Gazette* thereby bringing the Finance Bill, 1999 signed earlier on 11 June 1999 into legal force provisionally and not otherwise. The respondent's letters marked TRA 1 and TRA 2 collectively have no legal status to warrant the appellant to start charging VAT on the international courier services which were zero-rated prior to the Finance Bill, 1999 under the First Schedule to the Value Added Tax Act. We therefore maintain that the appellant had no law to comply with in connection with VAT until on 22 October 1999 when the relevant Act was published in the *Gazette*.

In addition to that, the conduct of the respondent essentially at all the material correspondences insisted to comply with the requirement of the law, such conduct was not backed up with the law which required that all the acts of the executives (the respondent) must be justified in the eyes of law. Thus the appellant would not comply with the law, which was as such not in force.

Honorable Vice-chairperson and members of the Tax Revenue Appeals Board, rejoining the issue that the assessment is invalid, the appellant still maintains that it was made hopelessly out of time as required under s 43 (4) of the Value Added Tax Act.

In further opposition, the appellant strongly submits that he relied on version borrowed from the words of Dr Luoga FD Makinyika, in his book *A Sourcebook of Income Tax in Tanzania* DUP (1996) Ltd (2000), on p 183, is not applicable as the version itself is the mere opinion of the author as he sees the assessment process and is not binding to this Honourable Board. Further reading of the relied on version, provides the better option which would have been quickly adopted options in the Dr Luoga's version includes visiting the taxpayer's premises where it considered necessary and such other things as may be necessary to verify the truthfulness of the statement contained therein.

In addition to that Dr Luoga's version does not suggest carrying out an assessment hopelessly out of time when there is uncertainty in the truthfulness of the liability of the return. The respondent is as such missing this point.

Furthermore, the respondent ought to have seen this matter of necessity since it is clear that the matter of assessment as strictly required under s 43 (4) of Value Added Tax Act involved a great deal of money in a developing country like Tanzania which affects her economic development and which are both therefore matters of public interest. Thus we are made to understand that there was no reason to fail to conduct an audit within the shortest possible time that is to say within one year and verify the returns and assess forthwith instead of waiting for a solid three years over and above of the prescribed time span to do assessment.

The provisions of s 43 (4) of Value Added Tax Act are very clear and the Parliament did not intend to entertain the laxity in the time span in making the assessments.

Regarding the relied on case of *Gunda Shubaya v CIT* (supra) at ps 22–24 obviously gives a necessary approach which ought to have been taken by the respondent to facilitate the assessment properly within time and correctly. The respondent is misconceptualizing the holding in favour of the appellant. However the respondent on the basis of this holding would have chosen to call even witnesses within a required period to clear the doubts cast upon the returns of the appellant.

Furthermore, the plain interpretation of s 43 (4) of Value Added Tax Act applied to the word "shall" to mean that in no way, the assessment made out of the prescribed period of one year can be entertained. All the incorrectness and inadequacies would have been sorted out within one year and not otherwise.

We therefore, maintain that the actual disputed assessment was that dated 5 March 2004 which is out of time, invalid, void and of no effect.

Honourable Vice-chairperson and members of the Board, in reply to s 25 (2) of the Value Added Tax Act, we reply that the period of five years is for keeping records by the taxpayer and not period for conducting of an assessment. It is therefore a total confusion of the submission by the respondent. This section requires the taxable person to keep records for a period of five years or such longer period which the Commissioner may require in writing in a particular case.

The section is clearly providing the time span for a taxable person to keep the records for as a period of five years. In order to have useful findings of the audit then the respondent should have done the audit within one year in order to be in compliance with s 43 (4) of the Value Added Tax Act which expressly and mandatory requires assessment to be within one year. However, if the audit was seen to be an important element to determine the assessment then the respondent ought to have made the audit within one year as required under ss 43 (4) of the Value Added Tax Act. It should be noted that s 43 (4) and s 25 (2) of Value Added Tax Act are two independent provisions which are not derivative. Assessment, audit and period to keep records are quite different things in the eyes of the cited provisions.

We therefore maintain that, the relevant and dispute assessment is that of 5 March 2003 and not of 3 April 2004 to sufficiently amount to assessment.

Honourable Vice-chairperson and members of the Board, in replying to the second part of the respondent's submissions in connection with the retrospective concept, we submit that art 64 of the Constitution of the United Republic of Tanzania, 1977, legislative powers are vested in parliament and the usual procedure of passing an Act involves Publishing a Bill in the *Gazette* at least 21 days before the National Assembly convenes to consider a Bill. The Bill is passed if the required majority of Members of Parliament vote for it and when it is assented to by the president and published in the *Gazette* or any other date cited in the Act or any other written law as the commencement date. Section 10 (2) of the Interpretation of Laws and General Clauses Act states:

> '10 (2) every Act shall come into operation the date of its any law retrospective publication in the gazette or if it is provided either in such act or any other written law that it shall come into operations on some other date, on that date.'

This means any law with retrospective effect is unconstitutional and therefore is void.

We still maintain that the law should not be with retrospective effect when it affects the individual rights or creates obligations. To dispose of this part of the retrospective effect of the law, we refer to the recent unreported case of the High Court of Tanzania, Dar es Salaam Main Registry on the constitutional matter involving *Nassor Athuman Gogo and Jessy William Lugiana and Others v The Board of Trustees of the Parastatal Pensions Fund and Another* (Misc Civil Cause 76/03), unreported in which the petition was allowed and the legal principle was set that the statute with retrospective effect is unconstitutional, and their lordships were of the general views at pp 9, 10, 11, 12, 13, 14 and 15 that the retrospective application of statute is generally not favoured. Also this general rule is however, that remedial statutes i.e those, which do not crate, enlarge diminish or destroy vested rights are favoured by the courts and their retrospective operation is not obnoxious to the spirit and policy of the law (see at pp 13 and 14 of the attached decision marked as annex R where it was held that interpretation of statues should be to the effect that:

> 'No rule of construction is more firmly established than this: that a retrospective operation is not to be given to a stature so as to impair an existing right or obligation otherwise than as regards matter of procedure…'

It was further stated that:

> 'Every statute which takes away or impairs vested rights acquired under existing laws or create a new obligation, or imposes a new duty or attaches a new disability in respect of transaction or considerations already passed must be presumed out of respect to the legislature, to be intended not to have a retrospective operation'.

We are of the humble submission therefore that, this Board should have special regard to the consequences of the retrospective effects of any statutes specifically the provisions of the Provisional Collection of Tax and Duties Act and GN 233 of 1999.

In summing up, the appellant submits that this Board should properly allow the appeal on the basis of the main submissions and key settled principles of law cited above in support of the appeal.

We so humbly pray.

JUDGMENT

In the present appeal, the appellant DHL Tanzania Ltd, is represented by Mr Alex Balomi, learned counsel and the respondent Commissioner General is duly represented by Mr Shigela, legal counsel.

The two parties opted to proceed by way of written submissions of which by starting off with the appellant through the learned counsel is to the effect that the bone of contention is the VAT assessment made under s 43 of the Value Added Tax Act, as amended, to the tune of Tshs 132,785,065 which was alleged to have been not accounted for by the appellant on international carriage of parcel in the period from 1 July 1999 to 6 December 1999. On 1 April 2004 the appellant lodged a notice of objection to the respondent as per s 12 (1) of the Tax Revenue Appeals Act objecting the assessment which has ended up in this appeal.

A The grounds of appeal being two in number as follows:

First and foremost, the assessment issued on 5 March 2004 is time barred and
secondly, in the alternative, even if the assessment was to be accepted as valid
then the tax charged from 1 July 1999 should not have been chargeable because
the change in the Value Added Tax Act had no legal force until the stated date of
B publications of the Finance Act, 1999 which was on 22 October 1999.

On this ground, the appellant submitted in writing that s 43 of the Value Added
Tax Act is based on the powers vested on the Commissioner to asses or demand
tax from a registered person if there is incorrectness or inadequacy of a return
within one year after the Commissioner General first had reason to believe it was
incorrect or inadequate.

C The appellant further explained that taking the events of this matter the
appellant was notified by the respondent on 28 January 2000 that he had not
charged VAT from 1 July 1999 to 6 December 1999 and so under s 43 (4) of the
Value Added Tax Act, the respondent had one year from that date to issue an
assessment to quantify and recover the unpaid tax but the respondent made the
assessment on 5 March 2004 which was more than one year and so time barred
D invalid and had no legal force.

Be that as it may the letter dated 5 March 2004 (document 1) which accom-
panied the disputed assessment does not disclose any previous claim or proof to
show that an assessment had been issued. On this fact it is obvious the letter itself
does not disclose the material aspects of the dispute. Even if the letter of 3 March
2003 is taken into consideration the appellant further explained that it only goes
E to show that the respondent had issued no assessment up till the time of the letter
which was a three-year lapse, where as it is in evidence that the actual assessment
in dispute was issued on 5 March 2004 and from the computations the delay is
almost four years and so hopelessly out of time.

The appellant further submitted that the respondent had no good cause which
stopped him from carrying out the audit excise within the prescribed period of
F one year so as to establish the existence of incorrectness or inadequacy of the
appellant's return.

As for the second ground the appellant submitted that as there were omissions
from the Finance Bill, 1999 the provisional charging of the tax allowed by the
Provisional Collection of Taxes and Duties Act did not apply, and the
retrospective charging suggested by the wording of the Finance Act, 1999 does
G not have any legal power.

On elaborating on this point the appellant submitted that no tax is chargeable
from 1 July 1999, because the change in the Value Added Tax Act had no legal
force until at the earliest, the stated date of publication of the Finance Act 1999,
which was 22 October 1999.

Furthermore as the changes made in the Finance Act were not introduced first
H in the Finance Bill their retrospective enforcement was not legal, notwithstanding
the statement in the Finance Act that its effective date was 1 July 1999.

Even considering the order under the Provisional Collection of Taxes and
Duties Act, cl 10 of Order No. 233 of 6 August 1999 of which mentions
amendment in Part XI of the Finance Bill, 1999 which had effect from 1 July
1999 did not mention anything as regards to the amendment to the First Schedule

and so no changes could be effected under the Order of 1 July, and so by this A
omission the simple statement in the Finance Act that all amendments therein have effect from 1 July 1999 has an irretrospective application which is contrary to the provisions of s 10 (2) of the Interpretation of Laws and General Clauses Act and parliament has no power to legislate retrospectively and change the character of past lawful acts or omissions to unlawful acts or omission.

In responding to the above submission the respondent as regards the first B
ground of assessment being time barred, explained that the respondent's officers performed an audit between January and February, 2003 and notice of the audit was sent to the appellant on 3 April 2003 and so in term of s 43 (4) of the Value Added Tax Act the respondent became aware and had reason to believe that the VAT returns submitted by the appellant were incorrect or inadequate. C

It follows from the above that the demand note (assessment) made on 5 March 2004 was well in time as the latest date of issuance of the assessment would have been 2 April 2004. The respondent further explained that the law only talks of the issuance of the assessment within one year but does not restrict the audit to be within one year.

As to the second ground of appeal that the appellant was not liable to pay VAT, D
from 1 July 1999 to 6 December 1999 the respondent argued that this does not hold water. This is so because the Finance Bill, 1999 before was passed into law by the parliament was printed on 10 June 1999 and published in the *Gazette* No. 23 vol. 80 dated 11 June 1999 and the implementation of the said Bill before being passed in law was with effect from 1 July 1999 by virtue of the Provisional Collection Order GN No. 233 10 (2). E

The event that followed before the Finance Bill, 1999 was passed into law, there occurred an amendment in Part XI of the Bill by way of schedule of amendments made by the Minister for Finance and these were forming part and parcel of the Bill as they are made before the Bill is passed into law, this amendment did include international courier services as it deleted the words "exported from the United Republic of Tanzania". F

As they were part and parcel of Finance Bill, 1999 they had the effect of bringing into taxation the International courier services business with effect from 1 July 1999 by virtue of GN No. 233 cl 10. The issue that these services were zero-rated during that period does not hold water.

Having gone through the well-argued submissions from both parties we
considered the first ground, as to whether or not the assessment issued on G
5 March 2004 was time barred. In determining this ground we had in mind the events as narrated and not disputed by any of the parties. These are as follows:

(a) The dispute occurred sometime in 1999.
(b) The audit by the respondent was carried out from January to February 2003.
(c) The appellant was issued with the notice of audit on 3 April 2003. H
(d) The assessment was issued on 5 March 2004.

From the above the appellant alleges that it took the respondent more than three years to carry out the audit, well out of time and so even the subsequent assessment was time barred.

A In our view we find that the underlying provision governing the assessment process as also pointed by the two parties is s 43 (4) of the Value Added Tax Act of which states:

> 'Notwithstanding the foregoing provisions of this section, an assessment based on incorrectness or inadequacy of a return shall be void and of no effect if it is
> B not made within one year after the Commissioner General first had reason to believe it was incurred or inadequate'.

In the dispute before us the assessment was issued on 5 March 2004 after an audit was carried out between January to February 2003 and notice sent out to appellant on 3 April 2003.

The wording first had reason to believe found in s 43 (4) are of great
C significance as these project as to when the counting of time should start.

On this we concur with the argument of the respondent that the time when the respondent first had reason to believe that the return was correct or inadequate was after the audit was done. This is the time the respondent could be satisfied that he had enough evidence to rely upon in order to establish any incorrectness or inadequacy but not otherwise. It is from here then that one can
D start counting the period of one year and in this case the latest time would be sometime in early April 2004. So by issuing an assessment on 5 March 2004 we find the respondent was still well in time and so the issue of time bar does not arise.

The issue of the audit to be within what time does not arise in this case as the time of keeping the records and accounts for a taxpayer is within five years as per
E s 25 of the Value Added Tax Act. We therefore answer the first issue to the effect that the assessment issued on 5 March 2004 by the respondent upon the appellant was well within time.

As to the second issue of whether or not the appellant was liable to pay VAT on international carriage of parcels and courier services from 1 July 1999 to 6 December 1999 we answer this in the affirmative as illustrated hereunder.

F The provision governing the dispute is to be found in the Finance Bill, 1999 of which the Provisional Collection Order GN No. 233 cl 10 (2) provides that the applicability of the said bill is with effect from 1 July 1999.

The Finance Bill, 1999 was printed on 10 June 1999 and gazetted on 11 June 1999 and was passed in the National Assembly on 6 August 1999 and assented to on 25 October 1999.

G We are in agreement that the international courier services up until 11 June 1999 were zero-rated and this was before the law was passed which was to be effective from 1 July 1999 by virtue of the Provisional Collection Order GN No. 233 in particular cl 10 (2).

It should be noted that there was an amendment sought in Part XI of the said Bill which included international courier services by way of a schedule of
H amendments before the Finance Bill, 1999 was passed into law. These schedules of amendments were of 21 July 1999 before the Finance Bill, 1999 was passed in the parliament. These were automatically forming part and parcel of the Finance Bill, 1999 which already had to take effect from 1 July 1999. It is then that on 6 August 1999 that the National Assembly passed the Finance Bill 1999 as law and assented on 20 October 1999.

It follows therefore that the Bill comprised the schedule of amendments which had by virtue of the parent Bill, 1999 taken effect from 1 July 1999 bringing into taxation the international courier business carried out by the appellant.

The retrospective aspect argued by the appellant as being unconstitutional, we state with due respect to the appellant's counsel that this Honourable Board is not the proper forum to determine that aspect.

As already pointed out we are in agreement that the appellant is liable to pay VAT on international carriage of parcels and courier services from 1 July 1999 to 6 December 1999 as was demanded by the respondent.

In follows therefore that the appeal is dismissed for lack of merits and each party to bear own costs.

Right of Appeal explained.

Read this day of 25 May 2005 in presence of Mr Alex Balomi learned counsel for appellant and Mr Shigela for the respondent.

DR WILBERT B KAPINGA v COMMISSIONER GENERAL

TAX REVENUE APPEALS BOARD

DAR ES SALAAM

(INCOME TAX APPEAL: CASE NO. 7 OF 2004)

27 January 2005

BR Mutungi, *Vice-Chairperson,* F Mteteleka and D Mwaibula, *Members*

Appeals—Waiver of the condition to deposit one third of the assessed tax pending determination of objection—Failure by Commissioner to give reasons for refusal to waive the condition—Whether Commissioner General's decision proper—Tax Revenue Appeals Act, 2000

The appellant was on 31 December 2003 served with a notice of additional tax assessment of Tshs 14,272,366. He lodged a notice of objection and requested for waiver of payment of one third of the tax pending the determination of his notice of objection. The respondent simply replied that the request had not been successful without ascribing any reasons.

Held:

The Commissioner was duty-bound upon refusal for waiver to give reasons. Failure to do so rendered his decision a nullity.

Appeal allowed.

Case referred to:

Nimrod E Mkono v Commissioner General (Tax Appeal 6/04), unreported

Tanzania Air Services Limited v Minister for Labour, Attorney General and The Commissioner for Labour [1996] TLR 217 (HC)

Cpt. Kameja, for the appellant.
Mr Mkwawa, for the respondent.

10 January 2005:

Captain Kameja, for the appellant: We are ready to proceed with the appeal. Your Honour, the matter in issue in the appeal before you are on all fours in the matters which were in issue in *Nimrod E Mkono v Commissioner General* (Tax Appeal 6/04), unreported, (copy attached) as the respondent except of course for the appellants who are different. In view of that situation the appellant and the respondent agree to have your Board to enter a consent order in this appeal that the order made by the Board in appeal case No. 6 of 2004 be adapted *mutatis mutandis* to the appeal before you No. 7 of 2004. We feel that it would not be in the interest of justice to go through the notions of arguing this appeal on matters which the Board has applied its mind and made a decision. We pray that the Board be pleased to enter the consent order as agreed between the parties and should the Board agree to the parties' request, we pray that an order be made ordering the respondent to admit and decide on the notice of objection raised by Dr Wilbert Kapinga (appellant) *vide* letter dated 13 January 2004, which is already on record as annex 5 to the statement of appeal and that each party bears owns costs.

Mr Mkwawa, for the respondent: Your Honour, I have no objection to the submissions made by the appellant's counsel and I pray the same as prayed by the appellant's counsel.

Order: Ruling on 11 January 2004 at 9.00 am.

RULING

This ruling is in respect of a prayer made by Captain Kameja for the appellant to the effect that this Honourable Board be pleased to make an order, ordering the respondent to admit and decide on the notice of objection raised by Dr Wilbert Kapinga (appellant). The prayer made by Captain Kameja is so made basing on the fact that as the Board has already made a decision in appeal No. 6 of 2004 an appeal which is similar both in facts and reasons for appeal then the said decision should be adopted *mutatis mutandis* to this appeal. On the other side Mr Mkwawa for the respondent had no objection to this prayer.

In going through the prayer made by Captain Kameja, learned counsel, we find that what the counsel is praying for is for an order from this Honourable Board to direct the respondent what to do. As the appeal has not been heard on merits it goes without saying that no order has been made by the Board in this appeal. By quoting appeal No. 6 of 2004 to us this stands as an authority or reference for the parties but it cannot be transferred into this appeal just because it is based on the same facts and circumstances. It is our opinion that the Board is ready to register what the parties have jointly agreed between themselves or consented obligation agreed between the parties but not an order from the Board giving out orders to any of the parties. In view of the foregoing, it is upon the parties to register their consent agreement over the matter or the appellant to withdraw the matter; whichever will be favourable to the parties to reach the ends of justice without any delay.

Right of Appeal explained.

Read this 11 January 2005 in presence of Captain Kameja for appellant and Mr Mkwawa for respondent.

Captain Kameja, for the appellant: We are asking for a short adjournment so that we discuss among our selves what to do. I pray for 30 minutes' adjournment.

Mr Mkwawa, for the respondent: No objection.

Board: Prayer granted and matter adjourned to 10:00 am.

Quorum: As before at 10:00 am.

Captain Kameja: Your Honour, having considered the basis and effect of the Board's ruling we are of the view that the best way to proceed is for the appeal to proceed to hearing so that the Board can then make the decision on merits and make the consequential appropriate orders and that subject to the Board's consent since the parties are not in dispute over the facts material to the determination of the appeal, we will request the Board to be pleased to allow the facts not in dispute so that the calling of witnesses can be dispensed with the matters to be argued. Then will be matters of law which we would request leave of the Board to argue by way of written submissions but under a schedule which would not exceed the time set by this Honourable Board of hearing this appeal, that is, 14 January 2005.

Mr Mkwawa: No objection to the submissions made by the learned counsel.

Order: (1) Submission by appellant by today 11 January 2005.
(2) Reply by 13 January 2005 from the respondent.
(3) Reply to reply if any by 14 January 2004.
(4) Deliberations on 18 January 2004 at 2:00 pm.
(5) Judgment at 9:00 am on 21January 2005.

Appellant's submissions
(Pursuant to the Order of the Board dated 11 January 2005)

Honourable Vice-chairperson and members of the Board, the High Court of Tanzania in its landmark ruling in the case of *Tanzania Air Service Limited v Minister for Labour, Attorney General and Commissioner for Labour* [1996] TLR 217 (HC) (Tanzanair case) (copy attached) Samatta JA (as he then was) laid down the law regarding the mandatory obligation for public authorities to give reasons for their decisions, and the consequences of such authorities failing to discharge the obligation. The learned judge stated, at p 222 of the ruling as follows:

> "It seems to me that the interests of justice call for the existence, in common law, of a general rule making it mandatory in matters of importance for public authorities, a term I use to include statutory and domestic bodies, to give reasons for their decisions. But what are E matters of importance? It is neither desirable nor possible to define that term, but certainly it should be taken to include all matters in which the liberty, livelihood or reputation of the individual is concerned or in which proprietary or pecuniary rights or F interests are at stake. In any other situation the decision-maker should be bound to give reasons only if he is requested by a party to do so".

The learned judge continued at p 223:

> "It is intolerable in a democratic society that the law should allow a decision maker … to make his decision without giving reasons why he has reached that decision".

At p 224 of the ruling the learned judge stated, further, as follows:

> "In my considered opinion, a duty to give reasons and a right to them should be recognized by our law and treated as being of decisive importance in administrative justice."

Honourable Vice-chairperson and members of the Board, in the appeal now before you the parties thereto are not in dispute on the facts relevant to the appeal. In Particular, the parties to the appeals are agreed that:

(1) On 5 January 2004 the appellant received from the respondent a Notice of Assessment of additional tax in relation to the appellant's year of Income ended on 31 December 2000. (Part of annex 3 to the Statement of Appeal).
(2) On 13 January 2004 the appellant lodged a Notice of Objection to the assessment (annex 5 to the Statement of Appeal) and simultaneously submitted a written request to the respondent for waiver of the requirement to pay one-third of the assessed tax pending final determination of the objection to the assessment (annex 4 to the Statement of Appeal).
(3) On 20 January 2004 the respondent under annex 1 to the Statement of Appeal informed the appellant that his request for the waiver had not been successful.
(4) In making and delivering his decision of 20 January 2004 to the appellant, the respondent did not give any reason (s) for his decision.

Therefore, in this appeal, there are three issues for the Board's determination, viz:

(1) Whether in making his decision on the request made to him by the appellant for waiver of the requirement to pay one-third of the assessed tax pending the final determination of the disputed assessment, the respondent was under obligation in law to give reasons for his decision.
(2) If he was so obliged, what are the consequences of his failure to do so?
(3) What reliefs the appellant entitled to.

The respondent's decision on the appellant's request for the waiver was communicated to the appellant through his tax consultant, Messrs Tax Professionals, on 20 January 2004 by letter of the same dated (annex 1 to the Statement of Appeal) signed by the Regional Revenue Officer, Ilala, on behalf of the respondent. It was as brief as it was arbitrary and, with due respect, arrogant. We quote it in extensor:

> "I refer to your letter of objection dated 13th January, 2004 and a further one of an even date addressed to the Commissioner for Income Tax to consider waiving the requirement to pay tax not in dispute in respect of the above named. I am directed to inform you that your request has not been successful. Please advise your client to pay one third of the tax assessed to facilitate the final determination of the assessment under dispute".

As stated hereinabove, the first issue for the Board's determination is whether in making his decision on the appellant's request for the waiver the respondent was under obligation in law to give reasons for his decision. It is the appellant's humble submission that the respondent was so obliged.

The test as to who in law is under a mandatory obligation to give reasons for decisions was categorically laid down in the *Tanzanair* case (supra), at p 222. All public authorities who make decisions in "Matters of importance", that is to say "matters in which the liberty, livelihood or reputation of the individual is concerned or in which proprietary or pecuniary rights or interests are at stake" have a mandatory obligation in law to give reasons for their decisions.

The respondent is the head of the Tanzania Revenue Authority (TRA), which is the public authority responsible for administration of the government's revenue regime. The matter on which the respondent was required to render a decision was a "matter of importance" in that it concerned the livelihood and pecuniary rights and interests of the appellant. The appellant was slapped with an assessment for additional tax in the amount of Tshs 14,272,366.00 for the year 2000 in respect of which he was aggrieved. The colossal amount of tax demanded concerned and affected not only the appellant's livelihood but also his business and, therefore, his pecuniary interests.

The appellant lodged an objection against the assessment but, so that he could be heard, he requested the respondent to waive the requirement to pay one-third of the assessed tax (that is, Tshs 4,757,455.30). If the respondent refused to grant the request for waiver, as he did, and the appellant failed to pay the one-third of the assessed tax, the respondent could take enforcement measures for recovery of the assessed tax. It cannot be overemphasized that such measures would severely and adversely affect the appellant's livelihood and pecuniary interests, especially given the magnitude of the claim.

In the *Tanzanair* case, (supra) the Labour Commissioner was requested to decide whether or not to confirm the order of the Conciliation Board of Dar es Salaam ordering the reinstatement of an employee to his employment with the applicant. The decision to be made by the Labour Commissioner affected the livelihood of the employee as it concerned his employment. It also affected the pecuniary interests of the applicant as it concerned its business. In the circumstances, the Labour Commissioner was adjudged by the court to be a public authority under a mandatory obligation to give reasons for his decision in the matter.

We humbly submit that, except for the fact that the respondent in this appeal was making a decision in a revenue rather than a labour matter, which distinction is of no legal consequence, the respondent in this appeal is in a similar position in which Samtta JK (as he then was) found the Labour Commissioner to have been in the *Tanzanair* case. Like the Labour Commissioner in the *Tanzanair* case the Commissioner General of the TRA, the respondent herein, was required to make a decision in a "matter of importance", in which the livelihood and pecuniary interest of the individual, the appellant herein, were at stake. Like the Labour Commissioner, the respondent herein was under a mandatory obligation to give reasons for his decision of 20 January 2004 refusing to grant the appellant's request for the waiver. That he did not do so is not in dispute.

The second issue is what, is the effect of the respondent's failure to give reasons for his decision.

Honourable Vice-chairperson and members of the Board, the effect of the respondent's failure to give reasons for his decision of 20 January 2004 is that it renders the said decision a nullity in law. In the Tanzanair case, cited supra the learned judge, having found that the Labour Commissioner had failed to give reasons for his decision in a matter of importance, had no hesitation in holding that "the Commissioner's failure to give reasons for his impugned decision is a serious irregularity which makes that decision a nullity in law" (p 223 of the ruling). In similar vein, we invite the Honourable Board to hold that the respondent's failure to give reasons for his decision of 20 January 2004 in a matter of importance rendered the decision a nullity in law, ab initio and forever.

The decision in the *Tanzanair* case was followed by this Honourable Board in *Nimrod E Mkono v Commissioner General* (supra), in which the facts and issues of law were on all fours with the facts and issues of law in this appeal, save for the appellants and the amount of tax assessed and objected to, which dissimilarities are irrelevant to the determination of the appeal before you.

In *Mkono* (supra), this Honourable Board held, (at p 22 of the judgment), that "the respondent had a legal obligation to give reasons for his refusal for waiver of one-third of the assessed tax", and that "with no reasons advanced by the respondent who was making an administrative decision then the decision is a nullity". In the premises, the respondent was ordered to admit and decide on the notice of objection raised by the appellant without payment of any deposit.

The third issue is to what relief the appellant is entitled. The appellant has prayed for orders setting aside the respondent's decision of 20 January 2004 and directing the respondent to waive the requirement upon the appellant to pay one-third of the tax assessed pending determination of the appellant's objection to the assessment.

We humbly submit that the reliefs sought by the appellant are, in the circumstances, the only just and efficacious ones. The Tanzania Revenue Authority Act, 1995 and the Tax Revenue Appeals Act, 2000 do not provide for review, revision of or reference from the respondent's decision refusing to grant a waiver under s 12 (3) of the Tax Revenue Appeals Act. Even if there were such provisions, given the arbitrariness and arrogance with which the respondent disposed of the appellant's request for waiver, it cannot be envisaged that the respondent would deal with the request with an impartial mind if the matter was referred back to him and, doing so, would not be in accord with the long-cherished principle that justice must no only be done, but also should be seen to be done. There is no other authority to which reference can be made of the respondent's decision. It is only this Honourable Board which can make just and effective orders in this matter and, in our humble opinion, the grant of the orders prayed for would be the most just and effective remedies in the circumstances of this appeal but, of course, this Honourable Board may make such other order (s) or grant such other relief (s) as it may deem fit. We, therefore, pray that as was the case in *Mkono* (supra), the respondent be ordered to admit and decide on the notice of objection raised by the appellant without payment of any deposit.

It is humbly submitted

Respondent's submission
(Pursuant to the order of the Board dated 11 January 2005)

Honourable Vice-chairperson and members of the Board, in the appeal before you, it is not in dispute that, the respondent issued a letter dated 20 January 2004 with ref. no. 30-1/01/03/80678B to the appellant, which informed him that his request for a waiver to deposit one-third of tax in dispute pending determination of his objection had not been successful.

Honourable Vice-chairperson and Members of the Board, the said letter dated 20 January 2004, is valid and competent under the law. The Tax Revenue Appeals Act hereinafter is clear on legal the requirement of depositing the tax.

Section 12 of the Act states as follows:

> "12. (1) Any person who disputes an assessment made upon him by the Commissioner-General may, by notice in writing to the Commissioner-General, object to the assessment.
>
> (2) Subject to subsection (3), where a notice of objection to an assessment is given, the person objecting shall pay the amount of tax which is not in dispute or deemed by subsection (6) of this section not to be in dispute, or pay one third of the assessed tax, whichever is greater, pending the final determination of the assessment.
>
> (3) Where a notice of objection is given under subsection (1), and the Commissioner-General is of the opinion that, owing to–
>
> (a) uncertainty as to any question of law or fact; or
> (b) considerations of hardship or equity; or
> (c) impossibility, or undue difficulty or expense, of recovery of tax,
>
> the person objecting the assessment is unable to pay the tax due and payable by him in accordance with the provisions of subsection (2), the Commissioner-General may allow the person objecting the assessment to pay the lesser amount as is reasonable in the circumstances, or not to pay tax until the assessment or liability to pay tax is finally determined".

Honourable Vice-chairperson and Members of the Board, the law states that unless the Commissioner General, forming the opinion as to the uncertainty to the question of law or fact, consideration of hardship or equity, or impossibility or undue difficulty or expense of recovery of the tax he may waive the requirement to pay tax prior to determination of the objecting payment of one third of the demanded tax is statutory requirement, the respondent under the law is not required to assign any reason for ordering the appellant to pay the same.

The respondent served the appellant with a notice of assessment. The appellant's letter requesting for waiver is the statutory requirement of paying one-third of the tax (annex E to the Statement of Appeal) did not explain the question of law surrounding the assessment to the respondent to consider waiving the statutory requirement. Whatever submission that was made by the appellant on the said matter of the law which the respondent refuted to exist, were made prior to the issuance of the notice of assessment.

No such submissions were made when the appellant stated the objection process to the respondent, that is, the Commissioner of Income Tax as shown on annex E to the Statement of Appeal.

The law does not require the Commissioner General to give any reason whatsoever, for any decision taken by him. It is only the duty of the appellant to satisfy the Commissioner General, in order to perform and assist the respondent to reach a decision.

There is no uncertainty as to the question of law or fact or consideration of hardship or equity, or impossibility or undue difficulty or expenses of recovery of tax, which can make the respondent to consider the request of waiver of payment of tax in terms of s 12 (3) of the Act, and to give reason for refusing to grant that request.

Honourable Vice Chairperson and Members of the Board, taxation legislations are to be strictly construed to give the words the sense in which they are ordinarily used. This means that in taxation you have to look simply at what is clearly stated in the law, there is no room for any intendment or presumptions as to tax. Nothing is to be implied, but you have to look fairly at what is said and what is clearly said, and that is the law.

The appellant has prayed for orders setting aside the respondent's decision of 20 January 2004 and directing the respondent to waive the requirement upon the appellant to pay one-third of the tax assessed pending determination of the appellant's objection to the assessment.

In his letter requesting for waiver of tax no good reason was given to the Commissioner General to satisfy him to exercise the discretion of waiving the one third tax stipulated under the law.

Therefore I pray to this Honourable Board to dismiss this appeal with cost.

It is humbly submitted.

Appellant's reply to the respondent's submissions
(Pursuant to the Order of the Board dated 11 January 2005)

Hounourable Vice-chairperson and members of the Board, having studied the respondent's submissions in reply we understand the respondent's case to be as follows:

(1) That "The law does not require for [sic] Commissioner General to give any reasons whatsoever, for any decision taken by him" (para 1, p 3 of the respondent's reply).
(2) That in his letter requesting for waiver the appellant did not give any good reason to satisfy the respondent to exercise his discretion to waive payment of one third of the tax assessed.

Honourable Vice-chairperson and members of the Board, the respondent, in A
para 1 on p 1 of his reply, admits to having made the decision on 20 January 2004 denying the appellant's request for waiver. What he does not add, but which he does not dispute either, is the fact that the respondent did not assign any reason for his decision.

The appellant contends and has submitted in his primary submissions that because of the respondent's failure to assign reasons for his decision, the said B
decision is in law a nullity and cannot stand. The respondent's answer, at para 1 p 3 of the reply, is that his decision of 20 January 2004 is valid because in his own words:

> "The law does not require for Commissioner General to give any reason whatsoever, for any decision taken by him".

C

But what is the law governing the respondent's decisions? According to the respondent, "The Law" as he defines it (para 2, p 1 of the reply) is "the Tax Revenue Appeals Act 2000 (No. 15 of 2000)". The respondent's concept of the law is clearly misconceived.

The term "Law" has been defined in *Black's Law Dictionary* (6th edn) at p 884, (copy attached) as follows: D

> "The 'law' of a state is to be found in its statutory and constitutional enactments, as interpreted by its courts, and in the absence of statute law, in ruling of its courts.
>
> Word 'Law' generally contemplates both statutory and case law".

True, the Tax Revenue Appeals Act is silent on the respondent's obligation to E
assign reasons for his decision. That does not mean that there is no law binding the respondent to give reasons for his decisions. Through judicial decisions the courts have developed law (case law) which binds the respondent to give reasons for certain decisions. That law was categorically laid down in the *Tanzanair* case cited in the appellant's primary submissions. At the risk of repetition, and for the sake of clarity, the law as laid down by Samatta JA (as he then was) is in summary F
as follows:

(a) Where public authorities make decisions on matters in which the liberty, livelihood or reputation of the individual is concerned or in which proprietary or pecuniary rights or interests are at stake it is mandatory for such authorities to give reasons for their decisions; G
(b) Where such authorities fail to give reasons for their decisions, such failure is a serious irregularity which makes the decision concerned a nullity in law.

As we amply demonstrated, we hope, in our primary submissions (pp 2 and 3) the request for waiver was a "matter of importance" as it concerned and affected the appellant's livelihood and pecuniary interests. In deciding on that "matter of H
importance" the respondent was in law, as laid down in the *Tanzanair* case, under a mandatory obligation to give reasons for his decision refusing to grant the request for waiver. That the respondent did not give reasons is not disputed. The consequences of the respondent's failure to discharge the mandatory obligation to give reasons is, quite clear; the decision is a nullity in law.

A The bold assertion by the respondent that the law does not require the respondent to give any reason whatsoever, for any decision taken by him is astounding. It smacks off and reflects the high handedness, arbitrariness and arrogance with which the respondent dealt with the appellant request for waiver as is evidenced by the respondent's curt and dismissive reply to the appellant that "your request has not been successful". Obviously, the respondent believes he is above the law. This
B Honourable Board which has powers to vary or set aside decisions of the respondent and make other orders it deems fit on appeal from decisions of the respondent is bound by law to give reasons for its decision; yet the respondent believes, and has the temerity to assert, that he is under no similar obligation to give reasons when making decisions over other person's "matter of importance" affecting such person's livelihood and proprietary rights or pecuniary interests.

C The respondent's other argument is that the appellant did not in his letter of request for waiver give "good reason" to satisfy the respondent so as to exercise his discretion to waive the requirement of payment of one-third of the assessed tax. In particular, it is contended that the appellant did not explain the question of law surrounding the assessment to the respondent and that whatever submissions were made on this matter by the appellant were made prior to the issuance of the
D notice of assessment.

Honourable Vice-chairperson and members of the board, this argument need not detain you, as it is misconceived and irrelevant to the appeal before you. For purposes of the appeal before you, whether the appellant had good reasons for requesting for the waiver and/or whether the respondent had any reason for not granting the waiver are irrelevant. This is not an appeal against the merits of the
E respondent's decision. It is an appeal against the respondent's failure to give reasons for his decision, irrespective of whether such decision had merit or not.

The appellant is simply saying:

(1) That he had a right in law to be given reasons by the respondent as to why the latter had refused to grant his request for waiver;
F (2) that the respondent had a mandatory obligation in law to give the reasons,
(3) that he failed to give the reasons; and
(4) that the failure rendered his decision a nullity in law.

In the premise, we reiterate our arguments in the primary submissions and pray to this Honourable Board to make the orders prayed for namely that:

G

(a) The respondent's decision contained in his letter ref: 30-1/01/03/1/90678 dated 20 January 2004 be overturned;
(b) The respondent be directed to admit and hear the appellant's objection without deposit of the tax assessed; and
(c) Any other directions/and orders as this Honourable Board may deem fit.

H

We humbly submit.

JUDGMENT

In the present appeal matter No. 7 of 2004 the appellant Dr Wilbert B. Kapinga is represented by Captain Kameja, learned counsel. In representing the appellant through the statement of appeal and written submission Captain Kameja explained that on 5 January 2004 the appellant received from the respondent a letter with ref. no. 30-1/01/03/1/90698 dated 31 December 2003 and with it was attached a notice of assessment dated 30 December 2003 for an amount of Tshs 14,272,366.00 purportedly being an additional tax assessment. On 13 January 2004, the respondent lodged a notice of objection as against the additional assessment and went further requesting for waiver of payment of one-third of the tax assessed pending the determination of the appellant's notice of objection. To this, on 20 January 2004 vide letter with ref. no. 30-1/01/03/1/906788 the respondent informed the appellant that his request for waiver of the requirement to pay one-third of the assessed tax had not been successful.

On the basis of this reply contained in the said letter the appellant had to rush and appeal to this Board as the reply (decision) was incompetent on the grounds that no grounds or reasons were given to support the decision.

Captain Kameja proceeded to state that the issue of or mandatory obligation for public authorities to give reasons for their decisions and such consequences of such authorities failing to discharge the obligation has long been determined in the case of *Tanzania Air Services Limited v Minister for Labour, Attorney General and Commissioner for Labour* (supra).

The learned counsel in supporting his argument depicted the following phrases from the said ruling "... It is intolerable in a democratic society that the law should allow a decision maker ... to make his decision without giving reasons why he has reached that decision" and "In my considered opinon a duty to give reasons and a right to them should be recognized by our law and treated as being of decisions importance in administrative justice".

According to Caption Kameja, the respondent was a public authority making decisions in "matter of importance" of which as per the cited case these involve matters of liberty, livelihood or repartition of the individual or proprietary or preliminary rights when they are at stake. Going by law, even in this appeal the respondent as the head of Tanzania Revenue Authority was making a decision on a "matter of importance" in which the livelihood and pecuniary rights and interest of the appellant were at stake. The effect of making a decision which contained no decision is that the respondent was acting with arrogance and arbitrariness and was thus a nullity in law. To this end Captain Kameja cited *Nimrod E Mkono v Commissioner General* (supra), in which this Honourable Board had decided on a similar issue containing the same facts.

In conclusion, Captain Kameja prayed that the Board should find the decision a nullity with the consequences being that the appellant's objection be heard and determined without depositing any payment.

On the other side Mr Mkwawa legal officer for the respondent Commissioner General, admitted in both the reply and in his submission that it is true the respondent issued the letter dated 25 January 2004 with ref. no. 30-1/01/03/90678B to the appellant which was informing him of the unsuccessful request for waiver of depositing one-third of the tax assessed. According to Mr Mkwawa the said letter was well within the ambit of s 12 of the Tax Revenue Appeals Act.

Still urging basing on the same section but under s 12 (3) Mr Mkwawa stated that the respondent had found no uncertainty as to law or fact or consideration of hardship or equity, or impossibility or undue difficulty or expenses of recovery of tax, which could make the respondent consider the request of waiver of payment.

In short as the matter stood there was no good reason given to the respondent to warrant him to exercise his discretion of waiver in respect of the appellant's request.

To cap it the entire respondent's counsel urged that all in all, the respondent under the law has no legal obligation of giving reasons to the decisions he makes.

In making our decision we have observed that the letter dated 31 December 2003 with ref. no. 30-1/01/03/1/90698, written by the respondent and addressed to the appellant does not given reason for the refusal of granting waiver to the appellant but it simply states that the request had not been successful.

We have also observed that the matter before the respondent was a matter of importance as it was to affect the livelihood and pecuniary interests of the appellant.

From the above, we find that the decision in the case of *Tanzania Air Services Limited v Minister for Labour, Attorney General and Commissioner for Labour* (supra), which binds us is of great relevance. Although a labour case, it was talking of a Government Authority like the respondent and laying down a legal authority that while making decisions the relevant Authority should give reasons why he/she has reached that decision.

As found by Samatta JA (as he then was) in the above-cited case of which is also our finding, we are now living in a fast-growing democratic society of which matters of administration of justice are very touchy to an individual. As a result those in the decision-making positions should be very careful and the only way to do this is to give reasons for the decisions they make.

We find it very absurd at this point in time or history to hear the respondent arrogantly stating that the law does not allow him to give reasons to his decisions. Letting this to proceed would be dangerous to the course of administrative justice.

From the foregoing we find that the decision by the respondent vide his letter had no reasons and as we have already valuated this issue his decision was a nullity. He was duty-bound upon refusal for waiver of one-third of the assessed tax to give reasons. It follows that by this decision we accordingly order the respondent to proceed with the determination of the appellant's objection without payment of any amount of money as deposit. The appeal is hereby upheld and each party to bear its own costs.

Right of appeal explained.

Read this 27 January 2005 in presence of Captain Kameja for the appellant and in absence of respondent duly notified.

MR ELIEZA KISIMBO, MS FATUMA RAMADHANI, MR ATHUMANI SAID v COMMISSIONER GENERAL

TAX REVENUE APPEALS BOARD

DAR ES SALAAM

(CONSOLIDATED INCOME TAX APPEAL: CASES NO. DSM 8 OF 2004; 62 OF 2003 AND 11 OF 2004)

11 May 2005

RKB Meela, *Chairperson*, J I Dallushi, *Members*

Employment—Income—Terminal benefits—Taxation principles applicable—Income Tax Act, 1973

Employment—Income—Employee Awards—Long service awards and golden handshake upon retrenchment—Limitation period for assessment of income tax on them—Income Tax Act, 1973, s 5 (2) (a) proviso (2), s 85 (1), and First Schedule para 9A

All the three consolidated appeals were on the taxing of employment terminal benefits by the respondent. The first appellant, Elieza Kisimbo, an ex-employee of TIPER upon being retrenched was awarded a lump-sum terminal benefit of Tshs 13,771,756 on which the respondent assessed a tax of Tshs 3,208,130. The second appellant Athumani Said an ex-employee of the Parastatal Pensions Fund (PPF) was awarded Tshs 52,829,200 which was taxed at 16,051,485. The third appellant Fatuma Ramadhani was awarded Tshs 43,494,000, taxed at Tshs 13,048,272. The appellants considered the taxed amounts as excessive and covering items, which ought not to be taxed.

Held:

(1) When dealing with taxation of an employee's terminal benefits, a balance should be struck by ensuring that exemptions are granted to ensure that such income is not eroded by strict interpretation of the law.

(2) Long service awards and golden handshake are payments in consideration of past service and not compensation for termination of a contract of service.

(3) Long service awards and golden handshake are at par with gratuitous payments under proviso (2) to s 5 (2) (*a*) subject to limitation under s 85 (1) and the partial exemption under para 9A in the First Schedule to the Income Tax Act, 1973

(4) Since the Group Endowment Assurance Scheme was not approved by the Commissioner, proceeds therefrom should be treated as gratuitous payments.

Appeals allowed.

Mr F Busigara, for the appellants

Mrs S Salim, for the respondent.

21 February 2005:

Chairperson: The Parties are addressed as per the observation of this Board as hereunder contained. The respondent's counsel, Mrs Salim is asked her opinion as regards the Preliminary Notices of Objection as filed in the Income Tax Appeals Nos. 8 of 2004 and No. 62 of 2003.

The Board Members, upon meeting in the Chairperson's Chambers on the day scheduled for commencing the hearing of Income Tax Appeals No. 8 of 2004, Mr Elieza Kisimbo (appellant) and the Commissioner General (respondent) and Appeal No. 62 of 2003 Mr Athuman Saidi and the Commissioner General (respondent) made the following considered observations:

> "We are of the considered opinion that the Notices of Objection proposed to be raised by the respondent if they are based on the non-attachment of the decisions by the Commissioner General for the notices of objection filed by each respective appellant in Income Tax Appeals No. 8 of 2004 and No. 62 of 2003, as required under rule 7 (2) of the Tax Revenue Appeals Board Rules, 2001 (GN No. 57/2001); then such objections are superfluous, this is mainly on the reason that the appellant tax consultant has informed this Board that the Commissioner General never issued the appellant the said decisions as required under subs (4) of s 13 of the Tax Revenue Appeals Act.
>
> According to the Statement of Appeal, the appellant assumes that since the respondent acted on the appellant's notice of objection and made a partial refund, he/she acted on the appellant's Notice of Objection; and since the appellant was not satisfied, he had to file a notice of Appeal to this Board and thus here we are to hear him.
>
> Therefore, the Notices of Preliminary Objection, if the same are based on the fact that there is no proper decision of the respondent, the said preliminary objection should be disallowed, and the respondent should be called upon to produce the said decisions now not formally annexed to the Statements of Appeal in the two appeals, showing how the respondent dealt with the notices of objection as filed by the two appellants severally, and eventually made them the refund as he did."

Mrs Salim, for the respondent: Honourable Members of the Board, I have heard and considered the observations of the Board and I am of the opinion that the preliminary objections raised by the respondent may be dropped or may not be entertained. This is because the respondent did not issue to the appellants the necessary documents which were supposed to be attached to the appellants' Statements of Appeal.

I request that the respondent be given time to issue to each of the appellants the said documents before the commencement of the hearing of the respective appeals.

That is all, Your Honour.

Mr Busigara, for the appellant: Honourable Chairperson, I agree to the request by the respondent's counsel to provide the appellants with documents supposed to have been filed with the Statement of Appeal to be allowed.

Board: The prayer by the respondent's counsel is allowed on the following conditions.

(1) The respondents' counsel is to file the respondent's reply to Appeal No.11 of 2004 and serve the appellants' representative as soon as possible before the Hearing on 23 February 2005.
(2) The respondent's counsel is to file to the Board the decisions of the Commissioner General giving rise to the present three Appeals.

Order: The hearing of the three appeals is to be consolidated on 23 February 2005.

23 February 2005:

Board: As earlier proposed during the previous adjournment, there are three appeals to be consolidated for the purpose of hearing and they are Appeal No. 8 of 2004, Elieza Kisimbo v Commissioner General, Appeal No. 11 of 2004, Ms Fatuma Ramadhani v Commissioner General, and Appeal No. 63 of 2003, Athmani Saidi v Commissioner General. These three appeals are hereby consolidated to be heard together unless there is a fresh objection to the contrary.

Mr Busigara, for the appellant: I confirm that I received most of the documents except that I did not get a decision in respect of Athmani Saidi's appeal.

Mr Busigara: I pray to make an addition that I did not get a decision in the form of the computations on the tax assessment.

Mr Shigela, for the respondent: Honourable members of the Board, it is true that the appellant was not served with the computation in the appellant's case, Athmani Saidi, but was based on the decision of the Commissioner General based on the legal principles upon which the refund was made to the appellant. However, he was as well served with the refund analysis or breakdown on which the refund was made to Athmani Saidi, the appellant.

In our view, the decision of the Commissioner General was given basing on the legal principles that could easily guide the appellant's tax consultant to cross check as to whether the Commissioner General did make a correct refund. In so doing, Honourable Members of the Board, we were forced by the circumstances that the matter was determined long ago as the computations in the appellant case could not be easily traced due to the backlog of the documents involved.

However, it is our belief that this fact cannot prejudice the appellant's tax consultant, as submitted above that he can adopt the decision of the respondent basing on the legal principles served on him. It is our belief that the issue of computations cannot bar him from cross checking as to whether the refund made to the appellant by the respondent was correct.

We so submit.

Mr Busigara: Honourable Chairperson, as I have already said, I have made a written submission in which I am making a number of comments, some of which touch on what has been explained by the respondent's counsel. For that reason, I pray that I be allowed to present a submission on the first aspect.

A Secondly, I would request that the allegation made by the respondent's counsel that there was a decision made by the Commissioner General based on the legal principles be proved.

That is all.

Board: The counter replies for the three appeals are formally filed and the
B respondent's counsel served.

The second observation would be taken care of by the respondent's counsel when making reply submissions to the appellants' submissions in chief later to be advanced before this Board. We can now start to hear the appellant's tax consultant's submissions in chief upon going through the preliminaries.

C *Appellants' submissions in chief*

Mr Busigara, for the appellant: Honourable Chairperson, having agreed that we present the issues jointly, I would like to highlight the common issues: the modality of taxing, long service award, the golden handshake, and the employer's contribution to the Group Endowment Assurance Scheme. The respondent wishes
D to tax the golden handshake as a payment for loss of office under s 5 (2) (c) of the Income Tax Act, under proviso (ii) instead of applying s 5 (2) (a) proviso (ii) because employment income is assessable as income of the year in which the services are rendered.

The golden handshake was paid in relation to past services and cannot therefore be taxed as though it were paid in respect of the unexpired period to which
E s 5 (2) (*c*) proviso (ii) applies.

We advance the same arguments in relation to the long service award. We also submit that these payments are entitled to a partial exemption granted under para 9A of the First Schedule to the repealed Income Tax Act.

We further submit that where such payments are allocated to the years of income which expired more than five years from the year of receipt, they should
F be taxed with reference to the limitation provided for under s 85 (1) of the Income Tax Act, now repealed.

We also submit that the provisions of s 85 (1) and proviso (*b*) to that section are inapplicable to such cases; otherwise, it will re-open time barred assessments in the case of employment income. We have in the written reply demonstrated the effect of doing so.

G The other general point regarding the tax treatment given by the respondent to contributions made in respect of years of income which had become time barred by the time assessments made were issued. It is the appellants' submissions that contributions should be deemed received in the year of contribution and be accordingly assessed. In this case, it was improper for the respondent to apply the provisions of s 85 (1) proviso (*b*) and assess contributions basing the time
H limitation of three years from the years of income 2001 as if those contributions were received in that year of income.

I think those are the common issues involved in the three appeals, and I submit that the respondent's decision dealing with those issues should be reversed, and the orders prayed for in the separate appeals be granted by this Honourable Board.

In the case of Ms Fatuma Ramadhani, I suspect that it could be the same with the case of Athmani Saidi because I did not get the respondent's computations in the Athmani Saidi's case. The respondent has taxed house allowance paid to Ms Fatuma Ramadhani, contrary to s 5 (2) (*a*) proviso (IV) of the Income Tax Act. We submit that it is illegal and that the respondent's decision should be reversed. A

That is all, Honourable Chairperson.

B

Mr Shigela, for the respondent: Honourable members of the Board, I pray to make some remarks if it pleases the Honourable Board. We pray that the matter be adjourned so as to enable us to prepare a reply to the submissions made by the appellants' tax consultant. I further pray that as I am engaged in three criminal matters in which I am the prosecutor for tomorrow and the day after tomorrow, I propose that the hearing of the respondent's replies be heard next Monday. C

That is all, Your Honours.

Mr Busigara: Honourable members of the Board, I have no objection provided that the Appeal cases finish on 1 March 2005 as I have other engagements earlier fixed. D

Board: The respondent will make reply submissions tomorrow Thursday 24 February 2005 at 11:00 am, as consented to by the respondent's counsel and sanctioned by the Board.

24 February 2005: E

Respondent's reply submissions

Mrs Salim, for the respondent: Honourable members of the Board, the respondent wishes to make a reply to the appellant's submissions on the three general issues raised, namely: long service award, golden handshake and the employer's contributions to the Group Endowment Assurance Scheme. F

We will also make a reply to the appellant's submission on the specific issue of taxation of house allowance for Fatuma Ramadhani.

I start with the issue of the Long Service Award. As far as this issue is concerned, we submit that this is not applicable in the three appeals present before this Board, as none of the appellants was paid long service award at the termination of the contract of employment. The respondent wishes to submit in evidence Form IT 390 for Elieza Kisimbo and Fatuma Ramadhani, PPF letter no. PPR/PF/20/C of 1 October 2000 that is the retrenchment letter of Athmani Saidi, to prove the foregone submission. G

Chairperson: Received as exhibits are photocopies of four documents. H

- RE 1 Notification for Fatuma Ramadhani of lump sum payment;
- RE 2 Benefits from PPF following termination of service;
- RE 3 "Kupunguzwa Kazi"—termination letter for Athmani Saidi, and
- RE4 Notification of lump sum payment IT 390 for Elieza Kisimbo.

A Mrs Salim: [Continues] However, one of the appellants, Athmani Saidi, was paid a retirement award which the respondent taxed under s 5 (2) (*c*) (iii) of the Income Tax Act because it was paid as compensation for termination of contract. The appellant's tax consultant did not dispute this tax treatment.

In the alternative, we submit that the respondent treated the long service award as a gratuity taxable in the year of receipt under s 5 (2) (*a*) of the Income Tax Act, B read together with para 9A of the First Schedule to the same Act as requested by the appellant. However, the respondent declined to apply proviso (ii) of s 5 (2) (*a*) of the Income Tax Act, because no evidence was submitted to him to prove that the regulation providing for such payment was properly implemented, and what was the appellant's basic salary at the time the payments were due and payable as per the Regulations.

C The second issue of the golden handshake was raised in the case of Elieza Kisimbo only. However, it is evident in the records that there was no dispute regarding the issue of the golden handshake at the level of the notice of objection. It is evident in the notice of objection the appellant lodged to the respondent on 16 August 2002, which is app 1 of the Statement of Appeal. Note of discussion containing the discussion between the appellant tax consultant and the respon- D dent's officers dated 8 May 2003, which is now annex TRA 1 in the respondent's reply to Appeal No. 11 of 2004 of Fatuma Ramadhani and the appellant's tax consultant's letter confirming the existence of the discussion, are also found in this annex, that the disputed issues raised by the appellants tax consultant were taxation of the Group Endowment Assurance Scheme, the taxation of the Long Service Award and the time limit for making assessments under s 85 of the E Income Tax Act.

According to the tax consultant's letter and the note of discussion referred to in the foregoing submissions, the parties agreed on the taxation treatment of Group Endowment Assurance Scheme benefits and that the Long Service Award be treated as gratuity taxable under s 5 (2) (*a*), read together with para 9A of the First Schedule to the Income Tax Act.

F The non-agreed issues were the application of proviso (ii) of s 5 (2) (*a*) of the Income Tax Act in taxing long service award and time limit for issuing assessments under s 85 (1) of the Income Tax Act. These facts prove that taxation of the golden handshake was not disputed by the appellant at the level of the objection and at the time of the discussion held by the parties.

The refund made by the respondent to the appellants was based on the G agreement reached on the discussion, whereby the appellant's tax consultant was satisfied with the resolutions made in those discussions. The appellant's tax consultant confirmed through his letter referred in the foregoing submissions that he was going to appeal on the two non-agreed issues. It is therefore, the respondent's submission that this Honourable Board should not consider this issue for the reasons submitted above.

H In the alternative and without prejudice to the respondent, treating the golden handshake as retrenchment benefit taxable under s 5 (2) (*c*) (iii) of the Income Tax Act was spread forward as prescribed in this provision because it is a payment for compensation for termination of employment contract. Such payment has no relationship to the past service as alleged by the appellant's tax consultant. This payment cannot be treated as gratuity taxable under s 5 (2) (*a*) (ii)

of the Income Tax Act, read together with para 9A of the First Schedule to this A
same Act, as there is no contract between the appellant and his employer that provides for specific duration of time and compensation payable on termination of such contract.

We also submit that there is no evidence submitted to the respondent and to this Honourable Board to prove that the said payment is taxable under s 5 (2) (*a*) (ii)
of the Income Tax Act. It is therefore the respondent's submission that the partial B
exemption provided for under para 9A of the First Schedule does not apply to the golden handshake paid to the appellant, as the same is not gratuity, and it was paid out of contract of unspecified term which does not amount to compensation on termination.

The third issue is Group Endowment Assurance Scheme. This is the only issue
which is common in all the three appeals. However, the appellants' tax consultant C
did not make any submissions in relation to this particular issue, save for the submission made on the limitation of time under s 85 (1) of the Income Tax Act, whose reply would be made separately. It follows therefore that the appellants' representative is barred from making fresh submissions on which the respondent would not have chance to respond to.

I request that Mr Lukoo should make an alternative submission to this issue. D

[Chairperson: Mr Lukoo is permitted to proceed with the respondent's reply].

Mr Lukoo: [Continuing the reply] Honourable Chairperson, for the two PPF employees, that is Fatuma Ramadhani and Athmani Saidi, PPF had a scheme
operated under the National Insurance Corporation. The PPF was contributing E
100% of the premium determined by the National Insurance Corporation (NIC) towards the scheme. This scheme operated for three years only, and after that PPF decided to withdraw. After the withdrawal, PPF decided to pay the benefits to its employees, but no special fund was set aside for the obligation. The amount was provided from the yearly budget of terminal benefits. The respondent knowing
that there were no special funds set aside, taxed the benefits as terminal benefits, F
rather than endowment scheme benefits.

These benefits are after the withdrawal, after the surrender values of the three years premiums were paid, the respondent did not tax these benefits because they were already surrender value. I have got the letter of withdrawal which is annex TRA 2; letter with ref. no. PPF/DF/54/108 dated 28 August 2001. [Appeal No. 11
of 2004]. G

That is all, Your Honour, on this issue.

Mrs Salim: [continues]: The respondent, in taxing the benefits replied to by Mr Lukoo, applied s 5 (2) (*c*) (iii) of the Income Tax Act.

I pray now to proceed with the issue of the application of s 85 (1) of the
Income Tax Act. As regards this issue, we submit that the legal provision H
applicable in the determination of time available for making tax assessments is s 85 of the Income Tax Act. We further submit that the provisions of s 85 do not make any reference specific to the provisions of s 5 which deals with taxation of employment income. It rather sets limits of time for making assessment in relation to all gains and profits from employment or service rendered, that are

taxable under the Act, without taking an account the specific types of gains or profits outlined under s 5 of the Income Tax Act.

The appellants' submissions that payments received by the appellants were allocated to the years of income expiring earlier than five years from the years of receipt, and therefore the provisions of s 85 (1) proviso (*b*) of the Income Tax Act, are not applicable, is wrong in law. We submit that s 85 (1) proviso (*b*) is the only relevant legal provision in determining time limit for making assessment in relation to any gains or profits from employment or service referred, and that commencement of time limit should start in the year of income in which the gains or profits are received.

Such counting goes forward and not backwards as alleged by the appellants' tax consultant.

It is therefore the respondent's submission that the assessments were made within the time prescribed under the law, that is s 85 (1) proviso (*b*) as amended by the Finance Act, 2000.

In the case of the PPF employees, the employer taxed the payments without notifying the respondent and therefore no original assessments were made by the respondent, and that the respondent just re-computed the amount when the appellants asked for refund. Therefore, the issue of time limit for employees of PPF is not applicable.

Now we move to the last issue which is the taxing of house allowance to Fatuma Ramadhani. We submit that this is a completely new issue that is raised for the first time before this Board, and the respondent did not make any determination on it. That may be the subject of review by this Honourable Board.

Honourable Chairperson and members of the Board, in view of what we have submitted, the respondent's taxation treatment of the disputed items was made in accordance with the law. We therefore pray that the appeals be dismissed with costs.

That is all, Your Honours.

Mr Busigara, for the appellant: Your Honours, I pray for an adjournment to marshal our rejoinder submissions. I pray that we start at 11.00 am tomorrow.

Order: (Board): The prayer for adjournment is granted. Counter reply or rejoinder submissions scheduled for tomorrow, Friday the 25 February 2005 at 11.00 am in as prayed for by the appellant's representative, Mr Busigara.

25 February 2005:

Rejoinder submissions by the appellants

Mr Busigara, for the applicant: Honourable Members of the Board, I pray to make rejoinder submissions to the respondent counsel's reply submission. For the record, I want that the following be noted:

(i) This is a consolidated rejoinder in respect of Appeal Case No. 8 of 2003, Mr Elieza Kisimbo, Appeal No.11 of 2004, Mrs. Fatuma Ramadhani and Appeal No. 62 of 2003, Mr Athumani Saidi.

(ii) That the Honourable Board allow written submissions to be submitted in respect of the said three appeals in addition to oral submissions related to the common issue concerning the modality of taxing the following items: A

- the long service award;
- the employer's contributions made to the Group Endowment Assurance Scheme; and B
- the housing allowance payment taxed on Ms. Fatuma Ramadhani of PPF and probably on Mr Athumani Saidi, whose tax computation could not be traced by the respondent.

It is therefore the appellants' understanding that the written counter reply duly admitted in respect of each individual appellant would form the basis of this C Honourable Board's orders as prayed.

I having said so, let me now respond to the respondent's submissions.

Concerning the long service award for Mr Athman Saidi of PPF, he received a retirement award in appreciation of his long service with the PPF and perhaps it would have been appropriate to discuss this item under the heading "Long Service and Retirement Award". If possible, the item could be amended D accordingly and be decided by the Honourable Board in the light of para 3.2 of the Statement of Appeal in Appeal No. 62 of 2003 and cl 3.12 (ii) of annex VIII appended thereto.

The respondent has in their submissions confirmed that the Retirement Award was taxed under s 5 (2) (*c*) proviso (iii) of the Income Tax Act. We submit that this is illegal, because retirement awards are not payable as compensation for E termination of contract, but are payable as a token of appreciation of the employee's long service by the employer. The Honourable Board is kindly requested to compare and contrast the case of Mr Athmani Said who retired (Appeal No. 62 of 2003) and of Ms Fatuma Ramadhani (Appeal No. 8 of 2004), whose services were terminated.

In the alternative, the respondent has submitted that they taxed the long service F award as gratuity taxable in the year of receipt under s 5 (2) (*a*) of the Income Tax Act, read together with para 9 (A) of the First Schedule to the same Act as requested by the appellant. The appellant wishes to dissociate himself from the allegation, because the appellant consistently maintained that the retirement and Long Service Awards are gratuitous payments which fall to be taxed under s 5 (2) (*a*) proviso (ii), read with s 85 (1) and para (A) of the First Schedule to the G Income Tax Act.

The appellants' submission that the respondent failed to apply s 5 (2) (*a*) proviso (ii) of the Income Tax Act, because the appellant did not submit evidence to prove that the regulation providing for such payment was properly implemented is not clear, because it does not specify the applicable regulation.

As for the golden handshake, I agree with the respondent's submission that the H question of improper taxation of this golden handshake was not made reference in the appellant's notice of objection. However, the circumstances under which this happened are fully explained in the appellant's submission in chief and this is why the Board ordered the respondent to serve these respondent's decisions to the appellant during the course of this hearing before this Board.

A Actually, the respondent initially acted contrary to s 84 of the Income Tax Act, and subsequently to s 13 (2) or (4) of the Tax Revenue Appeals Act. The Honourable Board has been requested to make appropriate orders regarding non compliance or omission.

The respondent should be barred by this Honourable Board from making this to be an issue as it was entirely of his own making.

B The improper taxation of the golden handshake was raised immediately after the appellant's tax consultant discovered that it was taxed under s 5 (2) (*a*) proviso (iii), through subsequent meetings and correspondences. The basis of the payment of the golden handshake was disclosed in the statement submitted by the appellant that it was one month's salary for each year of service. Reference to IT 390 tendered by the respondent as exh RE 4 shows that the golden handshake
C paid to the appellant, Elieza Kisimbo, was a Tshs 3,704,100 which is equal to 20 years times his monthly salary. Those figures are shown in forms which were in IT 390 already explained above. This confirms that the golden handshake was paid in respect of past years, which makes it liable to tax in accordance with the proviso of s 5 (2) (*a*) proviso (ii) of the Income Tax Act, subject to s 85 (1) and the partial exemption granted to gratuity payment under para 9 (A) of the First
D Schedule of the Income Tax Act.

It may be well for the Honourable Board to note that the word gratuity is used in the Act without being defined. It therefore assumes its ordinary dictionary meaning which according to the *Collins Pocket Dictionary* means a gift of money or gift of money especially the one given for a service rendered, or tip. So the golden handshake is a gift of money and qualifies for partial exemption under
E para 9 (A) of the First Schedule to the Income Tax Act.

Now we move to the Group Endowment Assurance Scheme. Annexure TRA 1 is evidence that proves that it was unanimously agreed between the respondent and the appellant not to tax Group Endowment Assurance Scheme benefits; this is therefore an agreed item. The question which has not been agreed upon, and which is not a common issue, is whether the Group Endowment Assurance
F Scheme previously operated for the PPF by the National Insurance Corporation of Tanzania, ceased to exist after it was withdrawn from the National Insurance Corporation by the PPF. We have adequately covered this point in the written replies made in respect of the individual appeals for the two ex PPF employees namely Mr Athmani Saidi and Ms. Fatuma Ramadhani; and the question of being barred from raising this point fails to rise.

G The next item is the application of s 85 (1) proviso (*b*) of the Income Tax Act. the appellant is still of the opinion that s 85 (1) proviso (*b*) of the said Act only applies to employment income which is not deemed to relate to a year of income different from the year of income in which it was paid. We have demonstrated in the written replies in Appeal No. 62 of 2003 the effects of not making this distinction. However, we leave it to the Honourable Board to
H decide.

Next follows the taxation of employer's contribution to the Group Endowment Assurance Scheme. The respondent did not respond to this point, and the appellants assume that the employer's contribution to assurance scheme actually contributed during the years of income which were time barred when assessments were made could not be taxed.

The next item is the house allowance. The taxation of this item was raised during the hearing of the Appeals, because the appellant was without tax computation until on 22 February 2005 following the Board's orders. It was therefore impossible for the appellants to have raised this point earlier than now and would pray the Honourable Board, the matter be included in the deliberations and be decided upon accordingly. This prayer is being made on the understanding that after this hearing the appellant would be barred from raising this issue, as afterwards the assessment would become final.

It is evident from Form IT 390 tendered as exhibit RE1 by the respondent that Ms Fatuma Ramadhani was paid house allowance Tshs 600,000 during the first half of year of income 2000 which was taxed by the respondent, contrary to s 5 (2) (*a*) proviso (iv) of the Income Tax Act.

[Mrs Salim: We are objecting as the appellant is submitting on a point or item which was not raised before the respondent when the notice of objection was raised or filed.]

Mr Busigara: The item objected to by Mrs. Salim can be excluded from my rejoinder submissions.

We submit that the three Appeals be upheld by this Board. We thank the Honourable Board for its attention.

Board order: We are through with the hearing of the three Appeals, and thereafter the Honourable Members will deliberate on the proceedings, have the judgment composed by the Chairperson and accordingly delivered when ready.

Deliberations by the Board Members will be on Monday 28 Feberuary 2005.

Judgment will be on Tuesday, 8 March 2005 at 2.30 pm.

8 March 2005:

Chairperson: I have not written the judgment due to work pressure, and for that reason, I formed the opinion that it is prudent to inform the parties that the judgment is not due for delivery today as scheduled.

Order: Judgment will be on Friday the 18 March 2005. All Parties have been duly notified.

Board: The judgment is not yet completely composed due to work pressure and the same is briefly adjourned up to Friday this week, the 6 May 2005 at 2.30 pm. Any inconvenience caused to the Parties is highly regretted.

JUDGMENT

(Delivered 11 May 2005)

This is a judgment in respect of three consolidated income tax appeal No. 11 of 2004, wherein the appellant is Ms Fatuma Ramadhani, appeal No. 62 of 2003, the appellant is one Mr Athumani Saidi, and Appeal No. 8 of 2004 wherein the appellant is one Mr Elieza Kisimbo. The respondent in all the three appeals is the Commissioner General of the Tanzania Revenue Authority (TRA). The three appeals were consolidated for the purposes of hearing and disposal thereof, on the main reason that they are all concerned with the legal provisions of the Income Tax Act, on the principles of taxing employment income. This legal fact was accepted by the three appellants' representative Mr Busigara, a tax consultant and the respondent's representatives Mrs M Salim and Mr Shigela both learned counsels. In fact all the three appeals concern the taxing of employment terminal benefits of the three appellants by the respondent's Employment Tax Region, Dar es Salaam.

According to the filed appeal No. 8 of 2004, the Statement of Appeal shows that Mr Elieza Kisimbo is an ex-employee of TIPER who upon being retrenched, was awarded lumpsum terminal benefits variously sourced amounting to Tshs 13,771,756 on which the respondent tax authority charged a tax amounting to Tshs 3,208,130. Mr Busigara in terms of s 19 (1) of the Tax Revenue Appeals Act served a notice to this Board to the effect that together with Mr Elieza Kisimbo a listed number of 33 ex-employees of TIPER had their respective terminal benefits taxed on the same principle and for that reason any decision affecting the taxing of Mr Elieza Kisimbo also affected those employees, and for that reason any relief granted by this Board should also be granted to them.

Moreover, as regard Appeal No. 62 of 2004 Mr Athumani Said, appellant, it is claimed by the appellant in the Statement of Facts, the appellant's gross terminal benefits paid to him by his former employer, the Parastatal Pensions Fund (PPF) was Tshs 52,829,200 out of which the respondent charged tax totaling Tshs 16,051,485. And the appellant Mr Athumani Said being aggrieved by the amount of tax charged raised an objection as he felt that the charged tax was excessive, for the appellant was neither served with any tax assessments nor any computation showing how the respondent had arrived at the charged tax.

Mr Athumani Said further claimed that the respondent had not specifically responded to his notice of objection, but the respondent did exchange a number of correspondences with the appellant and eventually refunded him Tshs 4,076,025 but never gave any reason as to why the respondent did not refund the appellant the claimed sum of Tshs 12,918,000.20. Accordingly, this appeal is a result of the appellant being aggrieved by the respondent's decision of not refunding him his total claim.

In the reasons in support of Appeal No. 62 of 2003, Mr Athumani Said, the appellant gives three main reasons as to why he is aggrieved by the respondent Commissioner General's failure to:

(1) Make full refund to the appellant without the respondent assigning any reason thereof contrary to s 13 (2) (*b*) of the Tax Revenue Appeals Act. 2000;
(2) To amend the assessment in the light of this appellant objections; and also the failure of setting out such amendment and serving a notice thereof to the appellant contrary to the law—that is the Tax Revenue Appeals Act;
(3) In the absence of any notice from the respondent served on appellant as to how the respondent treated the appellant's notice of objection, the appellant assumed that the respondents applied wrong taxation principles in taxing his employment income.

In the third appeal which is Appeal No. 11 of 2004 Ms Fatuma Ramadhani, the appellant and the Commissioner General, the respondent, the appellant was also aggrieved by the respondent's taxation of her employment's terminal benefits in the same principles as the other appellants in three consolidated appeals. The appellant Ms Fatuma Ramadhani, an ex-PPF employee, upon the termination of her services on 20 June 2000, was paid terminal benefits totalling Tshs 43,494,000 of which the respondent charged a tax of Tshs 13,048,272. That the appellant suspected that the respondent had taxed endowment benefits of Tshs 29,836,590, which the appellant was of the opinion, was net of tax; the appellant lodged a notice of objection demanding a refund of Tshs 13,117,512 which was over charged.

According to the Statement of Facts, the respondent only refunded the appellant Tshs 5,075,990 instead of the claimed refund of Tshs 13,117,152. The appellant being aggrieved by the respondent's decision of effecting partial refund lodged the present appeal in this Board. The appellant was aggrieved by the respondent's decision on the following grounds.

As the refundable sum was only Tshs 5,076,990 instead of Tshs 13,117,152 the appellant presumed that the respondent believed the benefits paid out of the Group Endowment Assurance scheme are taxable, a belief which is wrong. The appellant submits that the respondent could only have charged tax on the premium paid by the employer in accordance with s 5 (2) (*f*) of the Income Tax Act.

In Appeal No. 11 of 2004, the appellant, Ms Fatuma Ramadhani, prays this Board to uphold this appeal and order the respondent not to tax the Group Endowment Assurance Scheme benefits and the respondent to effect correct refund to the appellant.

In each of the three appeals, the respondent filed replies to each of the appellant's statement of appeal. In respect of Appeal No. 8 of 2004 of Mr Elieza Kisimbo the respondent's reply is as follows:

> "1. The first ground is contested. The respondent states that the amount of tax refund of Tshs 829, 822 paid to the appellant was the correct amount refundable to him.
>
> 2. The second ground of the appeals is contested. The respondent states that the tax refund was effected after they had discussed and agreed with the appellant's tax consultant on the tax treatment of the disputed items namely group endowment assurance scheme, payment for compensation for loss of office, long service award cash in lieu of leave, cash in lieu of gas/electric cooker, one way transport and workers' terminal benefits. The said agreement is contained in the respondent's letter No. 30/30-1/01/07/6/16/ ELK dated 28 January 2003, now appended to the statement of reply and marked TRA 1.
>
> 3. The respondent also contests the third ground of appeal. The respondent states that the appellant's terminal benefits were properly taxed and in accordance with the law. That the contents of the third ground of appeal are based on assumptions which cannot be maintained in this judicial Board as basis of appeal. The issue of time limit for issuing assessments does not arise as the said assessments are issued at any time prior to the expiry of seven years after the year of income in which the gains or profits from employment are

received. Long service and golden handshake are not gratuity envisaged by the Income Tax Act, 1973 and the same are fully taxable.

4. That the fourth ground of appeal is contested by the respondent; for the recovery of tax from terminal benefits by the appellant's employer was not communicated to the respondent, and that this issue was not raised at the time of objection and hence the respondent did not make any decision on it, that may be reviewed by this Honourable Board."

The respondent prays for the dismissal of Appeal No. 8 of 2004 with costs.

The respondent's reply in respect of Appeal No. 11 of 2004 of Ms Fatuma Ramadhani is almost similar to the reply made in Appeal No. 8 of 2004 of Mr Elieza Kisimbo. The same applies for Appeal No. 11 of 2004 of Ms. Fatuma Ramadhani, where the respondent makes similar replies to the statement of appeal refuting the appellant's allegations of facts and prays this Board to dismiss the two appeals with costs.

In his submissions in chief, Mr Busigara, the appellants' tax consultant submitted that the joint issues in the three appeals are centred on the modality of taxing the long service award, the golden handshake, and the employer's contribution to the Group Endowment Assurance Scheme.

It is submitted by Mr Busigara that the respondent treated the golden handshake as a payment for loss of office under s 5 (2) (*c*) of the Income Tax Act, under proviso (ii) instead of applying s 5 (2) (*a*) proviso (ii). Mr Busigara submits that s 5 (2) (*a*) proviso (ii) is applicable due to the fact that employment income is assessable as income of the year in which the services are rendered.

As regards the issue of the golden handshake, Mr Busigara submits that the same was paid in relation to past services and cannot be taxed as if it was paid in respect of the un-expired period of employment tenure to which s 5 (2) (*c*) proviso (ii) of the Income Tax Act, 1973 applies. Mr Busigara also argues that this reasoning applies to the issue of long service award, for these payments are in the form of gratuity payments entitled to partial exemptions under para 9A of the First Schedule of the Income Tax Act, Mr Busigara submits that where payments for golden handshake and long service awards are allocated to the years of income which expired more than five years from the year of receipt, they should be taxed with reference to the limitation provided for under s 85 (1) of the Income Tax Act. Again, Mr Busigara submits that applying the provisions of s 85 (1) and proviso (*b*) to that s constitutes re-opening time barred assessments in the case of employment income.

Mr Busigara also further urges that the contributions made in respect of schemes made or aimed at providing employment terminal benefits should be charged to tax or assessable in the year in which such contributions are made in the year of income.

Accordingly, urges Mr Busigara, for the respondent applying the provisions of s 85 (1) proviso (*b*) of the Income Tax act, and basing the time limitation of three years of income 2001 as if those contributions were received in that year of income.

Also in the case of Ms Fatuma Ramadhani, Mr Busigara submits that the respondent erroneously taxed house allowance paid to the appellant contrary to the provisions of s 5 (2) (*a*) proviso (IV) of the Income Tax Act, and accordingly that decision should be quashed by this Board.

Mrs Salim, the learned counsel for the respondent, in making reply submissions started with the issue of Long Service Award, where she submits that none of the appellants in the three appeals had been granted long service award. Mrs. Salim substantiated this by exhibiting before this Board Form IT 390 for Mr Elieza Kisimbo and Ms. Fatuma Ramadhani's retrenchment letters.

It is further argued by the respondent that Mr Athumani Said was paid retirement award which the respondent says he taxed under s 5 (2) (*c*) (iii) of the Income Tax Act, 1973, the reason advanced by the respondent being that the payment was a compensation for termination of the appellant's employment contract. And he further argues that the tax treatment was not disputed by the appellant's tax consultant.

The respondent also submits that he treated long service award as gratuity taxable in the year of receipt under s 5 (2) (*a*) of the Income Tax Act, read together with para 9A of the First Schedule to the Act. That the respondent did not apply proviso (ii) of s 5 (2) (*a*) of the Act, as requested by the appellant, because the respondent was not provided with evidence proving compliance to the regulations governing such payments.

As to the issue of golden handshake, as raised in the case of Mr Elieza Kisimbo, Appeal No. 8 of 2004, the respondent's counsel submitted that the same was not included in the notice of objection as lodged with the respondent on 16 August 2002. And to prove thus Mrs. Salim referred this Board to the app 1 of the Statement of Appeal and the note of discussion between the respondent officers and the appellant tax consultant, where it is noted that this item of Golden handshake was not included, and accordingly it cannot form a ground of appeal in this Board for that is procedurally not tenable under s 16 (1) of the Tax Revenue Appeals Act, 2001.

Mrs Salim, counsel for the respondent, submits that as per the note of discussion and the appellant tax consultant's letter earlier referred to, the parties had agreed on the taxation treatment of the Group Endowment Assurance Scheme benefits, and that the long service award was to be treated as gratuity taxable under the provision of s 5 (2) (*b*), read together with para 9A of the First Schedule to the Income Tax Act.

It is further submitted by the respondent's counsel, Mrs. Salim that the non-agreed issues between the parties were the application of proviso (ii) of s 5 (2) (*a*) of the Income Tax Act, in the taxation of the Long Service Award. The second non-agreed issue was the time limit for issuing assessments under s 85 (1) of the Income Tax Act.

It is also further submitted by the respondent's counsel, Mrs. Salim, that the refund made by the respondent to the appellants was based on the agreement reached on the discussion between the respondent's officers and the appellant's tax consultant. Mrs. Salim avers that the appellants' tax consultant was happy with the outcome of the said discussions and as a result the appellant tax consultant wrote the respondent to the effect that they were to appeal to this Board on the two non-agreed issues.

Alternatively, it is submitted by the respondent's counsel that there is no evidence submitted to the respondent, and neither to this Board that the payment of golden handshake was taxable under s 5 (2) (*a*) (ii) of the Income Tax Act, and not taxable under s 5 (2) (*a*) (iii) as done by the respondent. This payment of

A golden handshake was not a contractual provision between the appellants and their respective employers, neither was it a gratuity payment.

As regards the third issue which involves the Group Endowment Assurance Scheme, Mrs. Salim submits that it is common to the three appeals, but noted that the appellant's representative has not made any submissions in its regard, save on that made on this particular issue regarding the applicability of s 85 (1) of the B Income Tax Act on limitation of time. For that reason, Mrs. Salim submits that the appellant's tax consultant is estopped from making fresh submissions when making counter reply as the respondent would have no chance for reply.

Mr Lukoo, who is the respondent's senior tax collection officer, who is assisting Mrs. Salim in these Appeals, made a brief submission on the tax treatment on the Group Endowment Assurance Scheme. He submitted that this C Scheme was operated by the Parastatals Pension Fund (PPF) for employees who included the two appellants, Ms Fatuma Ramadhani and Mr Athumani Said and that PPF contributed 100% of the requisite premiums as determined by the National Insurance Corporation (NIC) who were the insurers. That the scheme operated for three years whereby the PPF elected to withdraw and continue with the scheme itself through budgetary allocations each year as provided for staff D terminal benefits. Mr Lukoo closed his brief submission on this point by informing this Board that the respondent did not tax the surrender value of the three year premiums.

Mrs. Salim continuing the reply submissions, submitted that the respondent taxed the Endowment Assurance Scheme under s 5 (2) (*c*) (iii) of the Income Tax Act.

E As regards the issue of limitation of the period for the respondent to make assessment of tax, Mrs Salim submits that s 85 of the Income Tax Act is applicable to all gains and profits from various sources, whether it be employment or services rendered, and there is no specific provision under this s 85 applicable only to employment income under s 5 also of the same Act. It is submitted by Mrs Salim that the appellants' interpretation of the applicability of F the said s 85 (1) proviso (b) of the Income Tax Act, is wrong for the appellants' assertion that the payments received by the appellants to be allocated to the years of income expiring earlier than five years, but Mrs Salim submits that the counting of time limitation for assessment should start in the year in which the gains or profits are received and then counting forward and not backwards. Accordingly, so submits Mrs Salim, the assessments made on the appellants lump G sum awards were made within the prescribed time limit under s 85 (1) proviso (*b*) as amended by the Finance Act, 2000.

Finally, Mrs. Salim submitted that in the case of the PPF employees, it was their employer who taxed the payments without first notifying the respondent, which means that the respondent made no original assessment, for the respondent re-computed the amount of tax charged and deducted when the appellants made H refund claims. And accordingly, here in respect of these ex PPF employees, the issue of limitation of time for making and issuing assessment does not arise.

Mrs. Salim also submitted that as regards the issue of the taxing house allowances paid to the appellant Fatuma Ramadhani, this cannot be an issue before this Board as the same had not been objected to in the objection filed with the respondent and for that reason, the respondent has not made any decision on

it which can be reviewed by this Honourable Board in accordance with the A
provisions of s 16 of the Tax Revenue Appeals Act.

Mrs. Salim closed the respondent's reply submissions by praying this Board to dismiss the appeals, for the respondent in dealing with the disputed issues in the taxation of the appellants' terminal benefits, acted within the parameters of the law.

Mr Busigara, the appellants' tax consultant and representative in this Board B
made oral and written counter reply submissions to the respondent counsel's reply submissions. Mr Busigara submits that Mr Athumani Said of PPF (Appeal No. 62 of 2003) received long service award in appreciation of his long service with the PPF which award can be also treated as retirement award.

Mr Busigara submits further that the respondent's admission that it taxed the
retirement award under s 5 (2) (*c*) proviso (iii) of the Income Tax Act, is legally C
wrong for retirement awards are not paid as compensation but as token of appreciation.

The appellant representative Mr Busigara does not agree with the respondent counsel that in the alternative they had taxed the long service award as gratuity taxable in the year of receipt under s 5 (2) (*a*) of the Income Tax Act, read with
para 9A upon the appellant's request. Mr Busigara maintains that is not right for D
the appellants have all along submitted that retirement and long service awards are gratuitous payments falling under s 5 (2) (*a*) proviso (ii) of the Income Tax Act, read with s 85 (1) and para 9A of the First Schedule to the Income Tax Act. Also Mr Busigara submitted before this Board that it is not enough for the respondent to claim that they (respondent) failed to apply s 5 (2) (*a*) proviso (ii)
of the Income Tax Act, because the appellant did not submit evidence proving that E
regulations governing such payments were properly implemented for the respondent counsel in the reply has not specified them.

It is admitted by Mr Busigara that the appellants' notices of objection the issue of improper tax treatment of the appellants' golden handshake did not feature, but again Mr Busigara submits that that was caused by the respondent
Commissioner's failure to serve the appellants with his decisions under s 84 of F
the Income Tax Act, that is service of notice of assessment. And also notices under s 13 (2) and (4) of the Tax Revenue Appeals Act that notices of the decision for the appellants notices of objection as filed. In those circumstances, Mr Busigara prays this Board to rule on the said omissions by the respondent.

It is also submitted further in counter-reply that the appellant's tax consultant
upon discovering the improper taxation of the golden handshake by the G
respondent under s 5 (2) (*a*) proviso (iii) instead of proviso (ii) of the Income Tax Act, protested to the respondent through correspondences and meetings. Giving an example of Elieza Kisimbo, referring to Form IT 390 as exhibited by the respondent, the same shows that this appellant was paid a sum of Tshs 3,704,100 which is equal to the 20 years' served times his one-month salary, and
accordingly that shows the golden handshake was paid in respect of past years' H
service rendered. Mr Busigara submitted that the payment of the golden handshake being a gratuitous payment or gift of cash paid by the employer to an employee for past service should be taxed under s 5 (2) (*a*) proviso (ii) of the Income Tax Act, subject to s 85 (1) and given the partial exemption under para 9A of the First Schedule to the Income Tax Act.

Mr Busigara in his counter reply also submits that Annexture TRA 1 annexed to the respondent's Reply to the appellant's Statement of Appeal, is evidence that the respondent and the appellant's tax consultant, agreed that the Group Endowment was not to be taxed, meaning that was an agreed item. However, this said annexture TRA 1 in its item (i) reads: " (i) Group endowment assurance scheme — this is taxable". And according to app 3 to the Statement of Appeal — Appeal No. 8/2004, a letter of the 23 January 2003 written by the appellant tax consultant, who was replied to by the respondent on 28 January 2003, the tax consultant says: "That the group endowment assurance scheme benefits are in form of life insurance money and will not be taxed." Looking into the two annextures, it means the parties did not agree on the tax treatment of the Group Endowment Assurance Scheme.

As regards the application of s 85 (1) proviso (*b*) of the Income Tax Act, Mr Busigara still insists that this provision of the Act is applicable only to employment income which is not deemed to relate to a year of income different from the year of income in which it was paid.

In its deliberation on the proceedings of the three consolidated appeals, this Board is of the considered opinion that the dispute between the appellants and the Income Tax Department of the respondent was occasioned by first the modality/procedure of making tax assessments in respect of the appellants' lump sum payments, especially the tax treatment of each component of the payments by the respondent. And second, failure of the respondent to issue respective notices of assessment to each of the appellants or each of the employees interested in the present appeals whose lumpsum terminal benefits were notified to the respondent. The non-issuing of a formal notice of assessment to each of the appellants and their fellow employees interested in the present appeals is perhaps inherent in the procedure of assessing tax income from salary employment income, as practiced by the Income Tax Department of the respondent. The respondent in the present cases was notified via the Income Tax Department "Notification of Lump Sum Payment" form, by the appellants' employers either the PPF or TIPER of the fact that they paid lump sum terminal benefits to the appellants and their colleagues.

The said "Notification of Lump Sum Payment" standard form has notes to the employer, of which note (ii) requires that this form be filed with the Income Tax Department not less than 45 days before the date when the employer proposes to pay the lump-sum payments to the employees. In the present case, that was not done as the said employers of the appellants filed the "Notification of Lump-sum Payment" form accompanied by the respective taxes withheld from each of the appellants and their affected colleagues. This error by the respective employers, needless to say flouted the respondent's good intention that the "Notification of Lump-sum Payment" was to be provisional assessment of tax by the employer, whereby the respondent would have had assessed the payable tax and issued notice of assessment to each of the appellants and their fellow affected employees through the employer. This procedure would have been in compliance with s 80, the filing of provisional tax assessment, and then s 84, service of notice of assessment, both sections of the Income Tax Act. This process designed by the respondent and executed by the employer as the agent of the respondent does not involve the taxpayers like the appellants and their

A colleagues who are now interested in the present filed appeals in terms of s 19 of the Tax Revenue Appeals Act.

The procedure above outlined of assessing tax and actual tax collection as carried out by the appellants' employer as a tax-withholding agent of the respondent to a certain extent is unjust to the appellants and to salaried income earners at large who are not informed about tax treatment of their income by the respondent. The extent of the injustice done to the appellants is exemplified by B the fact that they almost failed to lodge notices of objection against the tax treatment of each respective appellant's lump sum terminal benefits or payments. Accordingly, the appellants each filed a notice of objection on the basis of assumed tax treatment of their terminal benefits, contrary to the provisions of s 12 (4) of the Tax Revenue Appeal Act which require notices to contain statements in precise form of the grounds in respect of which the C objection is made.

The appellants' efforts to find if their terminal benefits were properly taxed were further frustrated by the respondent's failure to determine the appellants' notices of objection in the manner and procedure provided for under s 13 (2) of the Tax Revenue Appeals Act. That is the fact that the respondent never issued any notice on how it proposed to amend the assessments or even the D notice of how the assessments were finally amended resulting into the refund of tax paid to each of the appellants by the respondent. As this Board makes a finding that the procedure adopted by the respondent occasioned injustice to the appellants as it frustrated the objection and appeals procedure, any tax treatment of the appellant terminal benefits which was not initially objected to by the appellants is open to objection, and the respondent is enjoined to E entertain the same and review it accordingly within 45 days from the date of this judgment.

Matters which can be re-opened for review by the respondent upon the appellants' tax consultant filing proper notices of objection are the issues of the golden handshake raised in the case of Mr Elieza Kisimbo, Appeal No. 8 of 2004. The respondent counsel Mrs Salim correctly objected to the inclusion of this issue F in this Appeal as it did not feature in the notice of objection and no decision was made on it by the respondent, now to be reviewed by this Board. That offends the provisions of s 16 (1) of the Tax Revenue Appeals Act. And also the issue concerning the taxation of the housing allowance paid to the appellant Fatuma Ramadhani can be re-opened upon the appellant tax consultant filing formal notice of objection with the respondent within 45 days from the date of this G judgment.

This Board has noted that the note of discussion between the respondent officers and the appellants' tax consultant is not verified, for each prepared its own version of the notes of the discussion, and for that reason neither version binds the other party who did not prepare the same.

The Board upon considering the parties' arguments as summarized earlier, is H of the firm considered opinion that in taxing employees terminal benefits a balance should be struck out in the spirit of the Income Tax Act, taxing terminal benefits by ensuring that various exemptions are granted in order to ensure that such income is not diminished by payment of taxes. Hence, accordingly, when dealing with taxation of an employee's terminal benefits, like the ones granted in the present appeals, the tax authority, the respondent, should make positive construction of the Income Tax Act, provisions with the spirit of ensuring the employee's benefits are not eroded by strict interpretation calculated to diminish the spirit of granting terminal benefits safeguarded by statutory provisions.

In the above spirit as regard the issues of long services award and the golden handshake, this Board agrees with the appellants' tax consultant that these two payments were made to the appellants in consideration of past services they rendered to their respective employers and not as compensation for termination of unspecified period of contract as submitted by the respondent counsel. That is why the individual payment of these two awards is proportional to the number of years served by each employee up to the time of termination. Accordingly, the long service award and the golden handshake payments be treated as gratuitous payments to be taxed under s 5 (2) (*a*) proviso (ii) subject to limitation under s 85 (1) of the Income Tax Act, 1973 and subject to the partial exemption granted under para 9A of the First Schedule to the Income Tax Act.

As regards the group endowment assurances issue, this Board is of the considered opinion that, since the said scheme was not specified, nor approved by the respondent's Income Tax Commissioner under the provisions of the Income Tax Act, the proceeds from that scheme should be treated as gratuitous payments. The Board has noted that the payment of the benefits of the scheme to the employees, the appellants' was also based on the number of years of service and not on the unexpired period of employment contract. The tax treatment of this group endowment scheme should be taxed under the provisions of s 5 (2) (*a*) proviso (ii) subject to the limitation under s 85 (1) and the partial exemption granted under para 9A of the First Schedule to the Income Tax Act, of course limitation period running from the date of such payments or notification of payments to the respondent.

There being a refund due to the appellants and their colleagues as listed in the present three appeals under the provisions of s 19 (1) under the provisions of s 19 (1) of the Tax Revenue Appeal Act, such refund should be with interest as provided for under the provisions of s 112A of the Income Tax Act.

Ultimately, the three appeals as consolidated are successful to the extent illustrated above. The respondent and appellants' tax consultant are called upon to work together to give effect to this judgment as soon as practicable.

Each party is to bear its own costs of the appeals. The right of further appeal lies in the Tax Revenue Appeals Tribunal.

The judgment is delivered to the parties representatives who are Mr Busigara for the appellants and Mr H Mkwawa, legal counsel for the respondent, this 11 May 2005, here at Dar es Salaam.

ENGEN PETROLEUM (T) LTD v COMMISSIONER GENERAL A

TAX REVENUE APPEALS TRIBUNAL

DAR ES SALAAM

(INCOME TAX APPEAL: CASE NO. 1 0F 2004) B

(ORIGINATING FROM TAX REVENUE APPEALS BOARD CASE NO 45 OF 2003)

8 July 2004

A Shangwa J, *Chairperson,* N Mbise and D Kinabo, *Members* C

Appeal—Tax Revenue Appeals Act—Failure to serve a notice of appeal on the respondent—Whether appeal can be struck for that failure—Tax Revenue Appeals Act, 2000, s 16 (3)

Appeal—Failure to file notice of appeal in the Board and serve a copy on the D
Tribunal—Failure to pay specific fees—Whether the failures are sufficient reason to strike out the appeal—Tax Revenue Appeals Board Rules, 2001, rules 4 (2) and 7 (1)

The respondent filed a preliminary objection asking the Tribunal to strike
out the appellants appeal for: E

1. Failure to serve a notice of appeal to the respondent, under s 16 (3) of the Act.
2. Failure to file the notice of appeal in the Board and serve a copy in the Tribunal (rule 4 (2)), and
3. Failure to pay specific fees under rule 7 (1). F

Held:

Failure to serve a notice of appeal to the opposite party under s 16 (3) of the
Act is not fatal to the appeal and cannot render it invalid so as to be struck out
or rejected, where such notice is filed directly in the Tribunal and a copy
served on the Board under rule 4 (3). In the latter case the Registrar of the G
Tribunal is also obliged to serve the respondent with the copy of the notice.

Preliminary objection overruled.

Mr Nyange, for the appellant
Mr Teemba, for the respondent.

H

11 May 2004:

Mr Aggrey Teemba for the respondent: By consent, we request to argue our preliminary objection by way of written submissions.

A Order: Request to argue the respondent's preliminary objection by way of written submission is granted. Written submission by learned counsel for the respondent to be filed before 18 May 2004. Reply submission to be filed by 25 May 2004. Rejoinder by 28 May 2004. Mention on 31 May 2004 at 10:00 am.

B

RULING

(Delivered 8 July 2004)

Shangwa J:

On 10 May 2004, the respondent filed a notice of preliminary objection to the
hearing of the appellant's appeal against the decision of the Tax Revenue Appeals
C Board in Income Tax Appeal Case No. 45 of 2003 in which it was held, among
other things, that the appellant company committed fraud in relation to its return
of income for the year of income 1998, and is liable to payment of additional
taxes chargeable under s 78 (2) of the Income Tax Act, 1973. This objection was
argued by way of written submissions presented by the parties' representatives.

Initially, the points of objection which were raised by the respondent against
D the appeal were that the appeal is incompetent for non compliance with s 16 (3)
of the Tax Revenue Appeals Act, 2000 (15 of 2000) hereinafter to be referred to
as the Act; and Rules 4 (2), 6 (3) and 7 (1) of the Tax Revenue Appeals Tribunal
Rules, 2001 herein after to be referred to as the Rules. But, in his rejoinder to the
submissions filed by Mr Nyange & Company, advocates on behalf of the
appellant, learned counsel for the respondent, Mr Aggrey Teemba conceded to the
E fact that the decision of the Commissioner General was attached to the appeal and
withdrew the point of objection relating to non compliance with rule 6 (3) (*c*) of
the Rules.

He urged the Tribunal to strike out the appellant's appeal with costs for non-
compliance with the rest of the provisions on which the respondent's objection
is based. He stated that the appellant was supposed to comply with these
F provisions at the time of instituting the appeal to the Tribunal. He submitted that
under s 16 (3) of the act, the appellant was supposed to serve a notice of appeal
to the respondent within 15 days following the date on which it was served on
the Tribunal; and that under rule 4 (2) of the Rules, the appellant was supposed
to file this notice in the Board and serve a copy on the Tribunal; ;and that under
rule 7 (1) of the Rules, the appellant was supposed to pay the appropriate fees
G specified in the Second Schedule to the Rules.

He said that the appellant did not serve the respondent with the notice of
appeal as it was supposed to do, and that the notice of appeal was not filed in
the Board as it was supposed to be done, and that there is doubt as to whether
Tshs 100,000 being fees for lodging the statement of appeal which were supposed
to be paid were paid, and that Tshs 20,000 being fees for preparation of the record
H of appeal which were supposed to be paid were not paid.

He contended that non-compliance with the provisions of law and rules which
the appellant was supposed to comply with is fatal to the appeal and that under
rule 7 (2) of the Rules, the Tribunal is not supposed to entertain an appeal where
the appropriate fees under the Second Schedule to the Rules have not been
paid and that in its absolute discretion, the Tribunal may reject it under rule 9 (1)

of the Rules for non compliance with some conditions in the institution of the A
appeal.

Learned counsel for the appellant Messrs Nyange & Company submitted that the notice of appeal was filed in the Tribunal by using Form TRT 1 after being so directed by the Registry Officer of the Board, and that it was received by the Registrar of the Tribunal who served a copy on the respondent and the Board.

It was further submitted on behalf of the appellant that although a copy of ERV B
No. 12577636 indicates in words that the amount which was paid as fees for lodging the statement of appeal is Tshs 50,000, the actual amount which was paid is Tshs 100,000 appearing in figures on it and that the amount appearing on it in words is a clerical error by the Tribunal's cashier which has already been rectified.

Learned counsel for the appellant contended that they prepared the record of C
appeal. They did not see any rationale for objection to the hearing of their appeal on grounds of non-payment of such fees.

Generally, they contended that the provisions of s 16 (3) of the Act and Rules were complied with by the appellant and that at any rate non payment of fees for preparation of the record of appeal put at Tshs 20,000 by the respondent is not an irreparable defect that can warrant the dismissal of any appeal. They further D
contended that the objections raised by the respondent are in law not preliminary objections but administrative and record matters.

The legal question which is involved in this preliminary objection is whether or not an appeal can be struck out or rejected by the Tribunal in cases where the appellant fails to comply with the provisions of s 16 (3) of the Act or rules 4 (2) and 7 (1) of the Rules. E

In our considered view, where the appellant has failed to serve a notice of appeal to the opposite party as required under s 16 (3) of the Act, such failure is not fatal to the appeal and cannot render it invalid so as to be struck out or rejected.

There are two ways in which the opposite party is expected to be served with a notice of appeal. The first one is through the appellant as provided for under F
s 16 (3) of the Act. The second one is through the Registrar of the Tribunal as provided for under rule 4 (4) of the Rules.

Where the opposite party gets a notice of appeal through the Registrar of the Tribunal such as the respondent did in this case, such notice will be considered to be sufficient for the purposes of an appeal. The sole purpose behind the two provisions which bear a similar command to the appellant and the Registrar is to G
make sure that the opposite party is informed about the intended appeal.

We now proceed to express our views with respect to the issue of non compliance with rule 4 (2) of the Rules. Under this Rule, it is provided that the notice of appeal shall be filed in Board and a copy served on the Tribunal. In this case, the appellant filed the notice of appeal in the Tribunal instead of filing it in the Board and a copy served on the Tribunal. Obviously, such filing was not done H
in accordance with this particular rule. Despite this fact, we are of the considered view also that the appellant's appeal cannot be struck out or rejected for non compliance with this rule.

Moreover, as we will soon show, the appellant company cannot be faulted for having filed its notice of appeal directly in the Tribunal. This is because of the fact that under rule 4 (3) of the Rules, it is required that the notice of appeal has to be made in Form TRT 1 prescribed under the First Schedule to the Rules, on which it is indicated that the notice of appeal has to be lodged in the Tribunal.

Here, we have experienced a conflict between the provisions of sub rules 2 and 3 of rule 4 (2) of the Rules. The intention of the Minister responsible for finance was to require the notice of appeal to be filed in the Tribunal and a copy served on the Board. So we construe rule 4 (2) of the Rules to mean vice versa. We also construe the conflict involved between the provisions of subrules 2 and 3 of Rule 4 of the Rules in favour of the appellant.

Concerning the last point of objection, we find that rule 7 (1) of the Rules was fully complied with by the appellant. The fees for lodging the notice of appeal and the statement of appeal totaling Tshs 110,000 were paid by the appellant. In fact, the amount which was paid by the appellant as fees for lodging the appeal is Tshs 100,000 appearing in figures on ERV No 12577636 dated 5 February 2004. It is not Tshs 50,000 only as it had erroneously been indicated in words by the Tribunal's cashier. The error was rectified so as it may read in words as Tshs 100,000 and there was no fraud committed.

On instituting the appeal in the Tribunal against the decision of the Board, the appellant was not supposed to pay Tshs 20,000 being fees for preparation of the records of appeal because it had already paid Tshs 10,000 in the Board for the same purposes before filing its appeal in the Tribunal vide ERV No. 18097189 dated 21 January 2004.

An amount of Tshs 20,000 for preparation of the records of appeal as specified under the Second Schedule to the Tax Revenue Appeals Tribunal Rules is not one of the appropriate fees to be paid by the appellant on institution of the appeal in the Tribunal. This amount is only supposed to be paid in the Tribunal for preparation of the records of appeal where one requires for the same to appeal to the Court of Appeal of Tanzania against the decision of the Tribunal.

In conclusion, we hold that this preliminary objection has no merit and we hereby dismiss it. As there is a noticeable overlap in some of the provisions of the Tax Revenue Appeals Act and those of the Tax Revenue Appeals Tribunal Rules which is likely to prompt a legally minded person to base some objection to an appeal such as it was done in this case by learned counsel for the respondent, Mr Teemba, we order that each party should bear its own costs.

Delivered in chambers at Dar es Salaam in the presence of the parties' representatives, this 8 July 2004.

GEITA GOLD MINING LTD v COMMISSIONER GENERAL

TAX REVENUE APPEALS BOARD

MWANZA

(VAT TAX APPEAL: NO. MWZ 8 OF 2004)

28 February 2005

BR Mutungi, *Vice-Chairperson*, Mwisijo and Mukasa, *Members*

Appeals—Limitation of time in which to appeal—Non-compliance with appeal rules on time limits—Effects thereof—Tax Revenue Appeals Act, 2000 and Tax Revenue Appeals Board Rules, 2001

The respondent raised a preliminary objection that the appellant had lodged his appeal out of time. He was served with an assessment of tax on 30 January 2004 and lodged a notice of intention to appeal on 10 June 2004.

Held:

Even if the two parties were corresponding concerning the assessment, the law and procedure that has been laid down should be followed when lodging an appeal.

Appeal struck out.

Mr Kibuta, for the appellant
Mr Teemba, for the respondent.

24 February 2005:

Mr Kibuta, for the appellant: Your Honour we have the appeal itself against which there is a preliminary objection by the respondent and there is also an application to bring the same appeal out of time filed by the appellant. I have spoken to my learned friend and we both agree that these three proceedings are so intertwined that it makes sense to consolidate and hear them together.

Mr Teemba, for the respondent: I wish to have it on record that there is an application to appeal out of time. I know there are other applications to this Board but not in relation to this appeal. I only came to argue the preliminary objection.

Board: The matter was set for the preliminary objection and this is what will proceed to be determined.

Preliminary objection

Mr Teemba, for the respondent: Your Honour, after the appellant had filed the appeal on 28 June 2004 we filed a notice of preliminary objection that the appeal was lodged out of time in contravention of s 16 (2) and (4) of the Tax Revenue

Appeals Act, 2000 (15 of 2000) and also contravention of rules 4 and 9 of the Tax Appeals Revenue Board's Rules, 2001 (GN 57/2001) and the following are the reasons for the objection.

Your Honour, the respondent assessed the appellant on 30 January 2004 and served him with our notice of assessment on 5 February 2004 as confirmed by him and evidenced by document No. 2 attached to the appeal. There is no evidence ever objected to this assessment and this is in contravention of s 12 (4) of the Tax Revenue Appeals Act, because after being served with our assessment was to lodge a notice of objection within 30 days on 10 June 2004. Now about four months after receiving a notice of assessment the appellant filed a notice to appeal before this Board. This was contravention of rule 4 (2) of the Tax Revenue Appeals Board Rules which stipulates a period of 30 days from the date of service of notice of liability to pay duty or tax. In other words the notice of objection and notice of appeal almost go together in case of a taxpayer aggrieved by the decision. He was at liberty to file the two at the same time, that is, within 30 days of notice of assessment.

Your Honour, this appeal was filed on 28 June 2004 that was also once again in contravention of a gentlemen's agreement between the two parties made after a sitting of the two parties. I am referring to document 6 attached to the appeal on which the acting Commissioner for Value Added Tax (VAT) in a letter dated 4 June 2004 addressed to the Chief Executive Officer Geita Gold Mining and received by them on 8 June 2004 as confirmed by the same document in which the appellant was required or requested to file this appeal within 14 days. Your Honour, simple arithmetic shows that the appeal should have been filed on 22 June 2004 but was filed on 28 June 2004. Even by going with this Gentlemen's Agreement the appellant contravened what was agreed upon, let alone the law.

It is my humble submission that this Board should not entertain this kind of negligence both in contravention of the law and in appliances of the gentlemen's agreement. What is clearly potrayed is that the appellant was not serious at all, so it is my submission that for the provisions of the rules and the law itself the appeal is incompetent and consequently should be struck out.

Mr Kibuta for the appellant: Your Honour, let me first make the statement that the preliminary objection is thoroughly misconceived. Four points have been made by my learned friend.

First, that the appeal was brought out of time.

Second, that there was no notice of objection filed against the assessment.

Third, that both the notice of objection and notice of appeal must be filed within 30 days.

Fourth: That even in the face of the gentlemen's agreement the appellant failed to file the appeal on time.

Let me start with the third point. I must confess, your Honour, that as I read the appeal rules every day, both the Tax Revenue Appeals Tribunal Rules and the Tax

Revenue Appeals Tribunal Rules in relation to this Board, this is the first time in my profession as a tax lawyer to hear one suggest that both the notice of objection and notice of intention to appeal must be filed within 30 days. The notice of objection is governed by s 12 (1) and under subs (4) of s 12 is clearly stated that it shall be received by the Commissioner General within 30 days from the date of assessment.

A specific time period is set by the law for bringing the objection within 30 days. The time period for determining the objection is not set by the laws. It is open handled and my friend will be the first one to agree with me that an objection filed by Commissioner can take as long as one year to be determined. So to suggested that it must be brought within the same 30 days is a practicable impossibility upon receiving the objection, Tanzania Revenue Authority (TRA) is required to review the assessment so as to determine whether the objection has merit or not. Once the objection has been determined by the TRA, a notice is issued to the taxpayer of the determination of tax. That notice following the determination of objection has come to be known as the "variation notice" or "confirming notice".

When that procedure is completed and right of appeal explained by the Tax Revenue Appeals Board Rules then subrule (2) of the rules of this Board specifically rule 4 (2) requires that the notice to appeal against that notification can be brought to the Board within 30 days. I think my friend is confusing these two procedures. So, I will say that there is no way that the notice of objection and notice of appeal can be brought within 30 days.

Let me turn to the question whether this appeal was brought out of time. I will start where my friend started, that is when, was the assessment of VAT and interest issued. This was issued on 30 January 2004 both of us are in agreement about that date.

Following that assessment a series of correspondence all of which objecting to the additional VAT assessment was sent to the TRA the respondent and my learned friend has acknowledged in his statement that as a result of that a number of meetings between the parties took place attempting to resolve the dispute. These meetings are reflected in the letters by TRA and also in letters by the taxpayer. So the question for this Board to ask is at which stage of this interchange did the TRA take a definite position to reject representations by the taxpayer and on which date did the TRA make the decision? This question is important because we count the days allowed to the appellant from the date the decision to the objection is made.

This is where the confusion has occurred leading to the preliminary objection; let me walk you through the documents. My learned friend has referred to the final meeting on 2 June 2004. If you go through the record you find that both the parties maintained their respective positions and as a result there was a breakdown. That is why on 4 June 2004 the Commissioner of VAT Mr Mally wrote to the taxpayer notifying the taxpayer of the failure to resolve to VAT dispute, and importantly explained the right of appeal to the tax payer, telling the taxpayer he has 14 days to file the notice of appeal. I want to pay particular attention to the letter. It is critical to this preliminary objection. The letter gave a critical decision to the taxpayer in this letter. Mr Mally is wrong in only one thing, assigning 14 days to appeal. That is not the law. We know the law is 30 days.

A I suspect that Mr Mally confused the time for appealing to the Tribunal with the time limit lodging notice of appeal to the Board. This is under rule 4 (2) of the Tax Revenue Appeals Board Rules Rules (30 days). So the appellant had 30 days from the communication of the TRA decision to lodge the appeal.

On 10 June 2004 taxpayer lodged a notice of intention to appeal (within six days) of the determination of the Commissioner of VAT and eight days of the
B break down of the dialogue. So the notice of intention was within time.

My learned friend stated that the statement of appeal was filed on 28 June 2004 again as per rule 6 (1) the time for lodging statement of appeal is 45 days from the date of the accompanying decision. The statement was filed within 24 days of Mr Mally's letter.

Among the documents I was showing the Secretary of the Board are the
C extension of filing out of time harbouring under confusion as to the critical date when the decision by the TRA was made, we proceeded to apply for extension of time and this application has partly misled the TRA. The application to appeal out of time only compounded the confusion and was totally unnecessary as the appeal was within time.

I therefore submit that the TRA's preliminary objection has no merit and
D should be dismissed so that this Board can proceed to hear the appeal on merit. Similarly the application for extension of time is necessary and so the application should be closed.

Mr Teemba, for the respondent, in reply: Your Honour, I still insist the appeal is incompetent for non compliance with the law and rules provided in Tax Revenue Appeals Act and the Rules made under the Act. Let me first respond to
E my learned friend on the two notices namely the notices of objection and that of appeal. There is no confusion in law in respect of the two notices (12) (1) and 12 (4) and rule 7 (1). The appellant on rule 7 (1) is the one who decides what document and 7 (2) shows all the necessary documents to be attached. As you may have realised there is no notice of objection by the appellant and none was filed in this Board. It has never been served to the Commissioner General.

F It is true that the period of determination of an objection is not provided by law. There was no notice of objection to determine. The appellant resulted to out of door meeting. The law provides that the notice of objection should be 30 days and notice of appeal. The appellant did nothing and this is his problem. The notice of objection has never been there. The appellant is to prove that he had these documents and not for the Board to guess.

G Your Honour, the meeting held on 2 June 2004 had nothing to do with non-compliance of s 12 (4) and rule 4 (2) of the Rules. It is human practice for the parties to see what can he done after complying with the law. The appellant were sitting on their rights hoping things will go their way and things did not.

My learned friend is confusing this Board. The decision on 2 June 2004 the communication was only on what they had agreed. It was not a decision from
H Mr Mally. This was agreed by both parties and so it was not a command from him. Still the appeal was late. There is a limit to tolerance so the letter by Mally was nothing near a final decision of the Commissioner. He was only communicating as to what they had agreed.

I am not aware on the application of extension of time and so I am not going to comment on this. I wish to repeat that the appeal is incompetent. (i) There was no notice of objection to Commissioner within time at all. (ii) Both the notice of extension to appeal and the appeal itself were filed out of time and consequently incompetent and should be struck out with cost. This is my humble final submission.

Order: (1) Ruling on 28 February 2005 at 9:00 am
(2) Deliberation on 25 February 2005

RULING

(Delivered 28 February 2005)

This ruling is subject to the preliminary objection raised by Mr Teemba learned counsel for the respondent, the Commissioner General in appeal case No. 8 of 2004.

The preliminary objection itself as against the appellant, Geita Gold Mining Limited duly represented by Mr Kibuta learned counsel is to the effect that upon basing on s 16 (2) and (4) of the Tax Revenue Appeals Act and rules 4 and 9 of the Tax Revenue Appeals Board Rules. The appellant has lodged his appeal No. 8 of 2004 out of time and this contravening the above laid down provisions. In support of the preliminary objection raised by the respondent Mr Teemba, learned counsel, submitted before the Board that after the appellant had been served with the assessment on 30 January 2004 he was duty bound to raise a notice of objection with the respondent within 30 days after he had received the said notice. The learned counsel continued to submit that the appellant never did this as envisaged by s 12 (4) of the Tax Revenue Appeals Act but instead he lodged a notice of intention to appeal on 10 June 2004 about four months later to this Honourable Board without taking into consideration rule 4 (2) of the Tax Revenue Appeals Board Rules. These rules also stipulate 30 days from the date of service of notice of assessment to pay tax. The above procedure if followed properly according to the learned counsel's submission meant that these at law go hand in hand. The learned counsel also informed the Board that despite the appellant being notorious in contravening the law but also went as far as contravening the Gentleman's agreement drawn up between the parties. The said agreement was requiring the appellant to file his appeal after 14 days after receiving the respondent's letter dated 4 January 2004. What the appellant did he filed his appeal on 28 June 2004 which was more than 14 days stipulated in the "Gentleman's agreement". In summoning up the respondent's counsel strongly emphasized that the appellant was acting out of sheer negligence and lacked seriousness, and that the only penalty would be to strike out the appeal.

In responding to the above submission Mr Kibuta, learned counsel for the respondent lamented that the preliminary objection was uncalled for as it was misconceived.

He started by arguing that under s 12 (1) and 12 (4) of the Tax Revenue Appeals Act a notice of objection is to be received by the respondent within 30 days from the date of assessment but the date of determining the objection is not prescribed by law. After the determination of the objection then one can come before the Board with a notice to appeal once again within 30 days as per rule 4 (2). With this

A procedure in mind Mr Kibuta, learned counsel, found it absurd for the appellant's counsel to state that the procedure for issuing a notice of objection to an assessment goes hand in hand with a notice of appeal before the Board. According to Mr Kibuta these are two different procedures. In reacting to the question of time bar Mr Kibuta, learned counsel, explained that the assessment by the respondent was issued on 30 January 2004 and what followed after this is a
B series of correspondences between the parties whose aim was objecting the additional VAT assessment. The learned counsel further explained that as a result of these various correspondences and meetings the respondent issued his final decision via the letter dated on 4 June 2004 by one Mr Mally, which also among other things informed the appellant that he had 14 days to appeal. To this Mr Kibuta commented that the 14 days were contrary to the law, which stipulates
C 30 days as per rule 4 (2). The 14 days are there for appeals going to the Tribunal. The learned counsel explained that the fact that the appellant lodged his notice of intention to Appeal on 28 June 2004 with the Board he was well within time period stipulated by law which is 45 days rule 6 (1) of the Tax Revenue Appeal Board Rules. Yet the appellant had only taken up 24 days.

In reply to the submission by Mr Kibuta for the respondent, Mr Teemba,
D learned counsel, averred that even by going by records under rule 7 (2) of the Tax Revenue Appeals Board Rules the appellant was bound by law to attach all the necessary documents, the notice of objection to the Assessment being one of them but in the present appeal this was not attached. The only explanation to the above is that it was never sent to the respondent. He further submitted that as there was no notice of objection, it follows then that the respondent had nothing to decide
E upon. The appellant sat on his rights and opted to carry out what the learned counsel termed as "out of door meetings" forgetting all about the legal procedure laid down by the law.

Commenting on the letter written by one Mr Mally, Mr Teemba, learned counsel, stated that, Mr Mally was only communicating to what the parties had agreed on and it cannot be termed as the final decision of the appellant and so the
F preliminary objection should be upheld.

In considering the preliminary objection in this appeal we had to go through the sequence of events as portrayed in the documentary and oral evidence before us. We find that it is not a disputed fact that the notice of assessment was issued by the respondent onto the appellant on 30 January 2004. We find that it is not also a disputed fact that what followed after this was series of
G correspondences and meetings between the two parties which ended into a Gentlemen agreement in June 2004. We also find that it is not a disputed fact that what came out as a result in the long run was the appellant filing a notice of intention to appeal to the Board on 10 June 2004 and eventually appealing on 28 June 2004.

It is from the above foregoing events that we find that the first step, that is for
H the appellant to file a notice of objection of assessment with the respondent missing. This falls under the ambit of s 12 (1) which clearly states that:

> "12. (1) Any person who disputes an assessment made upon him by the Commissioner General may, by notice in writing to the Commissioner General, object to the assessment."

We turned to the submission by Mr Kibuta, learned counsel, that the series of A correspondences and meetings were notice of objections. On this we find that s 12 (4) of the Tax Revenue Appeals Act is very clear. It lays down as to what a notice of objection should contain which is "a statement in a precise form, of grounds in respect of which the objection is made and is submitted and received by the Commissioner General within 30 days from the date of service of the notice of assessment." B

As we perused through the file we did not find anything of the like to be termed as a notice of objection to the assessment addressed to the respondent.

Even by invoking rule 7 (2) of the Tax Revenue Appeals Board Rules as suggested by Mr Teemba for the respondent in his reply we have failed to find any attachment of the said notice of objection to the respondent by appellant. This takes us down to the letter dated 4 June 2004 of which Mr Kibuta, learned C counsel, in his submission suggested to be a final decision of the respondent. After a thorough perusal of the said letter it defeated our imaginations how this letter (document 6) could be termed as a "decision". What we find is that this was a mere letter bringing to the attention of the appellant what had been discussed between the two parties. There is nothing to suggest that the respondent was making a final decision as to an objection raised by the appellant. If follows D therefore that s 16 (4) would not apply as there was no way of counting the 30 days of instituting a notice of appeal before the Board, which also include rule 4. It follows that in the same situation even the 45 days as is in s 16 (2) (*b*) have no basis as to where one can start counting from.

It follows therefore that we find that even if the two parties were corresponding but the law and procedure that has been laid down should have E been followed. We further find that had the appellant decided to follow the law then he should have invoked the procedure found under s 12 (4) of the Tax Revenue Appeals, before pursuing his appeal under s 16 of the Act.

With the above foregoing findings by this Honourable Board we uphold the preliminary objection raised by the respondent that the appeal is incompetent before the Board as it has contravened the provision in the Tax Revenue Appeals F ss 12 and 16. We accordingly strike out the appeal and order the appellant to follow the procedures found in s 12 of the Tax Revenue Appeals Act as amended by s 58 of Finance Act, 2004 (15 of 2004) within 30 days from the date of this ruling, with costs to the appellant.

Right of appeal explained.

Read this 28 February 2005 before Mr Teemba for respondent and Mr Kibuta G for appellant.

JAMES MATHAYO MANYINYI T/A SOKONI TRADING STORE v COMMISSIONER GENERAL

TAX REVENUE APPEALS BOARD

MUSOMA

(VAT TAX APPLICATION: NO. MSM 4 OF 2004)

9 July 2004

BR Mutungi, *Vice-Chairperson,* Missango and Nzungu, *Members*

Appeal—Extension of time to appeal—Factors for consideration in an application for extension of time—Tax Revenue Appeals Act, 2000 and Tax Revenue Appeals Board Rules, 2001

The applicant filed a Chamber Application for extension of time to appeal out of time. The applicant had sent his appeal documents by Scandinavia Bus Service instead of the normal postal system. He had also addressed the parcel to one Agnes Marwa's name instead of the Board Secretary's address. The applicant took 47 days to check with the said Agnes Marwa on the receipt of the documents and only then learnt that they had not been delivered.

Held:

(1) The reasons advanced by the applicant are not sufficient to warrant extension of time as sought since they portray the applicant as having been reckless in processing the appeal.

(2) It is, however, in the interest of justice to grant the appeal since the grounds of the intended appeal are worth the consideration of this Board.

Application granted.

Case referred to:

Attorney General v Said Juma Muslim Shekimweri (Civil Appeal 35/97), unreported

Mr Byabusha, for the appellant

Mr Songoro, for the respondent.

Proceedings

5 July 2004:

Mr Songoro, for the respondent: Your Honour, we filed our objection which relates to the fees and we have realized that the fees were paid and so we pray to withdraw our application so that we proceed with the hearing of the main application.

Mr Byabusha, for the applicant: I have no objection to the prayer of withdrawal of the preliminary objection.

Order: There having been no objection, the prayer is accordingly granted and the preliminary objection withdrawn.

Mr Byabusha, for the appellant: Your Honour, before you is an application which we have presented under rule 9 of Tax Revenue Appeals Board Rules, 2001. The application has been sworn to in the affidavit by me giving reasons why an intended appeal is out of time.

Honourable members of the Board, the refusal of the Commissioner General to entertain the objection was written on 19 February 2004 and received in my chamber on 23 February 2004.

This refusal is part of the applicant's annex A1. As soon as I received the refusal, I prepared the notice of intention to appeal and by 8 March 2004 it had been filed to the Board and numbered 13 of 2004 in the Board's registry. The filling of this notice of appeal was to be done at Dar es Salaam. The Tax Revenue Appeals Board is centralized at Dar es Salaam and taxpayers have to file documents of appeal at Dar es Salaam.

What I did is that I contacted the Board Secretary who referred me to Ms. Agnes Marwa who I suppose is an employee of the Board. I do not know her role and I have not come into contact with her. The Secretary gave me No. 0222128098. I contacted her and she advised me to send it by EMS. I enclosed all the documents and the notice and I sent them to her. Later, I received a copy of the notice and an exchequer receipt No. 612250 of 8 February 2004. After filing the notice of appeal through EMS, I contacted her and she advised me to send my documents through the Scandinavia Bus Service. In the parcel I was to include Tshs 50,000 cash and my telephone number so that she could contact me on delivery. I have attached the Statement of Appeal and marked it A5 dated 11 March 2004. May I be permitted by the Board to demonstrate what I did? I have the parcel and the number is enclosed on the top and I will demonstrate how I kept the money in an envelope. I contacted the Scandinavia office and left the parcel there. This was personally addressed to Agnes. After a few days, I was informed that Agnes was in Arusha so the parcel could not be delivered. I contacted the Board, a lady responded and she said she knew nothing about my appeal. This was how the appeal process was hijacked. I have annexed the Scandinavia receipt marked A4. The other receipt is the EMS A3 and A2 for the notice.

Honourable members of the Board, after I had lost contact with Agnes, I had nothing to do than to retrieve the parcel till when she came back on 29 April 2004. At that time we had already ran out of time slightly over 20 days. As I have said earlier, I do not know Agnes nor am I related to her. This was designed by the Board of which I complied with. You will note from the dates that this system appears to be efficient and Agnes appears to be faithful. Your Honour, it appears that the appeal is out of time for about 23 days. I have filed the application under rule 9. I request you to consider that rule in arriving at the decision. You have to take into account the circumstances of each case. I have been blamed by the learned brother that I was negligent but that is not true. The appeal process was hijacked for the reasons which I have narrated which are beyond my control. In the counter affidavit, my learned brother says that my conversation with Agnes was hearsay, but this was direct conversation between me and the Board. Such conversation is permissible as evidence under s 6 (2) (i) (*b*) of the Evidence Act, 1967. I was not stating hearsay at all in my affidavit. The applicant has been in a habit of being out of time in filing his appeal. This is the second time we are appearing in this Board. But you should not consider cases in the past. Lastly, may I say that the intended appeal will contain substantial points of law to be considered by the Board. They appear in annex A5 which has three paras.

If we are permitted to appeal and those points come to the Board, they are in my opinion, very important to be determined. Your Honour, may I refer you to the decided case of *Attorney General v Said Juma Muslim Shekimweri* (Civil Appeal 35/97), unreported : on p 5. The court stated that even if the reasons for the extension of time are inadequate still the Court of Appeal can grant the extension of time if there are legal points to be considered. Our humble prayer is that you be pleased to allow us our application and we be allowed to file our appeal out of time for the reasons I have advanced.

Mr Songoro, for the respondent: After hearing the reasons from the applicant, we pray for time to prepare our reply for the reasons that the applicant has introduced before this Board, facts which we need to consider before giving our reply. This should be for a span of three hours.

Order: Given the fact that the respondent needs time to prepare himself properly for about three hours, we have considered his prayer but this application has been fixed for a whole week, we adjourn the hearing till tomorrow morning at 9.00 am, to give the respondent ample time to prepare his reply.

6 July 2004:

Mr Songoro, for the respondent: Your Honour, the matter before you is that the applicant is praying for the following orders.

First: He is praying for the Board to exercise the discretion to grant him leave to file his appeal out of time.

Secondly: He is seeking for costs.

The said prayers are contained in his chamber application supported by an affidavit. They are not sworn by himself but Mr Byabusha as counsel. The Commissioner General opposes this application for extension of time and his objection is supported by an affidavit sworn by Agrey Teemba, who is a counsel in the respondent's office. The substance of this application wants this Board to consider this application basing on rule 9 of the Tax Revenue Appeals Board Rules. Rule 9 of the rules in essence stipulates that "this Board may upon writing by a party and depending on the circumstances of each case and after the opposite party has been given time to be hear…"

The interpretation of the respondent is that the rule gives this Board discretion to consider this application and taking into account the circumstances of this matter. It is the submission of the respondent that this discretion has to be exercised judiciously and fairly. We are insisting on this on the fact that basing on the affidavit sworn by the applicant, the applicant properly issued notice of appeal on 8 March 2004 and under rule 6 (1) of the Tax Revenue Appeals Board Rules the applicant was to institute his appeal within 45 days of the Commissioner

General's decision. From simple mathematics, the appeal was to be due by 5 April A 2004. The appeal was never instituted in accordance with the rules. In the affidavit in support of chamber summons, it is apparent that the applicant had all the documents to institute an appeal. The only reason advanced by the applicant in his affidavit is that he sent a parcel containing documents for an appeal and the parcel was addressed to Agnes Marwa, not even the Secretary of the Board. The method used was not even a postal method of sending such kind of documents, B which is Scandinavia Bus service. Your Honour, the manner in which the applicant sent his alleged parcel containing an appeal is negligence on the part of the applicant for the reason that no one can explain the way the Scandinavia Bus service can deliver a Memorandum of Appeal.

Your Honour, the rules require the appeal to be addressed to the Secretary to the Board. That rule may not be substituted by allegations that he addressed the C memorandum to Agnes Marwa. Even if Agnes Marwa is an official of the Board, she cannot be substituted for the Secretary to the Board, who is duly authorized to receive the memorandum of appeal.

Your Honour, since the applicant invented his own method by adopting his postal system through Scandinavia Bus Service and by sending the parcels containing the memorandum to Agnes Marwa in her individual capacity, that was D contrary to rule 4 and 5 of the Board's rules which require that the appeal be transmitted to the Secretary and no one else. In view of what I have stated above, that is why the applicant particularly acted recklessly. He was not prevented to file an appeal out of time but it was his negligence that contributed to his failure of filing an appeal. It is our submission that this Board should not exercise its discretion in the circumstances where the applicant failed to comply with the E mandatory rules of filing an appeal. It is the respondent's submission that there is nothing absolutely that made him not file his appeal in time but negligence and recklessness.

Furthermore, your Honour, we submit that even this application for extension of time filed on 13 April 2004 was filed too late, almost 47 days after the decision was made. Your Honour, the applicant advanced another reason that there is a F point of law worth the consideration of this Board. He also brought the Court of Appeal's decision emphasizing that this Board should exercise its discretion for the reason that there is a point of law to be discussed. The decision of the Court of Appeal was based on the Court of Appeal Rules and not rules of this Board. It only fits to the Court of Appeal when deciding on extension of time in filing an appeal. I would like to tender the rules of Court of Appeal so that the Board G compares the wording of the rules of the Court of Appeal and those of the Board. In the Court of Appeal it states that "where there is sufficient reasons", while this Board in rule 9 should be on the "circumstances of the case". It is my humble submission that this decision of the Court of Appeal was interpreting a different rule. Secondly, if you read this rule you can discover that some of the documents were not available. In this application he had all the documents and had all the H opportunity.

On p 4 of the Court of Appeal decisions there were special reasons that were touching the public interest. There was an issue of the powers of the president. In this issue there is no public interest. I submit that this should not be the basis of this Board to exercise its discretion. Coming to the circumstances of this case, it is my submission that if this Board peruses annex A5, you may easily note that the tax that is in dispute was of the year from July 1988 to September 2002.

If you consider annex A1, a letter from the respondent for which the applicant forwards his objection to the respondent for determination, the respondent told the applicant that he will not entertain his objection for reasons that he did not adduce sufficient reasons for not filing his objection in time. The reasons for which the respondent refused the objection are stipulated in s 12 (5) of the Tax Revenue Appeals Act.

It is our submission that looking at the substances of this application, it appcars that the applicant takes steps after time has expired. He is always late to take steps according to procedures.

In view of what we have submitted, it is our submission that since the applicant was not prevented to appeal within the prescribed period, this Board should not exercise its discretion to the applicant who has demonstrated sheer negligence and recklessness as the circumstances demonstrate.

We submit your Honour, that the decision cited by the applicant is not the basis to rely on for the reasons we have explained before.

We pray that this application be dismissed with costs.

On the prayer of costs, according to the chamber summons, it is our submission that the applicant had all the opportunities to file but through negligence he failed and now he is praying for costs. I pray that in any event, the costs should be refused. That is all.

Mr Byabusha, for the applicant: If I may be permitted to start from where my learned brother has ended, that is prayer for costs; the chamber application is clear in para 2. The costs of this application are to be in the course, there is nowhere the applicant prayed for costs. This is mainly for the reasons that the Board should not fault the procedure laid down by its Secretary and to lay blames on the applicant.

Your Honour, the learned counsel referred to rule 9 of the Appeals Board's rule that it was the party to make an application. I do not know where he was getting this idea from that as an advocate, I was not allowed to do so. Section 3 of the Tax Revenue Appeals Act defines a party to mean a person or a party duly authorized, so this affidavit was sworn by me – a duly authorized agent and so I was competent to do so. Coming to the delay in filing the appeal, the letter was written on 19 February 2004 to the Commissioner General. This took time to be received up to 23 February 2004. But even if we go by the dates, the time expired by 5 April 2004. This application is from the time of expiration of this, that is 5 April 2004, while the application was filed on 1 May 2004 but on 30 April the Secretary endorsed its filing.

The rule of lodging such an appeal is as per rule 6 (1) of the Tax Revenue Appeals Board Rules. It does not state that it is to be lodged to the Secretary of the Board as interpreted by my learned brother. My advice from the Secretary and my endeavour were to file the appeal at the registry and this was to be through Agnes Marwa. This Board has been referred to rules 4 and 5 but to my knowledge these rules are irrelevant to this application. The proper rules for this application are rules 6 and 9.

You have been referred to the Court of Appeal Rules and considerations different from this application. The Court of Appeal Rules provide for "sufficient reasons" but rule 9 of the Board states "circumstances of each case".

I invite the Board to consider the ratio decidendi and not the particular facts. We are considering the legal points touching the applicant personally and taxpayers at large. My colleague also referred to reason of 19 February 2004 refusing to entertain the objection. Reasons are best to be considered on appeal by this Board and not in this application. If we are granted time to appeal we will attempt to satisfy this to the Board. As to the habit of being late in our things, I invite the Board not to look at the past experiences but to look at the circumstances of each case as per rule 9.

With these words, I think that I have shown that we were not negligent and each party should bear its own costs. We were advised rightly and this is what we did, but we are not blaming the Secretary either. If a case was in Dar es Salaam the document would have been filed in time. That is all.

Order: The ruling will be on 9 July 2004 at 9.00 am. after deliberation on 8 July 2004.

RULING

(Delivered 9 July 2004)

The ruling is in respect to an application filed by James Mathayo Manyinyi t/a Sokoni Trading Store, applicant and represented by Mr Byabusha, learned counsel on one side, and the Commissioner General, represented by Mr Songoro, counsel, as the respondent on the other side.

The applicant has come by way of a Chamber Application supported by an affidavit. The orders prayed for in the chamber application are as follows:

First, the Board extends time to the applicant to appeal out of time.

Second: Provision of the costs of this application. Before this application could be heard, the respondent, represented by Mr Songoro, had a preliminary objection to the effect that the application for extension of time to file a notice of appeal was incompetent for failure to comply, inter alia, with rule 8 of the Second Schedule to the Tax Revenue Appeals Boards Rules. The rule talks of the fees to be paid while instituting the application.

At the hearing Mr Songoro dropped the preliminary objection and as a result, the Board proceeded into the merits of the application itself.

In his submission before the Board and deposition in the affidavit, Mr Byabusha explained at large that on 19 February 2004, via his letter with ref. no. TRA/CDD/VI, the Commissioner General refused to extend time for the applicant to lodge an objection on tax assessment, which Mr Byabusha received on 23 February 2004. He further explained that on 8 March 2004, he promptly filed a notice of intention to appeal with the Board and his appeal was registered as No. 13 of 2004 and this was transmitted to the Board by way of Expedited Mail Service (EMS).

From here he was advised by the Board's Secretary to contact one Agnes Marwa whom he talked through telephone and he was directed to send the appeal documents and a fee of Tshs 50,000 by Scandinavia Bus Service of which he did. After compiling the records in booklets, he attached Tshs 50,000 in an envelope

A in cash and dispatched the parcel on 11 March 2004. The parcel had Agnes's telephone number on it for efficient delivery via the Scandnavia Bus Service (receipts attached).

To his surprise, Mr Byabusha learnt on 27 April 2004 from the very Agnes that the parcel was never received. On inquiring from the Scandinavia offices, he was informed that Agnes could not be traced in Dar es Salaam as she was in Arusha.
B He further narrated that as he had lost contact with Agnes, he had to wait till 29 April 2004 to retrieve the parcel and was already out of time slightly over 20 days. He clarified to the Board that he never knew Agnes in person nor was he related to her. What transpired was that he followed the direction from the Board. Mr Byabusha had prayed to the Board to take into account the circumstances surrounding this application as per rule 9 of the Tax Revenue Appeals Board
C Rules, in arriving at its decision.

As to the fact that what he was stating was hearsay, Mr Byabusha relied upon the Evidence Act, s 6 (2) (1) (*b*) that he was in direct contact with Agnes herself. In regard to the habit of being late in their things, he explained that this was the second time they were coming before the Board and each case should be considered on its merits and not to go by past experiences.

D Lastly, the learned counsel pointed out before the Board that their intended appeal contained substantial points of law which should be considered by the Board. On this point the learned counsel referred the Board to the Court of Appeal's decision *Attorney General v Said Juma Mushim Shekimweri* (supra) which in principle stated that even if the reasons for extension of time are inadequate, still the Court of Appeal can grant the extension of time where legal
E points are at issue.

In reply, Mr Songoro, learned counsel, argued that the Commissioner General through his objection of granting the extension of time as sworn by one Agrey Teemba (counsel) in his affidavit strongly submitted that the Board should comply with rule 9 of the Tax Revenue Appeals Board Rules. This is to the effect that the Board should take into account the circumstances of this matter. Furthermore, the
F Board in exercising its discretion should do so judiciously and fairly.

Mr Songoro explained that going by the records, the notice of appeal was filed on 8 March 2004 and so automatically the appeal was due by 5 April 2004. Mr Songoro could find no reason of the applicant's failure to file his appeal on time as he had all the necessary documents in his possession and had all the time he needed.

G Mr Songoro was perplexed by the method used by the applicant in sending his appeal documents to the Board. First and foremost, he used the Scandinavia Bus Service instead of the postal system. Secondly, he addressed the parcel in Agnes Marwa's name instead of the Board Secretary's address. And that for any stretch of imagination Agness Marwa could not be substituted for the Secretary of the Board as per the Board's rules 4 and 5.

H Mr Songoro stated that it was apparent that the applicant had acted recklessly and negligently in addressing Agness Marwa in her personal capacity and by adopting his postal system through the Scandinavia Bus Service.

On the point that the applicant in his intended appeal had points of law to be determined as he had quoted the Court of Appeal decision to support his point, Mr Songoro stated that this was misdirection on his part. First and foremost, the Court of Appeal rules are quite different from those of the Tax Revenue Appeal Board

Rules. The wording in the Court of Appeal rules is, "where there are sufficient A reasons", whereas in the Board a rule is "should be on the circumstance of the case".

Secondly, in the Court of Appeal decision, some of the documents were missing whereas in this application the applicant had all the documents.

Thirdly, the Court of Appeal decision was touching on an issue of "public interest" that is there was a question of the "powers of the president", a fact that is lacking in this application. B

Mr Songoro also put to the attention of this Board in his submission that the applicant had formed a habit of taking steps too late where matters of procedures were involved. He substantiated this point by pointing out that even on addressing this issue to the Commissioner General he was late and now he was late again on pursuing his appeal.

All in all, Mr Songoro ended by praying before the Board that since the C applicant had demonstrated negligence and recklessness on his part, thus his application should be dismissed with costs.

In reacting to Mr Songoro's submissions, Mr Byabusha, learned counsel, dismissed the fact of referring the Board to rules 4 and 5, as being irrelevant and the relevant rules being 6 and 9.

As to where the appeals should be lodged, Mr Byabusha explained that going D by the rules this was to be done to the Board's registry and it had not been specifically provided that it should be to the Board's Secretary.

In clearing his points in relation to the Court of Appeal's decision cited, he argued that what were of interest were the ratio decidendi of the said decision and not the rest of the proceedings. So he observed that the matters in this application were not only touching the applicant but taxpayers at large and thus their E application should be granted. As to costs he commented that they were to be in the course.

After the above summary, this Honourable Board has gone through the events which led to the delay of the filing of the intended appeal. We are of the common opinion that as properly pointed out by the respondent, the applicant was negligent on his part, and more so, he was also reckless. F

We have considered in depth that the applicant in sending his notice of appeal used the EMS which was a formal way of delivery of parcels. He later departed from this system and opted to use the Scandinavia Bus Service, which he alleged to have been the advice from the Secretary of the Board.

Even if we take this to have been the case, it is on record that the Scandinavia Bus Service on 11 March 2004 accepted the said parcel but the applicant took G 47 days to check with Agnes Marwa (the addressee). By and large and by all standards, this amounts to recklessness. We would have expected the applicant to have made a follow up after two to three days. It beats our minds how the applicant sat down for 47 days expecting the appeal to have been filed from the blues without making any initiatives. It is also doubtful that Agnes Marwa, an employee of the Board, could have been away for 47 days from her office. The H only reasonable explanation to such attitude is that the applicant never made any effort to remind the addressee to collect the parcel on time. So, the Board, taking into consideration the above circumstances, the reasons advanced by the applicant, with due respect, are not sufficient to warrant the extension of time as sought by him.

At this juncture, I would depart from the finding of the two members on the conclusion or decision that the application should be dismissed. My departure is based on rule 9 of the Tax Revenue Appeals Board Rules, in which it is provided and I quote:

> "The Board may, upon the application in writing by a party and depending on the circumstances of each case and after the opposite party has been given opportunity to be heard,extend the time for instituting an appeal ...."

I have gone further to see if the circumstances of this case should be considered in either dismissing the application or granting the application. It is on record that in the intended appeal, there are legal or contentious points of law to be determined. These determined, would dcfinitcly bc in thc intcrcst of thc applicant or as put by Mr Byabusha, learned counsel, even in the interest of the taxpayers at large. I am of the opinion, after glancing through the grounds of the intended appeal, that they are worth the consideration of this Board on appeal and that it is in the interest of justice to grant the application.

After having been satisfied with the above view, it is provided in rule 9 of the Tax Revenue Appeals Board Rules that the extension of time for instituting an appeal if granted then there should be a specific time limit of which I find a month to be sufficient.

In conclusion, we are of a humble finding that on the question of costs, each party is to bear its own costs.

Order: The applicant is to file his intended appeal within 30 days from the delivery of this ruling.

Read this day of 9 July 2004 in the presence of Mr Magere (TRA), for the respondent and Mr James Mathayo, applicant in person.

KAHAMA MINING CORPORATION LTD v COMMISSIONER GENERAL

TAX REVENUE APPEALS BOARD

DAR ES SALAAM

(VAT TAX APPLICATION: NO. DSM. 6 OF 2004)

12 August 2004

BR Mutungi, *Vice-Chairperson*, F Mteteleka and D Mwaibula, *Members*

Assessment—Waiver of condition to deposit half the amount of tax assessed in order to appeal—Uncertainties on points of law and fact about the basis and

legality of issuing the assessment—Whether presence of such uncertainties A
may justify a waiver to be granted—Tax Revenue Appeals Act, 2000

The applicant is disputing the respondent's assessment of stamp duty of Tshs 2,496,000,005 in respect of a transaction that took place in Canada. In March 1999, Barrick Gold Corporation, a Canadian company acquired the shares of Sulton Resources Ltd, a Canadian Corporation, through a public take B
over bid completed in accordance with the applicable Canadian Securities legislation. At the time of acquisition, Sulton Resources Ltd was the sole shareholder of Romanex International Ltd, a Canadian Corporation which in turn was the owner of all the shares of Kahama Mining Corporation Ltd. The applicant submitted that the shareholders of Kahama Mining Corporation Ltd were unchanged as the result of Barrick Gold Corporation acquisition of Sulton C
Resources Ltd. and no shares of Kahama Mining Corporation were transferred in connection with the said acquisition, hence no justification of levying stamp duty. Notwithstanding the uncertainties on points of law and fact as to the basis and legality of issuing the assessment the respondent demanded payment of 50% of the assessed tax before the applicant's objection could be entertained.

Held: D

Where there are uncertainties of law and fact they should be heard and determined by the respondent before any liability of payment is imposed on the applicant.

Application for waiver granted.

Case referred to: E

Afrika Mashariki Gold Mines Ltd v Commissioner General [2004] 1 TTLR XXX

Dr Luoga, for the applicant
Mr Songoro, for the respondent

F

9 August 2004:

Dr Luoga, for the applicant: In this application the applicant is praying for waiver for payment of half of the disputed tax liability as demanded by the respondent. May I briefly give the circumstances under which this application is made? Your Honour, on 15 May 2004 the respondent issued an assessment demanding G
payment of Tshs 2,496,000,000. The assessment was raised as stamp duty in respect of a transaction that took place in Canada between the Canadian companies as follows: Barrick Gold Corporation brought from the shareholders of Sutton Resource Ltd. Their shareholding in another Canadian company called Romanex International Ltd. This second company is the majority shareholder in Kahama Mining Corporation (the appellant) and it is still the majority H
shareholder as it has not sold its shares to any other person. In raising the disputed assessment, the respondent alleges that the applicant is involved in the sale of its equities. The appellant was then aggrieved on five main grounds:

1. They have never been parties to any transaction involved in the sale of their parties or shares of any other company.

2. Under the law in Tanzania, they have no capacity to sale any of their shares or shares in any company in which they are not members.
3. The transactions purported to create liability do not involve disposition of any assets in Tanzania and it is an independent transaction between foreign parties carried out in accordance with laws in a foreign country.
4. Section 5 of the Stamp Duty Act that was relied upon by the respondent does not apply to the purported transaction. Even if assuming that the transaction could be subject to stamp duty in Tanzania, the respondent can first raise an assessment upon the appellant in view of the provision of s 40 (*k*) of the Stamp Duty Act, 1972, which specifies who is the person liable to pay stamp duty where share transfer is involved, that is the purchaser or transferee. Since the appellant did not purchase any shares and no shares have been transferred to them, it is incorrect to raise an assessment against them.
5. Even assuming that there is a purported instrument executed outside the United Republic of Tanzania still the appellant could not be subjected to stamp duty in view of the provisions of s 25 of the Stamp Duty Act, which requires such an instrument first to arrive in Tanzania before the time for payment becomes due. Your Honour, if there is any purported sale of shares, any instrument involving such sale is compulsorily registerable under the Companies Act (Cap 212), which prescribes the instruments of transfer of shares and which requires the filing of returns showing the change of ownership of shares. The requirement to file returns and to register the transfer will register the arrival of the instrument in Tanzania and s 25 would require payment of stamp duty within 30 days.

Your Honours, these grounds by the appellant clearly show that there are serious uncertainties on points of law as to the basis and legality of issuing assessments. The grounds also show that there are serious uncertainties on points of facts as regards to the identity of parties to the purported transaction. Furthermore the grounds show that the amount involved is not only colossal but will also lead to serious inequities if the appellant will be compelled to pay the amount before the objection is entertained.

Your Honour, in accordance with the procedures under the tax revenue Act, the appellant had duly raised an objection to the assessment with the respondent, and the same is appended as KMCL AP2 to the application. Your Honour, the appellant also made an application for waiver with the respondent as per the law. The appellant having lodged the said application for waiver, the respondent was under an obligation as contemplated under s 12 (2) of the Tax Revenue Appeals Act, to consider the application and make a determination. To the contrary, on 5 of July 2004 as shown in annex KLMC AP 3, the respondent decided to reject the application and demanded payment of half the assessed tax before the appellant's objection could be entertained. We humbly submit that the decision by the respondent to ignore and reject the application for waiver was made arbitrarily. If the respondent had considered that there were no uncertainties in law being a person required by law to act judiciously, he would have been duty bound to furnish reasons for the rejection.

Your Honour, the decision of the respondent is an appellable decision and this Board is vested with jurisdiction under s 40 of the Tax Appeals Board Act, which amends the Tanzania Revenue Act, 1995 by introducing s 5A and giving right to any person aggrieved by the decision of the respondent in the discharge of any further revenue laws to appeal to this Board. In conformity to the law, the appellant has already lodged a notice of appeal before this Board.

Your Honour, this application is very similar in all aspects within the application of *Afrika Mashariki Gold Mines Ltd v Commissioner General* (App 18/03), unreported, and I will draw the similarities between the two applications. In both applications foreign companies transacted in shares with another foreign company. But in both applications a Tanzanian company had not taken part in the said transaction.

In both applications the composition of shares had not changed at all and the issues raised in both applications on points of law and on facts were the same. That is:

(a) Whether any transaction subject to stamp duty in Tanzania had taken place;
(b) whether the Tanzania company can be visited with stamp duty liability to a transaction to which it is not a party;
(c) whether the facts did indeed disclose uncertainties regard to points of law, and
(d) whether the respondent, if it is established that uncertainties as to points of law do exist, can completely refuse to grant waiver of payment.

The ruling of the Appeals Board on p 36 (last para) of the printed ruling was to the effect that the facts in that case, which are similar to the instant case, disclosed uncertainties as to points of facts and law. The Board decided that the existence of uncertainties should have made the respondent grant waiver for the payments. Accordingly, the Board granted the application of waiver and allowed an application to appeal without lodging half of the payments. These two applications are so similar such that the ruling referred to in the *Afrika Mashariki* case (supra) should have a very high persuasive effect, and we humbly submit and enjoin this Board for the sake of consistency, it be pleased to adopt the same position in this application.

Your Honour, in that ruling we made a very lengthy submission on the points as to why the respondent could not competently refuse to grant waiver where there were clear uncertainties on points of law and fact. The arguments are still valid in the present application. Having pointed out that there exist uncertainties in law and fact, our first contention is that the respondent ceases to be a competent authority to resolve such question of law or facts. That competency lies with this Honourable Board. What happens is that in such a situation whereby the respondent has already made a decision through a notice of assessment and the appellant company contests that the respondent has not addressed the important points of law and fact, the two parties became equal parties entitled to impartial resolution of the contended questions of law and fact. If the respondent refuses to grant waiver in order to enable the applicant to assess the judicial remedy of appeal, he commits the wrong of acting as a judge in his own cause contrary to rules of natural Justice. He is already an interested party who is keen to impose his decision. Sections 12 (3) and 16 (6) cannot be read in a manner which permits the respondent to apply the law to his benefits where there are unclear uncertainties.

Your Honour, it would be very absurd if the legislature had intended to confirm powers upon the respondent which can be used contrary to rules of natural justice and in violation of constitutionally guaranteed rights. For example, if such were the case, there would be nothing to prevent the respondent from manufacturing an assessment against a taxpayer knowing the same to be incorrect under the law, and proceed to demand payment of tax before addressing the tax payer's grievances, and also proceed to block the taxpayer from accessing the jurisdiction of this board.

The respondent is entrusted with massive powers over the appellant. These are powers capable of occasioning injuries if improperly applied. In the instance case, we have submitted that the powers have been improperly applied by the respondent by deciding to ignore the implications of the existence of clear uncertainties on points of law. We humbly submit that it is trite law that a person should not be left to suffer an injury and seek remedies later. It is in this context that this Honourable Board was vested with the jurisdiction introduced by s 40 of Tax Revenue Appeals Act, to adjudicate over any dispute arising from a decision of the respondent in the discharge of the statutory functions of the revenue laws.

Your Honour, this provision was not there before. It was introduced to widen the scope of jurisdiction of this Board to deal with any possible application of the law in order that there can be timely intervention where a wrong is about to be committed, and to ensure that the cause of justice is not impeded with. In the instance case, the respondent can impede the course of justice. Our humble submission, your Honour, is that this Board be pleased to find that:

The application by the appellant discloses very clear and serious uncertainties as to points of law and fact in relation to the demand of stamp duty payment.

The respondent acted wrongly and arbitrarily by peremptorily rejecting to address and consider the uncertainties raised by the applicant.

The respondent acted in contravention of s 12 and s 20 (3) of the Tax Revenue Appeals Act in refusing to grant waiver and demanding payment before the objection could be entertained.

Grounds exist for granting waiver to the appellant so that the objection lodged by the appellant is entertained and thereby order that the appellant can lodge an intended appeal to the refusal without the payment of the tax demanded. We pray that costs should follow the event as this is an interim application.

Mr Songoro, for the respondent: Your Honour, the respondent prays that we be given time to prepare our reply.

Order: Reply by Mr Songoro is on 11 August 2004 at 9.00 am.

11 August 2004 at 2.00 pm.

Quorum

Mr Songoro, for the respondent: Your Honour, the respondent opposes this application for waiver of payment of part of the tax due as envisaged by s 12 (1) of the Tax Appeals Act. The respondent wishes to advance three reasons with the view that the application for waiver has no merits:

(i) This application is not supported by any evidence to show that the alleged transaction which gave rise to the claim of stamp duty took place out of Tanzania. According to the application para 2 of the application, the appellant states that the grounds are contained in annex KMCL AP2. A Looking at the said letter, the basis of the applicant's application, the counsel of the applicant in the said para only narrates or produces names of companies and their share structures showing the status of the corporations involved and the way their shares are being held.

Your Honour this Board was not shown any document that supports the B transactions stated in para 2. It is the principle of law that it is the duty of the applicant not to allege mere words but to substantiate the words with evidence. The argument put forward in para 1 and 2 of F K Law Chambers are mere words of the counsels before this Board and there is no proof from the counsel or appellant to support that the transactions are not the ones which stamp duty is payable. There is no evidence to show that the companies were not in Tanzania C or on the property which is not in Tanzania. The omission to support the assertions in para 1 and 2 is not an oversight on the part of the applicant. It means that the appellant has no proof of para 2 and 3 of the letter dated 8 June 2000. KMCL AP 2. This application as it stands, it has no convincing reasons to move this Board and waive the payment of tax envisaged by the law as stated in para 3 of the Tax Revenue Appeals Act. It is the respondent's submission that even when D the applicant requested a waiver to the respondent, there were no convincing reasons to show that the companies stated in para 2 and 3 and the shares were not giving right to the appellant under the Stamp Duty Act. For this reason, the respondent prays to this Board to hold that the application has no sufficient details to warrant the exercise of waiver.

E

(2) It is the respondent's submission that the claim of the stamp duty by the respondent is solid on the basis of s 5 (1) (*a*) of the Stamp Duty Act and art 60 (*a*) of the Stamp Duty on Instruments Schedule to the Stamp Duty Act. Your Honour, without going to the details, I would like to submit that s 5 of the Stamp Duty Act is explicit as to the jurisdiction. Section 5 (1) (*b*) is emphasized by the respondent. I am referring to this section because the F shares of the Kahama Mines or their mining licence or the mine itself are in Tanganyika or Tanzania mainland. I wish to draw the Board to app B which was signed by the Commissioner for Minerals. It is the respondent's submission that the transfer of shares took place in Tanganyika and if at all the Board finds that it did not take place here then s 5 (1) (*b*) is applicable.

G

Your Honour, I refer you to s 40 (*k*) of the Stamp Duty Act. Here it shows who is to pay the duty. It is the purchaser or transferee. Article 60 (*a*) of the Schedule to the Stamp Duty Act states that the relief should be sought within six months. The applicant did not seek for relief. It is the respondent's submission that in the absence of any evidence from the appellant, the respondent has demonstrate to this Board that there is a transaction which took place and it was accepted by the H Commissioner of Minerals, and looking at app A it is Kahama Mining which asked the Commissioner for Minerals for consent of the transfer of shares. Similarly in app C, there is a letter from the appellant's accountants to the TRA saying that there is a re-organization of shares. After the appellant had said all this to the TRA and Commissioner of Minerals, their submission before this Board

A that the transaction of transfer of shares does not attract stamp duty which so far is pending for appeal at this juncture should not have any merit at all. It is our submission that the respondent's documents tendered in the Board demonstrate that there are shares which were transferred and there is a prima facie evidence that under the Stamp Duty Act, stamp duty is payable.

Moreover, the ground of uncertainties cannot stand. The law is clear and the
B facts that the respondents has are very certain. We further submit that even on consideration of hardship and equity, this application cannot stand for reasons that they have not tendered evidence before this Board to show that their company has financial difficulties. They should have tendered the financial statements supported by the bank statement if possible, which they did not do. Taking into account that, the amount of tax demanded by the law is the amount
C not in dispute or one third of the assessed tax. The assessed tax is not stated "legally taxed" or "wrongly taxed". It is only mentioned as "assessed tax". We submit further that the applicant's submission that the demand of stamp duty is wrong or illegal is wrongly brought before the Board, as it is not envisaged by s 12 (2). The issue of right or wrong is a matter to be decided on an appeal, if any. It is my submission that all the arguments presented by the appellant regarding
D legality or illegality of the tax should be disregarded and we should only stick to what the law states.

On the basis of the respondent's submission on the law governing stamp duty and the facts, which the respondent has supported by documents including the consent from the Commissioner of Minerals and a letter of the applicant's accountant, PricewaterhouseCoopers, it is the respondent's submission that the
E application has no merits at all. We pray that as the respondent has already found that this case of waiver is not established by the applicant, then the Board should find the same.

I will now proceed to the matter brought by the applicant that it is similar to *Afrika Mashariki Gold Mines Ltd v Commissioner General* (supra). In that application it is true that the Board granted waiver to Afrika Mashariki Gold
F Mines. It is our submission that this application before you is not similar to the previous one. As I shall demonstrate hereunder, it is true that the Board considered uncertainties as to the question of law or fact. On p 36 of the ruling, the Board was convinced that there were uncertainties and the reason was very clear that the East African Gold Mines of Australia which had sold its share was an Australian company. However in that case the respondent did not produce
G consent transfer instruments as we have produced in this case.

In that application, they did not show that there was re-arrangement of shares but in this case we have a letter which went to the TRA at Ubungo showing re-arrangement of shares. We also produced a letter from Kahama Mines to the Commissioner of Mines seeking for consent. Furthermore in the said ruling on p 3 there was a certificate of registration tendered in the Board but in this case
H there is no document tendered. They did not show where Kahama Mines was in cooperated. In the previous application on p 5, the Board was informed of Afrika Mashariki shares structure. We submit that in the previous application the Board was moved by the evidence, which was available to demonstrate the questions of Law and fact. In this application, despite the fact that the applicant had all the opportunity but they did not tender any documents to demonstrate which facts are

in dispute and which law is in dispute. It is the respondent's submission that the previous case of Afrika Mashariki is competently distinct in fact and in evidence to this one.

We submit that the argument of the applicant that this application is similar to the other one and so there is strong reason for waiver has no merit at all. Even the amount which was involved in the previous application was a huge amount and so one third is a huge amount. In the instant application the claim of stamp duty does not even reach one quarter of the previous amount. Your Honour, I would like to submit further that the appellant by demonstrating that the companies are incorporated outside Tangayika is not sufficient at all. The applicant was under an obligation to show the manner of the transaction, which took place to show uncertainty. It is only by submitting the facts that one may see and think there was uncertainty. This was done in the previous application. In the instance case we have nothing apart from the submission of the counsel.

After distinguishing between the two applications I pray to seek for an adjournment so that the respondents may address you on the issue of financial statement of the applicant. All the TRA records are in Mwanza. These will give the Board a broader picture of the issues. The documents will be ready by tomorrow.

Dr Luoga, for the applicant: I have no objection to this.

Board: There having been no objection from the appellant, we accordingly grant the adjournment to 2.00 pm tomorrow.

Order: Submission by the respondents is to precede tomorrow 12 August 2004 at 2.00 pm

12 August 2004:

Mr Songoro, for the respondent, continuing: Your Honour, I have come to introduce the financial statement. This is on p 4 of app (ii) in the respondent's view the Bulyankuru (subject matter of this application) which is at Kahama. The transfer of shares in Kahama Mine relates to property which is situating in Tanganyika. It is our submission that if this Board found out that the transfer of shares (the whole transaction) was not performed in Tanzania, then part of it was performed in Tanzania. That brings this transaction on the four corners of s 5 (1) (*a*) or (*b*) of the Stamp Duty Act. On the appellant's submission that no instrument has been brought such as share certificate, we submit that so long as this transaction is a matter which was to be performed in Tanganyika, the tax is payable. The fact that there was sale or no sale does not arise. The mere transfer of shares as per s 40 (*k*) attracts a stamp duty. It is the purchaser or transferee who to pay this tax. In respect of the purchaser, we are submitting that, though this matter will be determined on appeal, it is the view of the respondent that Barrick Corporation is the holding company of Kahama Mines or is the ultimate owner of Kahama Mine Corporation. We further submit that even on p 14 of the document I have tendered today, there are the TRA receipts of capital tax which are clear that the physical address of Barrick Ltd, Kahama Mines and Sulton Ltd is PO Box 1081 Dar es Salaam c/o Kahama Mines Corporation. From the

A respondent's point of view, from the time the appellant brought his objection, the taxpayer was Kahama Mines Ltd. We are submitting that on the basis of the documents that the Commissioner had in his possession by the time the objection was filed to and there were no uncertainties on law or on matters of facts. We are submitting this because the crucial point is about what the Commissioner General had by then and what is being produced now in the application or on cross appeal.

B For the reason I advanced yesterday and today, I pray that the application for waiver before you be dismissed mainly for two reasons:

> The application itself is not supported with sufficient evidence to show uncertainties on the part of the law. The provisions of the Stamp Duty Act are very certain. The facts before the Commissioner General were also very
> C certain on the liability of the stamp duty. I pray that this application be dismissed with costs in favour of the respondents.

Dr Luoga, for the applicant, in reply: Your Honour, the respondent's counsel has argued that the stamp duty which is demanded and which gave rise to this application relates to the share transfer, transactions that are depicted in app's A–G and which the learned counsel tendered before this Board in the course
D of his submission. The learned counsel has also argued that the liabilities of which the stamp duty attaches were not concluded between foreign companies or executed outside the United Republic. The learned counsel has further argued that, on the basis of the appendixes submitted, it is very certain that the applicant's company is liable to stamp duty under s 5 (1) (*b*) which include para 5 (1) (*a*) as read together with s 40 (*k*) in accordance with the rates provided for
E in s 60 (*a*) to the First Schedule of 1972 Act. We humbly beg first to bring to light a few inconsistencies which are explicitly from the respondent's submission. First the letter forwarding app A–C tendered by the respondent introduces serious uncertainties of the facts in this application. Your Honour, the letter is dated 9 August 2004 and bears app A–C on p 1 titled: Statutory Declaration. The respondent gives misleading information in line 4 from the bottom of that
F p where he makes reference to consent of transfer of shares of Messrs Barrick Corporation. The respondent also makes the misleading statement on p 2 of the forwarding letter item 2 (i). In that para there is a statement concerning the transfer of shares from Messrs Kahama Mining to Barrick Gold Corporation. Your Honour, app B tendered by the respondent and which is the consent to transfer shares of Kahama Mining, attests to the fact that the transfer was from
G Romanex International Ltd to Kahama Mining Corporation Ltd and from Sulton Co. Services Ltd to Barrick Leiman (E) Ltd. These are not transactions executed by the appellant and the appellant being a Tanzanian registered private company, has no legal competency to transfer shares on the basis of the two documents. It can be seen that the respondent was not certain in their determination under s 40 (*k*) as to who is the purchaser or transferee.

H Your Honour, I will now make reference to Appendixes D and E. The Board will notice that these appendices disclose values of the assets involved in the transfers which the respondent maintains to be the basis of the stamp duty liability annex D and which relate to the transfer from Sulton Resources to Barrick Leiman (E) Ltd under item 1 para D (*c*) cl (ii). The value of the financial asset written by the respondent is Tshs 1,000 and the respondent in his own writing discloses thereby that the value is in accordance with cl 2 of the agreement. Similarly, looking at app E, the same item, the value disclosed is Tshs 4,999,000. Assuming that the respondent is correct, the stamp duty liability which is disputed by the appellant was based on these transactions and applying the rate of duty under para 60 (*a*) as submitted by the respondent the stamp duty chargeable on these transactions would be 4% of Tshs 4,999,000. It is unclear of how a small sum can produce a stamp duty of Tshs 2,496,000,000. We humbly submit that there is something terribly wrong that probably misled the learned counsel to make reference to a transaction on which the stamp duty disputed was not based. Your Honour, it is on account of the respondent's confusion and inability to establish facts that we filed these additional annex, which clarify the position as follows:

(i) That the transaction as stated by app A to C as tendered by the respondent were fully exempted from both capital gain tax and stamp duty in respect of the exemption from stamp duty annex KMCL–app 4 contains exceptions to stamp duty. These are the last three but one document appended to that annex. All the transactions referred to were exempted from stamp duty under s 39, and the respondent had full knowledge of the facts and was duty bound to unveil the truth to this Board.

Your Honour, it is surprising that the respondent has contested that the stamp duty that is disputed is in respect of the transaction that took part outside the United Republic of Tanzania and which does not involve transfer of shares in the appellant company by the appellant. The respondent made that fully aware of the contents in annex KMCL app 6. Your Honour, that annex is a letter by the respondent to the appellant informing the appellant that on the basis of information obtained from a daily newspaper of 11 April 2000 and 15 May 2000, is aware that there have been share transfers and he picked the figures in a daily newspaper to compute stamp duty liability. You will notice that the demanded liability of Tshs 2.4 billion is not based on the agreements referred to by the respondents. It is based on a newspaper article which appears as annex KMPL app 7. Your Honour, that article referred to a public take over bid over a listed foreign company implicitly the respondent was highly uncertain as to what a public take over bid entails and how share transfers take place.

In brief transaction in equities of a listed company involves a lot of shareholders. Barrick Leiman Corporation had to acquire lots of equities in Romanex International from many shareholders. For ease of understanding I can give a small example of any company wishing to take over the CRDB Bank in Tanzania today. First, such a company will not purchase its shares from CRDB, and second, there cannot be a single instrument of transfer of those shares. Strangely your Honour, after the respondent had become aware of the contents of the news paper reports and in a demonstration of ignorance or inability to comprehend facts as attested by annex KMCL app 5, the respondent wrote to the appellant demanding the applicant to reproduce the sale agreement. In so doing your Honour, the respondent created a lot of uncertainties as to questions of law. The first, being the status of the appellant in the public bidding of shares of Romanex International, outside this country. The second is whether there could be single sale agreement or not. The third, is whether an appellant who was not the one who sold or bought the share outside Tanzania can now be compelled to produce such an agreement or not.

A What surfaces from the respondent's demands is clear testimony that the
respondent himself could not put together the correct facts in order to identify the
place of sale, mode of sale, the manner of sale, the parties involved and whether
the laws of the United Republic of Tanzania do apply to that sale. The question
we humbly wish to pose to this Board is what on earth can be the most uncertain
than the inability of the respondent to see and make correct descriptions as
B demonstrated in these applications.

Your Honour, the learned counsel for the respondent did point out to a number
deficiencies in the manner the appellant's counsel prosecuted this application
particularly in respect of non submission of records to prove that Barrick Gold
Corporation, Sulton Resources Ltd or Romanex International are in fact foreign
companies. Your Honour, as counsels we appear before this Board as officers of
C this Board duty bound to assist this Board to arrive at a just decision. Before
appearing to this Board interactions between parties had already taken place. We
were entitled to assume that matters not disputed before the Board can
comfortably be left out so that this Board only addresses itself to issues in dispute
before it. Your Honour, as can be seen in annex KMCL app 4, the respondent had
official documents showing places of incorporation of these companies to be
D outside the United Republic of Tanzania. It is highly inconsistency for the
respondent to make reference to a postal address of convenience which the
respondent wrote for purposes best known to them and assert that the postal
address is actually the address of the foreign companies. The respondent is full
aware of the provision in the companies' ordinance requiring of a certification of
compliance before carrying out any business in Tanzania and is fully aware of the
E fact that you cannot obtain such certificate if you do not provide an address of a
resident person for purpose of service. That address cannot be validly used by the
respondent to substitute Barrick Corporation as purchaser or any other person
involved in seeking shares to Barrick Corporation in Canada with the name of the
appellant for the purposes of assigning the stamp duty. That it is very crucial
question of law between the respondent and the appellant that remains uncertain
F and that can only be resolved by this Honourable Board or the learned counsel
himself as he has quoted s 40 (*k*) and stated clearly that only the purchaser or
transferee in a share transfer transaction is liable to stamp duty. If the basis of the
stamp duty liability is disclosed in AP 6 there is uncertainty as to who is the
purchaser or transferee in this case. Again the respondent cannot resolve this
question and an impulse have developed between the two parties such that only
G this Board can clarify.

Similarly, the learned counsel at the end of his submission yesterday submitted
that the appellant should show how the transaction took place. This demand as
well raises serious uncertainties as to how one party has taken place. The
submissions by the respondent are replete with uncertainties. One deadly
uncertainty is the submission by the respondent that once the respondent demands
H half of the assessed tax, the same must be paid irrespective of whether there is a
complaint that the demand has been illegally or wrongly demanded. By making
that submission, the learned counsel introduced before this Board another serious
uncertainty of the law, specifically the application of s 12 (2) of the Tax Revenue
Appeals Act. That section begins with "subject to …" so before applying subs (2),
subs (3) should start first. This is a serious uncertainty in law. In view of the
disclosures made in the annex submitted today to clarify the basis of stamp duty

demand, this Board can now clearly see the similarities between this case and A *Afrika Mashariki* case I referred to in my main submission where a newspaper article triggered off stamp duty assessments like in this case.

Your Honour, what is important in this application is to determine whether the appellant has sufficiently brought to light uncertainties both in law and fact surrounding the demand of stamp duty. This Board will wisely look at the facts submitted, the records produced and the arguments made by the parties to B ascertain the existence or non-existence of the uncertainties. It is imperative that this Honourable Board should open its doors to allow the appellant to be heard on their grievances by allowing them to file their appeal without paying this highly and erroneous stamp duty liability. Your Honour, the law has given this Board very wide power in order to regulate misuse of powers sometimes through interest serving interpretations of the letter of the law by the respondent. The C legislature did envisage that possibility and decided to entrust the impartial regulation of the exercise of power by the respondent to this Board. It is in this context that, as a matter of fact, not only can an appellant apply for waiver before this Board, but the appellant could also have referred the rejection to be determined by this Board. The respondent does not have a free hand in dealing with the taxpayers. We pray for the demand for pre-payment before the intended D appeal is lodged is waived and the applicant be permitted to appeal against the Commissioner and bring objections for the decision of this Board. We also pray for costs in the course. In that context, we wish to rest our submission.

Order: (1) Deliberation will be on 16 August 2004.
(2) Ruling will be on 18 August 2004 at 2.00 pm E

RULING

(Delivered 18 August 2004)

This is a ruling upon an appeal by Dr Luoga, learned counsel for the appellant or applicant, Kahama Mining Corporation Ltd, brought under s 5A of the Tanzania F Revenue Authority Act, 1995 as amended by s 40 of the Tax Revenue Appeals Act, read together with s 12 (3) and (6) of the Tax Revenue Appeals Act, 2000 and rule 4 (4) of the Tax Revenue Appeals Board Rules, 2001.

According to the submission by Dr Luoga, the dispute between the appellant and the respondent in this appeal, the Commissioner General represented by Mr Songoro, learned counsel, is Tshs 2,496,000,005 which is stamp duty as G assessed by the respondent in respect with a transaction that took place in Canada.

In revisiting the circumstances which led to the said assessment, Dr Luoga learned counsel, averred before the Board that in March 1999, Barrick Gold Corporation, a Canadian company, acquired all the outstanding common shares of Sulton Resources Limited, a Canadian Corporation, through a public takeover bid completed in accordance with the applicable Canadian Securities legislations. H At the time of acquisition, Sulton Resources Limited, was the sole shareholder of Romanex International Limited a Canadian Corporation, which in turn was the owner of all the shares of Kahama Mining Corporation Limited. Dr Luoga clarified that the shareholders of Kahama Mining Corporation Limited were unchanged as a result of the Barrick Gold Corporation acquisition of Sulton

Resources Limited and no shares of Kahama Mining Corporation were transferred in connection with the said acquisition.

Being the case as above narrated, Dr Luoga then submitted that the events and transactions which transpired do not give rise to stamp duty liability in terms of s 5 of the Stamp Duty Act and this is why they approached the Commissioner General and raised an objection as to the assessment of the stamp duty on sale of the shares. The respondent agreed to entertain the objection on condition that half of the established stamp duty is paid. According to Dr Luoga, their objection is based on five major grounds.

1. The appellant has never been a party to any transaction involved in the sale of their shares or shares of any other company.
2. Under the law in Tanzania they had no capacity to sale any of their shares or shares in any company in which they are not members.
3. The transaction purported to create liability does not involve disposition of any assets in Tanzania. The transaction was an independent venture between foreign parties carried out in accordance to laws in a foreign country.
4. Even if the transaction could be subject to stamp duty in Tanzania, s 40 (*k*) of the Stamp Duty Act does not apply as liability to pay stamp duty where a transfer involved is on the purchaser or transferee. In this case the appellant did not purchase any shares and no shares have been transferred to them.
5. Section25 of the Stamp Duty Act, which requires such an instrument first to arrive in Tanzania before the time for payment becomes due was not complied with. In this case returns should have been filed as per the Companies Act (Cap 212) showing change of ownership and then this transfer is registered. This would have marked the arrival of the instrument in Tanzania.

After stating the above grounds Dr Luoga was of the view that there were serious uncertainties on points of law as to the basis and legality of issuing of assessment. That this also goes to the findings that even on points of facts the serious uncertainties are obvious. Dr Luoga further expressed his fears that even the amount involved if the appellant was to be compelled to pay before the objection was entertained, could lead to inequities. The objection raised is appended and adopted as app 2.

Dr Luoga further explained that their application also entailed the waiver by the respondent as per s 12 (2) of the Tax Appeals Act of which the respondent was to consider their application and make a determination. To their surprise the respondent on 4 July 2004 decided to reject their application and demanded payment of half of the assessed tax before their objection could be entertained. The learned counsel lamented before the Board that by all standards the respondent's act of ignoring their application and rejecting it was made arbitrarily. That all said, had the respondent found that there were uncertainties, then he should have been prudent enough and acted judiciously by furnishing reasons for the rejection. This is why they are before this Board as they are aggrieved by the respondent's decision and are seeking for waiver pending their intended appeal. Dr Luoga further cited *Afrika Mashariki Ltd v Commissioner General* (supra), an appeal lodged before this Board, which he pointed out that could have a persuasive affect in deciding this appeal. That also with this appeal in mind, the Board could maintain consistency in its decisions, as it is of a similar nature.

He moved the Board to adopt the decision in that appeal as there were a lot of similarities to the appeal at hand. He stated that the two applications both involved foreign companies transacting in shares with other foreign company. In both instances, the composition of shares had not changed at all and the issues raised in both cases on point of law and of facts were the same.

Dr Luoga also highlighted the arguments in *Afrika Mashariki Ltd* (supra) of which he stated that they were also valid in this appeal. The arguments were to the effect that the respondent had ignored the implications of the existence of clear uncertainties on points of law and facts and had misused his powers by improperly applying them, hence violating the constitutional guaranteed rights in which the respondent has acted as a judge in his own course forgetting that he is an interested party who is keen to impose his decisions. In summing up Dr Luoga cautioned the Board that it should intervene where a wrong was about to be committed and insure that the cause of justice is not impended. His prayers then before the Board are as follows:

(i) That the application by the applicant discloses very clear and serious uncertainties as to points of law and fact in relation to the question of stamp duty payment.
(ii) That the Board should find that the respondent acted wrongly and arbitrarily in failing to consider the uncertainties raised by the appellant.
(iii) That the respondent should be found to have contravened s 12 and 20 (3) of the Tax Revenue Act in refusing to grant waiver and demanding payment before entertaining the objection.
(iv) That the Board should order the objection raised by the appellant to be entertained and the appellant be allowed to lodge their intended appeal without payment of the tax demanded, and costs to follow event.

In reacting to the above submission, Mr Songoro, learned counsel, strongly opposed the appeal putting forth a lengthy submission. In totality, Mr Songoro did not find any merits in the application for waiver of payment of part of the tax due which is envisaged by s 12 (i) of the Tax Appeals Act. Mr Songoro in advancing his reasons before the Board, stated three major grounds of arguments which are as follows:

(1) That this application is not supported by any evidence to that the alleged transaction which gave rise to the claim of stamp duty took place outside Tanzania. Mr Songoro in relation to this point had in mind the letter annexed in the appellant/applicant's prayers which simply had the names of the companies, their share structure and their status. The letter which is the basis of the applicant's complaint cannot suffice to be a clear evidence of the purported transaction. The counsel reminded the Board of the legal maxim that who alleges must prove. As per the counsel's arguments the picture before the Board is that Dr Luoga was tendering just mere words but no proof at all, and the same story was before the Commissioner of which he

was not convinced and this is why he ordered that the applicant pay half of the assessed stamp duty.

(2) That s 5 (1) (*a*) of the Stamp Duty Act, s 40 (*k*) of the Stamp Duty Act and art 60 (*a*) of the Schedule to the Stamp Duty Act was properly utilized. Mr Songoro, learned counsel, submitted that with these sections in mind, the respondent had all the required facts which are that the shares of Kahama Mines, the mining licence and the mine itself are all in Tanganyika. Mr Songoro also prayed to the Board to turn to the letter from the Kahama Mines seeking for the consent of the Commissioner for Minerals of the transfer of shares (app A). He also pointed out (app C) to a letter from the appellant's accountants to TRA informing them that there was a re-organization of shares. With the above in mind then there is a prima-facie evidence that under the Stamp Duty Act, stamp duty is payable as there were shares which were transferred. Mr Songoro quoted s 40 (*k*) of the Stamp Duty Act which shades liability to pay stamp duty upon the purchaser or transferee, and art 60 (*a*) which gives six months for one to seek relief. In this matter the applicant never sought for any relief.

(1) That the prayer for uncertainties cannot stand in this application. Mr Songoro explained that the respondent was very certain of the facts and the law governing the stamp duty liabilities.

That even the prayer for hardship and equity cannot stand as the applicants have no proof whatsoever to show that they had financial constraints. One would have expected them to tender a financial statement or bank statement. Mr Songoro pointed before the Board that what was of interest in this matter was payment of stamp duty which is a legal right envisaged in the statutes and not its illegality or legality, that is an issue which could properly be dealt with in an appeal.

Having pondered on the three, grounds Mr Songoro then turned to the issue of similarities of which Dr Luoga was comparing *Afrika Mashariki Ltd v Commissioner General* (supra), an appeal which was determined by this Board and the present matter. To the contrary, Mr Songoro submitted that the two appeals were quite distinct. He elaborated the differences being that in the *Afrika Mashariki* appeal the consent from the Commissioner of Mines was missing. Even the proof of transfer of shares was missing, and even proof of re-arrangement of shares was also missing. But these are all to be found in this application. In the *Afrika Mashariki* case there was a certificate of registration but this is missing in this case. Mr Songoro summed-up this issue to the effect that in the *Afrika Mashariki* case the Board was moved by the evidence which was availed to it to demonstrate the questions of law and fact, but the applicant in this matter has failed to do so.

To shed more light and show clarity, Mr Songoro, learned counsel, tendered before the Board the appellant's financial statement. In the statement according to Mr Songoro, it shows that the properties of the appellant are situate in Tanganyika and so the Board should be moved to find that the said transaction, if not a part of it, was performed in Tanzania and so well in conformity with s 5 (1) (*a*) or (*b*) of the Stamp Duty Act. So, the issue of uncertainty does not arise for as long as there was a transfer of shares, the stamp duty was to be paid and the purchaser or transferee was to pay the said tax.

Mr Songoro also pointed to the fact that the TRA receipts of capital tax show the physical address being in Dar es Salaam c/o Kahama Mines Ltd of the Canadian Companies.

Having submitted at length, Mr Songoro prayed that with the evidence availed to the Commissioner General at the time of the objection, there was no uncertainty in law or in fact and so the prayer for waiver should be dismissed as the application itself is not supported with sufficient evidence to show that uncertainties and costs should be in favour of the respondent.

In reply to Mr Songoro's reply, Dr Luoga vehemently submitted in depth that the documentary annex A–C tendered by the respondent or relied upon in his arguments were misleading as they showed that the transfer of shares were from Messrs Kahama Mining Corporation Ltd to Messrs Barrick Corporation and the other transfer Messrs Kahama Mining to Messrs Barrick Corporation. That the appellant being a Tanzania's registered private company, has no legal right or competency to transfer shares and this is why the appellant submitted that the respondent did not know or was not certain as to who was the purchaser or transferee in the said transaction.

Dr Luoga upon relying on annex D and E, elaborated to the Board that the value of the financial assets was 1,000 Tshs and the value disclosed was Tshs 4,999,000. Therefore, even on the assumption that the appellant was liable to pay stamp duty; the duty chargeable on the transactions would be 4% of Tshs 4,999,000. Taking this computation in mind, there is uncertainty as to how the respondent came up with a big sum, which according to Dr Luoga, must have been due to the fact that there was confusion and inability to establish facts by the respondent.

Dr Luoga showed his disappointment before the Board in his reply that, according to annex A and C as brought forward by the respondent, it is clear that he knew that the transaction therein was exempted from capital gain tax and stamp duty under s 39 of the Stamp Duty Act, only that the respondent was hiding the truth.

Dr Luoga also made it very clear to the Board that the respondent relied on the agreements based on a newspaper article annex KMPL annex 7 which was in relation to a public take over bid. According to Dr Luoga, it seemed that the respondent did not know what a take over bid entails. The respondent obviously could not identify the place of sale, mode of sale, the manner of sale, the law involved and lastly the parties thereto.

In responding to the fact that the appellant had not brought documentary evidence, Dr Luoga explained that the appellant and respondent had prior communication before coming to the Board and matters in dispute and not undisputed had been communicated to each party. So, there was no need of going over into matters not in dispute. As to the postal address mentioned by the respondent, Dr Luoga made it clear that this was for convenience sake and also for the purpose of getting a certificate of compliance before carrying out any business in Tanzania.

In conclusion, Dr Luoga prayed before the Board that since there were uncertainties both in law and in fact in the present case, they should be granted waiver as they waited to lodge their intended appeal. As an ending note, Dr Luoga stressed that the respondent should not be left to have a free hand in respect of

A matters touching the tax payers, and this is why the Board was established to
regulate the respondent's enormous powers.

After going through the lengthy submissions, the Honourable Board went into
deep scrutiny of the matter. This has led us to the fact that the issue here is
whether the appellant is liable to waiver of the stamp duty imposed upon him by
the respondent which is half of the amount to be taxed before he could lodge his
B complaint. This is as per annex KMCL app 3 of which the respondent states "we
wish to inform you that the Tanzania Revenue Authority has decided to entertain
your objection on the condition that Tshs 1,240,000,000.50, which is half of the
established stamp duty liable amounting to Tshs 2,496,000,005, is paid as
required under s 12 (8) of the Tax Revenue Appeals Act".

Going through the lengthy submissions, one establishes that the matter boils
C down to another issue which is whether the appellant/applicant has sufficiently
brought to light uncertainties both in law and fact surrounding the demand of
stamp duty.

Upon these issues we had to look through various facts submitted by both the
appellant and respondent, and the records produced as annex. It is the common
finding of this Honourable Board that there are clear uncertainties on points of
D law and fact in this matter. As rightly put by the appellant the matter seems to
have triggered off after the news paper item showing a public take over bid.

There is a legal issue to be tackled in relation to the shares sold and the law
applicable. This is in reference to the foreign companies' involved (Canadian
companies) in the said transaction *vis à vis* the local company, Messrs Kahama
Mining Corporation.

E There is also an issue of the shares and the financial stand of the company
which are sorely matters of fact. We are of a common stand that had the
respondent first verified the uncertainties that now are obvious, the respondent
would have granted the application of waiver by the appellant.

As correctly put by the applicant/appellant, that the order of payment of half of
the stamp duty tax as assessed, if carried out, could lead to miscarriage of justice,
F a stand which we also adopt, we feel that these uncertainties should be heard and
determined by the respondent before any liability of payment is imposed on the
appellant, if any. With this said, we find in favour of the appellant to say that we
accordingly grant the application for waiver where they were to deposit half of the
assessed stamp duty as per s 12 (2), read together with s 12 (8) of the Tax Revenue
Appeal and s 16 (5), until such time that the Board has determined and decided the
G intended appeal in case the objection fails, we further order that the respondent
admits and decides the objection by the applicant/appellant.

As the waiver granted involves a large sum, we are of the opinion that for
avoidance of any delay, the applicant/appellant should, within 30 days from the
date of this ruling, make a follow-up to the respondent as regards the
determination of the objection at issue of which the respondent in his letter dated
H 14 July 2004 admits to be ready to entertain. As an obiter, in this application as
was in *Afrika Mashariki Gold Mines Ltd v Commissioner General* (supra), there
were arguments of a similar nature as regards the uncertainties in law and in facts
particularly on the pricking issue of stamp duty.

Right of appeal explained. Read this day of 12 August 2004 before Deo Mwanyika, for the applicant, and Mr Songoro, learned counsel for the respondent.

KOMBO HASSANI C/O MULTIMODAL FREIGHT CO. LTD v COMMISSIONER GENERAL (No. 1) A

TAX REVENUE APPEALS BOARD

DAR ES SALAAM B

(CUSTOMS AND EXCISE TAX APPEAL: CASE DSM 10 OF 2004)

26 May 2005

BR Mutungi, *Vice-Chairperson*, I Dallushi and J Karashani, *Members* C

Appeals—Notice of appeal—Must be filed within 30 days from date of service of decision of Commissioner General's decision to taxpayer—When the 30 days begin to run whether from date of Commissioner's letter or date of service of same to taxpayer

Appeals—Notice of appeal—Must be filed within 30 days from date of service of D *decision of Commissioner General to taxpayer—a party that alleges such service has the burden of proof*

The appellant filed an appeal against the decision of the Commissioner General. Before hearing of the appeal the respondent raised a preliminary E point that the appeal was not properly before the Board since it was filed 39 days after the date of service of the decision of the Commissioner General on the taxpayer, the appellant thus infringing the provisions of s 16 (3) of the Tax Revenue Appeals Act. The respondent further argued that the appellant offended the provisions of rule 4 (2) of the Tax Revenue Appeals Board Rules in that he filed the notice of intention to appeal against the F decision of the Commissioner General 39 days after service of such decision. The appellant argued that while the decision of the Commissioner General was dated 4 June 2004 it was served on him on the 15 June 2004 and so he was within time by filing his notice of intention to appeal and his appeal on 13 July 2004. The Board considered when the 30 days from the date of the decision of the Commissioner General began to run and who had G the burden of proving service of the Commissioner General's decision to the taxpayer.

Held:

(1) The wording of s 16 (2) of the Tax Revenue Appeals Act requires one to file his intention of appeal within 30 days from receipt of the decision of the Commissioner General; H

(2) the duty of serving a taxpayer with the decision of the Commissioner General is vested with the respondent;

(3) there is a reasonable doubt as to whether the appellant was served or not on 4 June 2004, a doubt which gives a benefit or advantage to the taxpayer, and

A (4) with lack of proof from the respondent as to when the appellant was served with the decision of the Commissioner General, we take the date of service as being 15 June 2004 and so the appeal is well in time and proper before the Board.

Preliminary objection dismissed; appeal to proceed on merit.

B No cases referred to.

Mr Mngoya, for the appellant
Mr Primi, for the respondent

25 May 2005:

C Mr Primi, for the respondent: The respondent has raised a preliminary objection to the effect that the appeal has been improperly brought before the Board as it is time barred in view of s 16 (3) of the Tax Revenue Appeals Act, 2000 read together with rule 4 (2) of the Tax Revenue Appeals Board Rules, 2001.

This is because the notice of appeal was filed out of time, the same was filed on
D 13 July 2004 and the decision which the said appeal alleges was delivered on 4 June 2004 so the notice was lodged about 39 days from the date of decision by the Commissioner General. According to s 16 (3) the appeal against Commissioner General's decision ought to be brought before the Board within a period of 30 days after the decision. Similarly according to rule 4 (2) of the Tax Revenue Appeals Board Rules a notice of intention to appeal against the decision of the Commissioner
E General out to be lodged to the Board within a period of 30 days from the date of service of the Commissioner General or decision of liability to pay any tax.

Since this appeal and notice of intention were lodged not within 30 days but within 39 days without leave of the Honourable Board, it is my humble prayer that the appeal is improperly brought and should be struck out. I beg to submit.

F Mr Mgoya, for the appellant: Your Honour, the notice of assessment was served to the appellant on 15 June 2004. He collected it from the Registry on 15 June 2004 and even in our notice of intention to appeal, we pointed that it was received on 15 May 2004 and endorsed that he collected it on 15 June 2004.

The respondent was not offered any proof that it was collected on 4 June 2004. We agree it was written on 4 June 2004 and the manner of service is a little bit
G strange, as the appellant was just called on the corridors and was just given and endorsed but nowhere did he sign in the respondent's registers. If we calculate from the date of collecting the notice of assessment and time of lodging the intention to appeal we believe we are within time, taking into consideration that the notice of objection was served on the respondent on 25 November 2003 and the decision came out on 4 June 2004. We consider that we are within time. We are not called here to
H prove, but on 15 June 2004 is the date when the appellant collected the letter of assessment. In the alternative we pray that the Board allows us to proceed on merit.

Mr Primi, for the respondent: Your Honour in view of the submissions by the appellant's counsel the submission that the notice of assessment or decision was served on 15 June 2004 puts the respondent to uncertain position as there is no evidence submitted on the manner on which the appellant was served. In such a

situation there is a reasonable doubt that the appellant might have been served on A
the date the decision was delivered, and in this way, this appeal will be out of time. It is my humble prayer that without such evidence, the respondent still insists that the appeal has been improperly brought before the Board. I beg to submit.

Order: (1) Ruling on 26 May 2005

B

RULING

(Delivered 26 May 2005)

In this matter the respondent, the Commissioner General, duly represented by Mr Primi, legal counsel has raised a preliminary objection to the effect that this
appeal is improperly brought before the Board as it is time barred in view of s 16 C
of the Tax Revenue Appeals Act read together with rule 4 (2) of the Tax Revenue Appeals Board Rules.

Mr Primi, legal counsel submitted that the appeal was filed on 13 July 2004 after the appellant was aggrieved by the respondent's decision delivered on 4 June 2004. According to Mr Primi this was within a period of 39 days contrary to
the 30 days envisaged by the law as per s 16 (3) of the Tax Revenue Appeal Act. D

He further submitted that the same argument goes to rule 4 (2) of the Tax Revenue Appeals Board Rules whereby a Notice of Intention to Appeal against the decision of the Commissioner General is to be lodged with the Board within a period of 30 days from the date of service of the Commissioner General's decision.

As a result of failure of complying with the law, the appeal and notice of
intention to appeal were filed after 30 days from the date of the respondent's E
decision. Mr Primi suggested that he would have expected that the appellant would have in the event sought leave from the Board to file their appeal and intention out of time.

In reply Mr Mgoya, legal counsel, representing the appellant Kombo Hassan responded by submitting that they are well in time as the notice of assessment was
served upon them on 15 June 2004 after the appellant was found roaming in the F
respondent's corridors.

He further submitted that the appellant had endorsed on the notice on 15 June 2004. The date was marked by himself as he was never made to sign anywhere by the respondent.

Mr Mgoya admitted that they had no quarrel with the date when the notice of
assessment was written, that is 4 June 2004 but they received the same on 15 June G
2004. The legal counsel further argued that it was upon the respondent to prove that they were served on 4 June 2004 and not 15 June 2004, the proof which has not been established before the Board.

In reply Mr Primi, legal counsel for the respondent reacted that with the appellant's submission, the respondent is left in a dilemma as to whether it is true
the appellant was served on 15 June 2004 as he has brought no evidence to H
substantiate the same. As a result this brings about a reasonable doubt that it was possible that the appellant had been served with the respondent's decision on 4 June 2004 and so the appeal is out of time.

Having the above in our minds and the wordings of s 16 (2) of the Tax Revenue Appeals Act, we agree with the respondent's counsel that the law

A requires one to file his intention of appeal within 30 days from receipt of the decision of the Commissioner General. It follows then, that the duty of serving a taxpayer with the said decision is vested with the respondent.

In this appeal before us, taking the submission of Mr Primi, legal counsel, it is obvious to us that the respondent has no knowledge as to when he served the appellant with his decision. He has come before this esteemed Board with no B proof at all as far as the date of service of the decision is concerned.

It beats our minds then as to what is the basis of the respondent's prayer that the appeal is time barred on grounds that s 16 of the Tax Revenue Appeals Act was not complied with. We proceed to concur with the respondent's feeling that there is a reasonable doubt as to whether the appellant was served or not on 4 June 2004, a doubt which gives a benefit or advantage to the taxpayer of which, we C accordingly accord him.

It follows then with lack of proof from the respondent as to when the appellant was served with the decision of the Commissioner General, we take the date of service as being 15 June 2004 and so the appeal is well in time and proper before the Board and we therefore order that the appeal should proceed on merit. In the circumstances the preliminary objection is accordingly dismissed with costs.

D Right of Appeal explained.

Read this 26 May 2005 in presence of Mr Mngoya for appellant and Mr Primi for respondent.

E

KOMBO HASSANI C/O MULTIMODAL FREIGHT CO. LTD v COMMISSIONER GENERAL (No. 2)

F TAX REVENUE APPEALS BOARD

DAR ES SALAAM

(CUSTOMS AND EXCISE TAX APPEAL CASE DSM 10 OF 2004)

G 3 June 2005

BR Mutungi, *Vice-Chairperson*, I Dallushi and J Karashani, *Members*

H *Compoundment—Compoundment of offences—Maximum import duty penalty prescribed at 300%—In imposing the penalty Commissioner General to exercise discretion judiciously—East African Customs and Transfer Management Tax Act, s 173*

The appellant appealed against the imposition by the respondent of a maximum import duty penalty of 300% against a revised valuation of his imported goods which had earlier been seized by the respondent. In the first

instance, the respondent compounded an offence against the appellant and A
imposed on him a fine of Tshs 9 million which was equivalent to 109% of the import duty. In addition to the fine, taxes and duties were also imposed. Upon appeal by the appellant the respondent made a corresponding review whose effect was to reduce the amount of taxes and duties payable but the fine remained at Tshs 9 million which this time meant 320% of the import duty. The respondent reduced the fine to 300% which is the maximum fine B
percentage he has discretion to impose. Aggrieved by the decision the respondent the appellant appealed to the Board challenging that decision as being arbitrary and not judicious.

Held:

(1) Although the respondent by law has discretion to prescribe any fine not exceeding 300% of the import duty, this should be done judiciously; C

(2) since the previous import duty penalty was on the basis of 109% then even after the revision that was made on the value of goods the corresponding penalty on the import duty should have been based on the 109% of which the appellant had no dispute with from the very beginning, and

(3) the respondent should not have, without any reasonable grounds moved the fine on import duty to the maximum of 300% without giving reason for D
vacating from his earlier decision of imposing 109% as fine.

Appeal upheld.

Mngoya, for the appellant
Primi, for the respondent

E

26 May 2005:

Submission for the appellant

Mr Mngoya, for the appellant: Our appeal has two grounds; that the Commissioner General erred in law in composing the maximum penalty of 300%, F
and secondly the respondent also erred in law in not refunding the access money paid to him.

Your Honour from the beginning, the appellant was one of several small businessmen who imported different items from Zanzibar through Bagamoyo port. At the Bagamoyo port the respondent seized all the items of all the businessmen and several notices of seizure were issued. G

Your Honour, we pray to rely on the photocopy of seizure, which we appended in our statement of appeal but not numbered.

Mr Primi, for the respondent: No objection.

Board: Admitted and marked P1. H

Mr Mngoya, for the appellant: On 20 March 2002, the appellant was required to pay a sum of Tshs 27.8 million and Tshs 8.2 million import duty and a fine of Tshs 9 million on the purported evaded import duty.

Your Honour, we pray to tender the calculation served on the appellant.

Mr Primi: No objection.

Board: Admitted and marked P2. The appellant was aggrieved and asked the respondent to review the calculation and proper values, as the import duty was excessive.

Mr Mngoya, for the appellant: The respondent complied with and revised the calculations on the items seized. On 30 August 2002 the appellant was required to pay about 15 million in total. Import duty was calculated at Tshs 2.8 million and this time the fine stood at Tshs 9 million as in the previous assessment.

The appellant paid under protest the whole of Tshs 16.8 million. Your Honour we pray to tender the assessment, which ordered the appellant to pay.

Mr Primi: I have no objection.

Board: Admitted and marked P3.

Mr Mngoya, for the appellant: We have come before this Board to put out that the second time on the served assessment (Tshs 9 million) is erroneous because the fine stands at 320% of the import duty, while in the first case, the same Tshs 9 million stood at 109%.

The respondent should have taken the 109% to the served assessment. In protest, the respondent decided to refund the excess of 20% and in his decision the respondent said that the Tshs 8 million was 300% of the evaded imported goods. The Board should consider the respondent's decision.

It is true that there is a provision of the law which is the Finance Act, 1994, s 11 but we believe this was misconstrued by the respondent.

The cruelty of this section is the word "conviction". In that year the same provision was enacted in the Sales Duty Act and Stamp Duty Act reading similarly. There is confusion in penalty and additional sum. There has to be a conviction, and convictions are done before merits of law and this provision of the law was enacted in several Acts to determine or prevent notorious evaders of import duty.

In our case in hand, regarding the appellant, it was his several importations and it was done in multi-model and had no record of being notorious. We now beg to re-consider the decision of the respondent bearing in mind the appellant's case.

Submission for the respondent

Mr Primi, for the respondent: It is my humble reply that the appellant's appeal is based on matters of law, and in essence, is challenging the decision of the Commissioner General in relation to a fine imposed on the appellant, which fine was prescribed at a rate of 300% of the customs duties that were found to be evaded by the appellant.

Before I come to the actual issue, I would like to point out that here we are talking of customs duty against Import duty.

According to the definition of customs duty under the East African Customs and Transfer Tax Management Act (Cap 27 of the Community Laws) as applied by Act No. 19 of 1997, customs duty means any duty, tax, levy or imposition collected through customs and in this case it includes all the taxes on goods and included VAT, import duty and excise duty. Import duty refers to customs tariff duty imposed under the Customs Tariff Act.

Your Honour, the brief history of this appeal is partly submitted by the counsel for appellant. In essence he does not dispute the fact that the goods imported by the appellant were seized at Bagamoyo by customs officers after being found to be uncustomed goods and upon seizure of the said goods. The appellant did admit to have committed an offence and requested the matter to be compounded under s 173 of the East African Customs and Transfer Tax Management Act. Under the said section the Commissioner of Customs is required, where he finds any person committed an offence against matters of law, and that person admits such an offence had been committed, the Commissioner may proceed to prescribe penalty provided under the relevant contravened provision of the law and after prescribing that penalty he may order to pay all the relevant duties and taxes that he had evaded. So in this case the appellant was found with uncustomed goods. According to s 146 of the East African Customs Transfer Tax Management Act, the maximum penalty prescribed thereunder is 300% of the duty evaded. Since the matter was compounded by the Commissioner, s 173 of the above-quoted law allows the Commissioner to prescribe any penalty but not exceeding the actual penalty prescribed on the contravened provision, so the Commissioner had power to prescribe any amount of monies but not exceeding 300%. Having the facts before the Board, it is not in dispute that in the first instance when this matter arose the Commissioner had demanded the appellant to pay customs duty amounting to a total of Tshs 27,838,156 including a penalty of Tshs 9 million.

This penalty of Tshs 9 million, was equivalent to 109% of the total duty evaded. It is also not in dispute that the Commissioner did revise the amount evaded to a total of Tshs 16,802,267 including a fine of Tshs 9 million, which upon grievances from appellant came to note an error on the penalty prescribed that came to be 320% of the duty evaded.

Since the law empowers the Commissioner to impose a fine not exceeding 300% the Commissioner in revising the penalty did reduce the fine of Tshs 9 million by deducting the 25% and refunding the appellant a total sum of Tshs 500,586, vide letter dated 4 June 2004 under reference TRA/CUS/DSM/LR/F.10/1 which is attached to the statement of appeal. In that letter the respondent tells the appellant specifically that the penalty has been revised to a percentage of 300% of the duty evaded which is in line with the law.

Your Honour, going to the argument by counsel of appellant that there is a confusion in law regarding the word “conviction”, it is my humble submission that in view of the provision of s 173 of the East African Customs and Transfer Tax Management Act, the Commissioner is empowered to exonerate one from being prosecuted in the court of law and being convicted by way of compounding the offence under the said section and this is what was done by the Commissioner in this case.

The issue of additional sum does not arise because s 146 of the East African Customs and Transfer Tax Management Act as amended by the provisions of s 11 (2) of the Finance Act, 1994 (16 of 1994). It is therefore my humble submission that the decision by Commissioner dated 4 June 2004 was in law correct and I humbly pray the appeal be dismissed. I beg to submit.

A Mr Mngoya, for appellant, in reply: Your Honour, the relevant section is not s 146 but s 148. The response by the Commissioner was given under s 148. I did not submit that there is confusion of the word "conviction" but I said the respondent erred in imposing 300% as fine. From the letter of 4 June 2004 he termed the Tshs 9 million as a fine; we submit that this is an additional sum of 300% percentage.

B Your Honour, the respondent by imposing 300% as fine was wrong. On the other hand, the calculations and assessment in total were done arbitrarily. How come the respondent imposed the 300% in addition to 320%, and not to the 109% imposed earlier on. It was not done judiciously.

We pray that the Board reconsider the decision, bearing in mind the differences I had pointed out.

C

Order: (1) Judgment on 3 June 2005 at 9.00 am.

JUDGMENT

(Delivered 3 June 2005)

D The appellant one Kombo Hassan duly represented by Mr Mngoya, learned counsel, has opted to appeal before this Board after being aggrieved by the calculation of the Commissioner General of the amount due for refund dated 4 June 2004 and received by the appellant on 15 June 2004. The events that have led to this appeal are that after the appellant's goods had been seized by the customs officials and the appellant having admitted to the commission of the E offence, the Commissioner General decided to compound the offence by ordering taxes and fine to be paid under s 173 of East African Customs and Transfer Tax Management Act. As a result of this, the value of goods came to Tshs 32,890,920, import duty Tshs 8,222,730,000 and penalty on import duty at a rate of 109% amounting to Tshs 9 million. According to the appellant this calculation came about due to the increase of value of the goods and the quantity of items by the F customs officials.

After complaints on the exorbitant amount by the appellant the customs officers revised the value and consequently revised the value as follows:

Import duty Tshs 2,833,138, value of goods Tshs 11,332,552 and penalty on import duty at a rate of 320% of the import duty amounting toTshs 9 million. It is upon the penalty prescribed on import duty that the appellant submits that as G the Commissioner General had issued a compoundment order prescribing a penalty of 109% of the inflated import duty then he ought to have adjusted the same on the same basis after revising, and come up with an amount of Tshs 2,833,138 instead of Tshs 8,222,730. The appellant further disputes the fact that the law prescribes a maximum penalty of up to 300% of the import duty in question, and the Commissioner may opt to prescribe any penalty but not beyond H the 300% of the import duty, still the penalty on the import duty so prescribed should have been maintained at the rate of 109% as had already been done and so the demand for Tshs 9 million penalty was clearly unfair and excessive. It was not enough for the Commissioner to refund the 20% in excess already paid amounting to Tshs 500,586.

The appellant in arguing the appeal submitted that he was not a habitual offender to warrant the Commissioner to charge a maximum penalty.

On the other side Mr Primi, legal counsel representing the Commissioner General argued that what the custom's officials did was well in line with the law. The law prescribes maximum penalty after compoundment of 300% and this is why after realizing the 20% in excess the respondent did refund the same to the appellant.

From the above submissions it is clear before the Board that the appellant's dispute lies with the maximum import duty penalty of 300%. On this we find that as narrated by the appellant and not disputed by the respondent, the first fine on import duty was at a rate of 109%. It is also not disputed by the respondent that the review was to be done on the valuation amount of the goods which was accordingly adjusted after the review but the fine on import duty was elevated to 320% and later after complaints by the appellant, reduced to 300%.

It should be noted here as we have noted that no reason was advanced by the respondent as to why the Commissioner opted to impose the fine at 300%.

We would have expected that using his discretion granted to him by the law, he would have revised the whole matter on the basis of a corresponding review. On the same footing then as the previous import duty penalty was on the basis of 109% then even after the revision made on the value of goods the corresponding penalty on the import duty should have been based on the 109% of which the appellant had no dispute with from the very beginning. It follows therefore that the respondent without any reasonable ground should not have moved the fine on import duty to the maximum of 300% without giving reason for vacating from his earlier decision of imposing 109% as fine.

It raises our suspicion as to why the Commissioner had raised the penalty to 320%. We are inclined to agree with the appellant that the percentage was raised either hastily or arbitrarily. The respondent by law has discretion to prescribe any fine not exceeding 300% of the import duty; but this should be done judiciously.

From the foregoing, this Honourable Board proceeds to uphold the appeal and orders that the respondent calculates the fine on import duty basing on the 109% formerly prescribed by him and the appellant be refunded the difference accordingly. Each party to bear own costs.

Right of Appeal explained.

Read this day of 3 June 2005 in the presence of Mr Mngoya for appellant and in absence of respondent duly informed.

MARIE STOPES (T) LIMITED v COMMISSIONER GENERAL (No. 1)

TAX REVENUE APPEALS BOARD

DAR ES SALAAM

(INCOME TAX APPLICATION: NO. DSM. 4 OF 2004)

6 June 2005

RKB Meela, *Chairperson*, I Dallushi and J Karashani, *Members*

Practice and Procedure—Preliminary objection—Preliminary objection raised just before the hearing of the application was to begin—When a preliminary point of law may be raised

Just before the hearing of an application began respondent prayed to raise a preliminary objection on a point of law. This prayer was resisted by the counsel for the applicant arguing that it should have been raised earlier. The Board considered the arguments of both counsel.

Held:

(i) As the preliminary objection is said to be based on a legal point which can be raised at any time during a hearing, it would be much convenient that the Board hears the same at this early stage before hearing the application itself;

Prayer granted.

Dr Luoga, for the applicant
Mr Songoro, for the respondent

6 June 2005:

Mr Songoro, for the respondent: Your Honour, the respondent has a preliminary objection against the Application.

Dr Luoga, for the applicant: Honourable Chairperson, we have no prior notice for the said preliminary objection, but we stand guided by the Board that, if the learned counsel has an important point of law which ought to be raised as a preliminary matter, it would be in the interest of justice that this Honourable Board should hear the point.

Chairperson: Mr Songoro is asked to explain the nature of the said preliminary objection and as to why they failed to give notice of the said objection when they filed their counter affidavit in this Board.

Mr Songoro, for the respondent: The preliminary objection, which I intend to raise, is based on the time frame under which such an application is to be made. I am of the view that the time within which it has to be made is 30 days, which are counted from the date the assessment was issued. That is the

position introduced by the Finance Act, 2004 which was effective from the A
1 July 2004.

This matter was assigned to Mr Kidaya of the TRA and he managed to file the counter-affidavit, and he is the one who handles the pleadings. Now the matter has been assigned to me this morning when I was informed by the Secretary to the Board (TRA) that Mr Kidaya has traveled. Upon reading the pleadings and the law that is the Finance Act, 2004 and the Tax Revenue Appeals Act, 2000, B
I am of the opinion that there is an important matter, which has to be considered by this Board. That is the reason why I have brought this matter of time frame this morning before this Board.

Dr Luoga, for the applicant: Your Honour, it would appear that the learned counsel has no good reason as to why he failed to notify this Board of the said C
preliminary objection. The Legal Services Department of the respondent is supposed to work as single solid team; the absence of an officer cannot suffice as the reason for not observing the due process or procedures.

The learned counsel has omitted to tell this Board which provision of the Finance Act, 2004 serves the time limitation and how this applied to the application at hand so that I could effectively assist the Board. The counsel D
simply told this Board that time runs out 30 days after the assessment, without telling the Board as to which assessment he is talking about. Perhaps that would have helped this Board to decide as to whether to hear the anticipated preliminary objection.

Mr Songoro, for the respondent: I tend to agree with Dr Luoga that the Legal E
Services Department is expected to work as a single solid team. But I also reply that it was through my research on the Finance Act, 2004 that I discovered that there was a time limit for bringing such application, which touches on assessment and collection of taxes.

Sincerely, we were bound to bring a notice of our preliminary objection but I lacked such time to bring the same this morning. Equally, I am bound to bring F
an objection even orally if there is a point of law. I think I would not be honest to the Board to conceal such point and raise it later. It was under such circumstances that I have been forced to raise it at this stage. That is all.

RULING

G

Mr Songoro, a learned counsel for the respondent, this very morning before the Board was about to start hearing the Application, submitted that he had a preliminary objection on the point of law, which he prays to raise against the application as filed. Dr Luoga, a learned counsel for the applicant, submitted that if the said preliminary point of law was for the interest of justice, then he stands to be guided by this Board.

H

Mr Songoro as required by this Board, informed this Board that the preliminary point touches on the time factor of bringing the present application as provided for in the Finance Act, 2004. Mr Songoro, also said that this matter was initially assigned to Mr Kidaya, also a learned counsel of the TRA, who filed the pleadings. But today he is absent for he has traveled, whereby the conduct of the application was assigned to Mr Songoro this morning, whereby he discovered

A the legal point he now intends to bring before this Board. Mr Songoro admits that the respondent was bound to bring a notice of preliminary objection before this Board, but only lacked time to do so. Nevertheless he feels obliged not to conceal such matter from this Board, for a preliminary objection can be raised at any time during the hearing of a cause.

This Board has been reminding the respondent to file replies to filed B statements of appeal and also file notice of preliminary objection at the earliest. As Mr Songoro submitted that having discovered the procedural lapse in the filing of this present application he was bound to raise the matter with this Board to decide as to whether to hear it or not. This Board has carefully considered both counsels' submissions and is of the view that as the preliminary objection is said to be based on a legal point which can be raised at any time during a hearing; it C would be much convenient that the Board hears the same at this early stage before hearing the application itself.

Although we are going to hear the preliminary objection on a point of law, as prayed by Mr Songoro, we insist that the respondent shall in the future raise such objections by way of notice to avoid ambushing other parties and to allow them time for preparation to argue the same.

D

MARIE STOPES (T) LIMITED v COMMISSIONER GENERAL
E **(No. 2)**

TAX REVENUE APPEALS BOARD

DAR ES SALAAM

F (INCOME TAX APPLICATION: NO. DSM. 4 OF 2004)

8 June 2005

RKB Meela, *Chairperson*, I Dallushi and J Karashani, *Members*

G *Applications—Applications and limitation period—Application lodged after expiry of time—Whether the application may be entertained by the Board*

Applications—Application made under s 7 of the Tax Revenue Appeals Act, 2000—Whether the section is subject to the provisions of ss 12, 13, 14 and 16 of the same Act—Tax Revenue Appeals Act, 2000, ss 7, 12, 13, 14 and 16

H

This was an application for declaration of status, which arose from a decision by the respondent refusing to grant a tax-exempt status to the applicant. The application was made under s 7, but without complying with the provisions of ss 12, 13, 14 and 16, of the Tax Revenue Appeals Act, 2000. The respondent argued that the application was not properly submitted before

the Board for failure to comply with statutory provisions and prayed that it A
be dismissed.

Held:

(1) The applicant's failure to comply fully with the procedures enacted in Tax Revenue Appeals Act has resulted into a peculiar procedure unknown to the Act, and the applicant is accordingly late because the time limit for questioning the respondent's decision of denying the applicant a tax-exempt B
status lapsed more than two years ago;

(2) the present application is hopelessly time barred.

Obiter: The applicant could have brought proceedings for a declaratory order concerning its tax-exempt status only and could argue not to be bound by limitation of time where the applicant had not commenced business but had C
first applied to the Commissioner for Income Tax to be granted tax exempt status under s 14 and para 5 of First Schedule to the Income Tax Act, 1973 and was refused.

Application dismissed.

Case referred to: D

Marie Stopes (T) Ltd v Commissioner General (Comm Case 10/04), unreported

Dr Luoga, for the applicant
Songoro, for the respondent

E

Submissions on the preliminary objection

Mr Songoro, for the respondent: Honourable Chairperson and members of the Board, the applicant filed the present application before this Board on 25 November 2004. According to the prayers in the Chamber Summons, prayer No. 4, the applicant is contesting that the respondent acted wrongly and unlawfully in assessing F
and collecting income tax from the applicant. It is on the basis of this wrongful and unlawful act in assessing and collecting tax that the applicant is applying in prayer No. 5 for the restoration of the wrongfully collected tax.

It is the respondent's submission that the issue of assessing and collecting of tax is pleaded in the applicant's application and Chamber summons. We are submitting that under the Finance Act, 2004 (15 of 2004), which repealed ss 12 G
and 13 of the Tax Revenue Appeals Act, and substituted them with new ss 12 and 13: any person who disputes an assessment in any manner, if the assessment is wrong, or unlawful, so long you dispute it, you have to raise an objection to the Commissioner General within 30 days upon the receipt of such assessments. And by virtue of s 16 (1) and (2) of the Tax Revenue Appeals Act, any person who is served by a decision or notice of the Commissioner General determining the H
objection, may appeal to this Board against the decision of the Commissioner General. Section 16 (1) (*a*) and (*b*) of the Tax Revenue Appeals Act, places a condition that the Board shall not entertain an appeal pursuant to this section unless the appellant had given prior notice to the Commissioner General that he intends to appeal against such decision, and the appeal is lodged with the Board

A with 45 days from the date of service of decision of the Commissioner General determining such objection.

It is the respondent's submission that firstly, there was no notice of objection served on the respondent 30 days since the assessment was made. Secondly, there was no notice of appeal given to the Commissioner General within 30 days from date of the Commissioner General's decision, as there was no such notice of
B appeal issued to the Commissioner General. Furthermore there is no proof that this application was filed within 45 days from the date of service upon the appellant of the notice under subs (4) of s 12 of the Tax Revenue Appeals Act.

It is the applicant's submission that this application seeking a declaration that the respondent acted wrongly and unlawfully in assessing and collecting income tax from the applicant, has been filed hopelessly out of time for the
C reason that s 14 (3) of the Tax Revenue Appeals Act emphasizes that the provisions of this Act relating to Appeals to the Board against assessments, and the provisions relating to further appeals to the Tribunal, shall take effect with respect to any appeal under this section as if such appeal were an appeal against an assessment.

It is the respondent's submissions that since the application is based on the
D legality and correctness, and whether the assessment was wrong or was unlawful, then the correctness, and whether the assessment was wrong or was unlawful, then the correct of procedure of contesting this is the one sated under s 14 (3) of the Tax Revenue Appeals Act which refers to the provisions relating to appeals to the Board as pointed out to be ss 12 and 16 of the Tax Revenue Appeals Act.

It is the respondent's submission and prayer that this application has been
E filed out of time contrary to s 12 (1) and (2) and contrary to ss 16 (1) and (2) (*a*) and (*b*) of the Tax Revenue Appeals Act, we therefore pray that this Board dismisses the same with costs. In the alternative, we pray that this Board dismisses this application because it was filed prematurely, as it was not accompanied by the decision of the Commissioner General as emphasized by ss 12 and 16 of the Act. That is all.

F

Dr Luoga, for the applicant: Your Honour and members of the Board, basically what the counsel for the respondent is alleging is that in lodging the application, the applicant did not comply with the procedure. He has submitted that the correct procedure would be to pursue an Appeal after duly complying with the provisions of ss 12, 13, 14 and 16 of the Tax Revenue Appeals Act, as amended by the
G Finance Act, 2004.

Honourable members of the Board, the basis of the applicant's assertion is that the chamber summons contained in para 5 of the orders sought, application for order, which bear on the correctness of an assessment to tax. It is for this Board to note that the respondent counsel has skillfully refrained from addressing the basic declaratory orders prayed for in paras 1, 2, and 3 in the Chamber Summons.
H What the counsel is attempting to do is to tinker paras 4 and 5 and give them undue primacy. This is wrong and an attempt to divert the cause of justice. Paras 4 and 5 are merely consequential orders, which the applicant did not even require to include in the Chamber Summons. It would suffice for this Honourable Board to address paras 1, 2, and 3 and give an order that would provide the redress sought. The inclusion of paras 4 and 5 is necessarily consequential, the question

is whether para 1, 2, and 3 stand independently or not and whether or not this Board has jurisdiction under s 7 of the Tax Revenue Appeal Act to entertain this application. A

Honourable Members of the Board, this is an application for the declaration of status, which arose from a decision by the respondent to refuse to grant a tax-exempt status to the applicant. The applicant has never contested any assessment but has been paying all the taxes collected because they could not object to any B assessment if their status remained unrecognized. It is not surprising that the counsel has not told this Honourable Board which assessment the appellant is aggrieved with.

Furthermore the counsel for the respondent has clearly attempted to conceal the fact that all the records forming the basis for the application evolve from the refusal by the respondent to grant tax-exempt status to the applicant. C

Honourable members, any person is entitled under the law. The applicant has claimed under s 14 of the Income Tax Act, 1973, read together with, para 5 of the First Schedule thereto, to be treated as an exempted person being a charitable organization. If the Commissioner refuses to accord such a status to which the person is legally entitled, the remedy is to get from a competent organ a declaration of the correct status so that both parties relate to each other and D operate according to the law.

Under the law, the only competent organ to make such declaration of status is this Honourable Board. The proper procedure to move this Honourable Board is through declaratory proceedings. These are taken under s 7 of the Tax Revenue Appeals Act. We have the advantage of a High Court decision on that point in *Marie Stopes (T) Ltd v Commissioner General* (Comm Case 10/04), unreported, E which in effect recognizes the wide jurisdiction this Board has, which include even to take declaratory proceedings under s 7.

Honourable Chairperson and members of the Board, s 7 does not operate subject to compliances under ss 12, 13, 14 and 16 of the Tax Revenue Appeals Act. The declaratory orders sought are not subject to objection proceedings. It is significant that the counsel for the respondent laboured hard to avoid calling this F application an appeal, because he was attempting to superimpose a procedure on this Application, which is not prescribed by the law.

We humbly pray that the preliminary objection be dismissed with costs for the following reasons: First, in that this application is not based on a complaint against an assessment. Secondly, the decision on which the application has been taken is not subject to the objections and appeals procedure. Third, that the G application has been competently taken under s 7 of the Tax Revenue Appeals Act. Fourth, that should this Honourable Board find that paras 4 and 5 in the Chamber Summons are in anyway offensive, dictates of substantive justice, we would enjoin this Honourable Board to strike out the offending paras and address the basic orders which are sought in paras 1, 2, and 3, but not to dismiss the application as prayed for, particularly when the respondent's counsel has not H challenged the competence of all the other orders which we have sought particularly in paras 1, 2, and 3, which are basic, and paras 6 and 7 are which routine redress paras.

We beg to submit.

A Mr Songoro, for the respondent, in reply: Your Honour, only a brief reply. First, the procedure, which the respondent is complaining was not followed, is a statutory mandatory procedure. The applicant has indicated this application is brought under s 7 of the Tax Revenue Appeals Act. In the actual fact the Chamber Summons quotes s 7 of the said Act, but s 7 is subject to s 12. It is the respondent's submission, that even if the applicant is pursuing an application before this Board B he cannot disregard the provisions of s 12 because their application refers to matters of wrongful and unlawful assessment.

Application contains civil matters, which arose from the revenue laws administered by the respondent. Therefore, by just citing paras 4 and 5, the respondent was not diverting from the course of justice. The respondent was showing what was the actual complaint of the applicant and what was the net C effect of the application if it succeeded. If the application is successful, the assessments will be seen by this Board that they were wrongly and unlawfully made. According to para 5 there will be a restoration of the wrongfully collected taxes.

Therefore, though the applicant has baptized the matter as application, the applicant is actually seeking this Board to sit on the decision of the Commissioner D for Income Tax and make other decisions.

I would further submit that this application must take the procedure as the one prescribed for appeals before this Board.

In other words, the applicant's contention that this applicant has its own procedure apart from that of appeal is not proper, for both applications and appeals are subjected to one procedure.

E The applicant has also contended that if the applicant had sought to seek the declaration of the status of the applicant, they could have done it easily by not introducing paras 4 and 5 and other matters in the affidavit, which deal with unlawful and wrongful collection of taxes. We further reply that this Board has undoubtedly wide jurisdiction to entertain matters arising from the revenue laws, but our objection is not based on the jurisdiction. It is rather based on the time F frame of filing the application; a non-compliance of statutory procedure, particularly when the assessment is said to be wrong and unlawful.

On the applicant's submission that the declaratory orders sought are not subject of objection procedure, the respondent submits that it is wrong for the orders sought relate to unlawfulness and wrongful assessments of tax. The respondent further replies that under s 14, even if it is a refusal to make any G refund of tax or any other dispute which is not necessarily an appeal, the procedure according to s 14 is the one followed in filing appeals.

On the applicant's submission that we have not challenged the rest of the orders, it is the respondent's submission that the procedure of filing the application is wrong and also the timing of filing the same was not proper as it was filed upon non-compliance with respective procedure.

H On the applicant's prayer that this Board should delete paras 4 and 5 if it is satisfied that the same offend, and the Board allow the application to proceed on grounds 1, 2 and 3, it is the respondent's reply that even if that is done, the application is made under s 7 and it does not meet the test of s 12 and on the basis of this application, it would not be possible to draw a line between paras 4 and 5, which are said that can be disregarded, and the rest of the other paras of the Chamber Summons.

It is the respondent's reply that this application be dismissed as a whole, and if the applicant wants to pursue the matter he can bring another application subject to the provisions of the Tax Revenue Appeals Act.

That is all Your Honours.

Board: Now we are through with the hearing of the preliminary objection. The time being almost 2.00 pm, the board members will deliberate on the submissions by the learned counsel this afternoon and thereafter the ruling will be composed and be delivered tomorrow 7 June 2005 at 12 noon.

7 June 2005:

Chairperson: I am not yet through in composing the ruling. It would seem that the Board needs more time to dispose of all the issues raised by the parties counsel in their respectful submissions. The chairperson respectfully regrets the inconvenience caused to the parties, counsels.

Order: The ruling will be tomorrow the 8 June 2005 at 2.30 pm.

RULING

(Delivered 8 June 2005)

In this application, the applicant is Messrs Marie Stopes Tanzania Limited and the respondents are the Commissioner General, of the Tanzania Revenue Authority and the Commissioner for Income Tax, Tanzania Revenue Authority. The applicant's representatives are Messrs FK Law Chambers who made appearance by its learned counsel, Dr FDAM. Luoga, while the respondent is represented by its officer a learned counsel Mr H Songoro.

This application is by way of chamber summons supported by an affidavit sworn by one Mr Edward Wambugu, the principal officer of the applicant. The respondent also filed a counter affidavit sworn by its Principal Officer Mr Emmanuel P Mahendeka.

The chamber summons pray this Board to issue the following declaratory orders in favour of the applicants:

1. That the applicant is and has always been a charitable organization;
2. That the applicant being a charitable organization, is under the Income Tax Act, 1973 exempt from payment of income tax;
3. That the respondents acted wrongly in not recognizing that the applicant is a charitable organization;
4. That the respondents acted wrongly and unlawfully in assessing and collecting income tax from the applicant;
5. That the applicant is entitled to restoration of the funds wrongly appropriated by the respondents purportedly being income tax due to the respondents;
6. Costs of this application;
7. Any such and further order as this Honourable Board may deem proper and just to grant.

Although the respondents had not filed a notice of preliminary objection in this Board, on the first day scheduled for the hearing, the respondent orally prayed to advance and argue a preliminary objection against the filed application. Mr Songoro, a learned counsel for the respondent told this Board that initially one Mr Ndanai Kidaya, a learned advocate, who had been assigned to represent the respondent and had filed the reply pleading was on safari and he, Mr Songoro was assigned to represent the respondent. Mr Songoro then told this Board that upon reading through the filed pleadings discovered defects of procedural nature in the applicant's application. The Board allowed Mr Songoro to make submissions on the preliminary objection on points of law.

In his submissions in chief for the preliminary objection, Mr Songoro submitted that the applicant, in filing the present application, failed to observe the procedure enacted in the provisions of Tax Revenue Appeals Act. Mr Songoro argued that according to prayers No. 4 and 5 in the Chamber Summons, the applicant is contesting that the respondents acted wrongly and unlawfully in assessing and collecting income tax from the applicant, and on that basis the applicant is now praying for the restoration of the wrongfully collected tax. Mr Songoro then submitted that according to s 12 of the Tax Revenue Appeals Act, as amended by the Finance Act, the applicant was disputing the assessed income tax and was bound to raise a notice of objection to the Commissioner General within 30 days from the date of service of the notice of assessment. Thereafter, the applicants upon being served with a final decision of the respondent, (Commissioner General) and if aggrieved, may appeal to this Board under the provisions of s 16 (1) and (2) of the Tax Revenue Appeals Act as amended by the Finance Act, 2004. It is provided that such an appellant shall give notice of appeal to the respondent within 30 days following the date of being served with the notice of the final determination of the assessment of tax and such appeal is filed within 45 days from the date of notice of final determination of the assessment of tax served on the aggrieved taxpayer.

Mr Songoro submitted that there was no notice of objection, nor notice of appeal given by the applicants to the respondent pursuant to the cited provisions of the Tax Revenue Appeals Act, as amended. It is submitted further that the present application seeking declaration that the respondent acted wrongly and unlawfully in assessing and collecting income tax from the applicant, has been filed hopelessly out of time, for the very reason s 14 (3) of the Tax Revenue Appeals Act provides that the provisions of this Act relating to appeals to the Board against assessments shall take effect with respect to any appeal under this section as if such appeal were an appeal against assessment.

Mr Songoro then prayed this Board to dismiss the application because the same was filed contrary to the provisions of ss 12 (1) and (2) and s 16 (1) and (2) *(a)* and *(b)* of the Tax Revenue Appeals Act.

Dr Luoga, a learned counsel for the applicant, when making his reply to the respondent's preliminary objection refuted the assertions and allegations made against the application. Dr Luoga submitted that according to the line of argument advanced by Mr Songoro, for the respondent, he was giving undue primacy to paras 4 and 5 of the Chamber Summons, while refraining skillfully from addressing the basic declaratory orders prayed for under paras 1, 2 and 3 in the Chamber Summons. Dr Luoga submitted that the prayers in paras 4 and 5 are merely consequential which the applicants could have not pleaded in the

Chamber Summons, and prays this Honourable Board to ignore them and A
address itself to paras 1, 2 and 3 and consequently issue orders would provide
the remedies sought by the applicant. Dr Luoga submitted that the issue is
whether the said paras 1, 2 and 3 can stand independently and this Board has
jurisdiction under s 7 of the Tax Revenue Appeals Act to entertain this
application.

It was further submitted by Dr Luoga that the present application is for the B
declaration of status, which arose from the decision of the respondent refusing to
grant a tax-exempt status to the applicant. The applicant had never contested any
tax assessment but was paying all the collected taxes because he could not have
objected so long as his status remained unrecognized by the respondent. Further
to that, the respondent's counsel had deliberately concealed the fact that all the
records forming the basis of this Application evolves from the refusal by the C
respondent to grant the applicant a tax exempt status.

It was also argued by Dr Luoga that any person entitled to apply for tax-
exempt status to the Commissioner of Income Tax under s 14, read together with
para 5 of the First Schedule on the ground that such person is a charitable
organization, where the Commissioner refuses such an application, such person
can apply to this Board as a competent legal organ for a declaratory order. Dr D
Luoga submitted that the correct procedure to move this Board is through
declaratory proceedings, which are taken under s 7 of the Tax Revenue Appeals
Act. Such legal procedure was stated by the High Court in its decision in *Marie
Stopes (T) Ltd v Commissioner General* where the High Court recognizes the
wide jurisdiction of this Board which includes taking declaratory proceedings
under ss 7 of the Tax Revenue Appeals Act. E

Dr Luoga further submitted that s 7 of the Tax Revenue Appeals Act does not
operate subject to compliances to ss 12, 13, 14 and 16 of the same Act. He added
that the declaratory orders sought are not subject to objection proceedings and
that the respondent's counsel has been attempting to superimpose on this
application procedures not prescribed by the law.

Ultimately, Dr Luoga prays this Honourable Board to dismiss the preliminary F
objection on the basis of the foregone advanced grounds, and where this Board
finds that paras 4 and 5 of the Chamber Summons were offended in any way,
to strike them out and address itself to the basic orders/prayers as contained in
paras 1, 2, and 3 and not to dismiss the application as prayed for by the
respondent's counsel who had not challenged the competence of these three
prayers which are basic to the present application and the rest of the prayers G
which are in paras 6 and 7 being routine redress prayers.

Mr Songoro, a learned counsel for the respondent in his rejoinder submissions,
emphasized the respondent's objection to this application. He submitted that the
basis of the respondent's objection is that the applicant has failed to comply with
statutory mandatory procedure. Mr Songoro submits that as the present
application is brought under s 7 of the Tax Revenue Appeals Act, it should be H
observed that s 7 is subject to the provisions of s 12. That as the application refers
to civil matters arising out of the revenue laws administered by the respondent,
the jurisdiction of the Board to adjudicate on the same is exercisable under s 7
subject to the procedure obtainable in s 12 of the Tax Revenue Appeals Act. Mr
Songoro argued that the respondent's objection is not based on the jurisdiction of

A this Board but on the procedure of filing matters before this Board and
particularly matters of time frame in taking certain steps where a taxpayer such
as the applicant wishes to come in this Board to challenge decisions made by the
respondent in the course of administering revenue laws. Again, Mr Songoro
reiterates the respondent's position that the application should be dismissed as
a whole for being incompetent before this Board, but the applicant could bring
B a fresh one after complying to the statutory provisions of the Tax Revenue
Appeals Act.

In its deliberation on the submissions by both counsel on the preliminary
objection raised by the respondent, the Board is of the considered opinion that the
main issue is whether or not the applicant in filing the present application was
statutorily required to follow the procedures enacted under ss 12, 13, 14 and 16
C all of the Tax Revenue Appeals Act.

This Board notes that the respondent's counsel Mr Songoro's objection can
simply be interpreted to be that the jurisdiction of the Board is conferred under
the provision of s 7 of the Tax Revenue Appeals Act but exercisable procedurally
subject to the provision of s 12 of the Act. The wording of the said s 7 of the Tax
Revenue Appeals Act provides:

D

> "7. The Board shall, subject to section 12, have sole original jurisdiction in all
> proceedings of a civil nature in respect of disputes arising from revenue laws
> administered by the Tanzania Revenue Authority."

There is no doubt that the applicant has a dispute with the respondent, and
precisely the Commissioner for Income Tax in that the applicant on 26 October
E 2001 applied to be granted a tax exempt status, and their application was not
granted for reasons communicated to the applicant vide the letter written by the
then Acting Commissioner for Income Tax dated the 22 May 2002, now annex
MSTL 6 to the affidavit. Again, it would seem that the appellants were not
satisfied with the respondent's decision and further asked him to reconsider its
decision whereby the respondent, Commissioner for Income Tax *vide* his letter
F dated 6 January 2003 confirmed the respondent previous decision, asserting that
"the assessed tax is legally due and collectable" and where the applicant were
aggrieved they could prefer an appeal to this Board.

According to the documents annexed to the Affidavit of the applicant officer
supporting this application, the applicant never heeded the advice to appeal to this
Board, since the Commissioner for Income Tax confirmed his decision on
G 6 January 2003 as per the provisions of s 13 (4) (*b*) of the Tax Revenue Appeals
Act, before its amendment by the Finance Act, 2004. That brief history of dispute
between the parties shows that the applicant were supposed to comply with the
provisions of s 16 of the Tax Revenue Appeals Act by appealing to this Board
whereby this Board would have had the opportunity of reviewing the
respondent's decision and declare whether the applicant had a legal right of being
H granted a tax exempt status under the provisions of s 14, read together with para
5 of the First Schedule to the Income Tax Act. According to this Board's
reasoning, the applicant's failure to comply fully with the procedures enacted in
the Tax Revenue Appeals Act has resulted into the adoption of a peculiar
procedure unknown to the Act, and the applicant is accordingly late as the time
limit of questioning the respondent's decision of denying the applicant a tax

exempt status has lapsed more than two years ago. Therefore, the present application is hopelessly time barred.

However, this Board is of the considered opinion that the applicant could have brought proceedings for a declaratory order concerning its tax exempt status only, and could argue not to be bound by limitation of time where the applicant had not commenced business but had first applied to the Commissioner for Income Tax to be granted tax exempt status under s 14 and para 5 of First Schedule of the Income Tax Act, and was refused.

This Board is ultimately of the finding that the respondent objection against the application as argued by Mr Songoro, his learned counsel, correctly interpreted the applicable provisions of the Tax Revenue Appeals Act as applicable in the circumstances of the application. The preliminary objections upheld and the application is dismissed in its entirety. The applicant if it wishes is advised to appeal out of time against the respondent's decision to refuse to grant tax-exempt status subject to complying with the provisions of the Tax Revenue Appeals Act.

Each party is to bear its own cost of the application. Appeal lies in the Tax Revenue Appeals Tribunal.

This ruling is delivered to the parties' counsel, Dr Luonga for the applicant, assisted by Mr Thomas, advocate and Law Externees Miss Rose, Mr Omary Ayub and Mr Songoro, advocate assisted by Mr E Mahendeka, Senior Tax Assessor for the respondent.

The ruling delivered this afternoon of the 8 June 2005 at Dar es Salaam.

NAMERA GROUP OF INDUSTRIES v COMMISSIONER GENERAL

TAX REVENUE APPEALS BOARD

DAR ES SALAAM

(VAT TAX APPLICATION: NO. 13 OF 2004)

18 May 2005

BR Mutungi, *Vice-Chairperson,* F D Mteteleka and D A Mwaibula, *Members*

Practice and Procedure—Preliminary objection raised to challenge the competence of an application against refusal by Commissioner General to admit notice of objection—Application must be accompanied by a statement of refusal by the Commissioner—Whether the law prescribes a format of the statement of refusal—Whether after refusal by the Commissioner the proper remedy is by way of application or appeal

Aggrieved by the decision of the respondent to refuse to grant the appellant waiver of payment of tax deposit pending final determination of the objection lodged by the latter, instead of filing an appeal to the Board the appellant filed an application before the Board. Before hearing the matter, counsel for the respondent raised a preliminary objection that the application was incompetent for lack of proof of payment of requisite fees and that there was no evidence of statement of refusal by the respondent, the Commissioner General. The Board considered the objections raised in light of the applicable law and whether a party to proceed by way of application or appeal.

Held:

(1) After refusal by the respondent to grant the waiver of payment of tax deposit pending final determination of the objection lodged by the appellant he ought to have come to the Board by way of appeal having paid the requisite fees;

(2) the law has not laid down a format of the "statement of refusal" of the Commissioner General;

(3) the two letters of the Commissioner General (annex C) constituted a statement of refusal by the respondent Commissioner General, and

(4) there was a refusal for waiver and so the proper course to follow was for the applicant if aggrieved to file an appeal against that refusal.

Preliminary objection upheld.

Mr Rugazia, for the appellant
Mr Teemba, for the respondent

16 May 2005:

Mr Teemba, for the respondent: We have not raised a formal preliminary objection but there are two documents I would like to know about:

(1) Evidence of payment of fees.
(2) Statement containing refusal by Commissioner General to admit the notice of objection.

Mr Rugaziya, for the appellant : The appellant paid fees on November 2004 and the same was paid to the Secretary of the Board to the sum of Tshs 20,000.

As to the second document the decision not to waive is contained in annexture C TRA/CG/V.I of 27 September 2004.

It was subsequent to that refusal by the Commissioner General that the applicant through our advice chose to file an application against that refusal.

Mr Teemba, for the respondent: There is no evidence of payment of fees in respect of filing notice of appeal amounting to Tshs 5,000. The Tshs 20,000 is for extension of time and there is no such application before this Board and no fees for payment of appeal to this Board. The effect of this failure is for this appeal not to be entertained and I pray that the matter be struck out as incompetent.

There is no statement containing the refusal of the Commissioner General to admit the notice of objection. What my friend is stating was a letter but not a statement. The result is the same that the appeal is incompetent for want of this statement.

For these two reasons the appeal is incompetent and ought to be struck out.

Order: (1) Deliberations today 17 May 2005.
(2) Ruling tomorrow morning 18 May 2005 at 9.00 am.

RULING

(Delivered 18 May 2005)

This ruling is in respect to a preliminary objection raised by Mr Teemba, legal counsel for the respondent, immediately before the commencement of the hearing of application No. 13/2004.

Mr Teemba was disturbed by the fact that for any appeal to be heard there must among many requirements be two things mainly:

(1) Evidence of payment of fees.
(2) A statement containing the refusal by the Commissioner General to admit the notice of objection.

Mr Teemba, having shown his concern on the two above prerequisites, submitted that these two items were missing in the present file. According to Mr Teemba what is to be found in the file is only payment of Tshs 20,000 which is fees payable in respect of filing an application; yet no fees for filing an appeal is evident.

As regards the refusal by the Commissioner General, Mr Teemba reacted that what is in the file is merely a letter but not a statement of refusal by the Commissioner General. In totality Mr Teemba was of the finding that the matter as it is stands before the Board is incompetent and should be struck out.

On the other hand, Mr Rugazia learned counsel for the appellant Namera Group of Industries (T) Limited, responded by stating that what they had paid before the Board is Tshs 20,000 for filing the application for waiver of payment of tax deposit pending final determination of the objection and this had come into being after the respondent vide annexture C (Ref: TRA/CG/VI dated 27 September 2004) had refused the appellant the waiver for depositing before the objection is finally determined.

Having the above salient submissions by both parties in our minds we had to put matters right as follows:

According to us we find that what necessitated the appellant to come before this Board was the respondent's refusal to grant him waiver to deposit tax pursuant to a notice of objection lodged by the applicant. On this we find it was proper for the applicant to have paid the Tshs 5,000 with the Board as fees for the notice of intention to appeal as he was aggrieved by the decision of the respondent. The proper way as we have already stated was to come before the Board by way of an appeal; we have found on record that the appellant paid this fees as per exchequer receipt No. 20097950 dated 1 November 2004.

What we could not comprehend is why after this he opted to file an application for waiver before this Board instead of pursuing his appeal of which the proper fee would have been Tshs 50,000. The only reason we give to this act of the applicant is that there must have been confusion on his part in going about the matter ending up in filing an application instead of an appeal.

As to whether there was a statement of refusal from the respondent or not we would first and foremost state that the law has not laid down a format of the "statement of refusa". On the same basis we adopt annex C as a statement made

A by the respondent and from the said exhibit the last para which state "please advice your clients to either pay the demanded tax or comply with the provisions of section 12 (2) of the Tax Revenue Appeals Act, 2000 to enable their objection to be accepted" is obviously a refusal duly signed by the Commissioner General himself. It follows therefore that we find there was a refusal for waiver and so the proper forum to follow was for the applicant if aggrieved to file an appeal against
B that refusal.

This brings us to making a ruling in agreement with Mr Teemba's prayer that the application before the Board is incompetent and we accordingly strike it out with liberty to the appellant to file a fresh appeal with appropriate fees, if he so wishes. The preliminary objection is accordingly upheld. Each party to bear own costs.

C Right of appeal explained

Read this day of 18 May 2005 in presence of Mr Rugaziya for applicant and Mr Teemba for respondent.

D

RUNGWE FREIGHT (T) LIMITED v COMMISSIONER GENERAL (No. 1)

TAX REVENUE APPEALS BOARD

E

DAR ES SALAAM

(CUSTOMS AND EXCISE TAX APPEAL: NO. 13 OF 2004)

20 June 2006

F

BR Mutungi, *Vice-Chairperson*, I Dallushi and J Karashani, *Members*

Practice and Procedure—Preliminary objection—Jurisdiction of the Board is challenged—Whether Board to hear the matter and decide on jurisdiction on the basis of the evidence

G

This was an appeal seeking an order for refund of customs duties paid as a result of a compoundment order issued by the respondent. The respondent raised a preliminary objection challenging the jurisdiction of the Board in this matter in that it was of a criminal nature and that the compoundment order was
H like a decree of the High Court on which the Board had no jurisdiction. Counsel for the appellant argued that the issue before the Board was not new in that the Board had earlier on decided that it had jurisdiction to entertain a matter arising out of a compoundment order. Such decision had however been overturned by the Tribunal but on a different grounds. Counsel for the respondent argued that this matter was new before the Board and that the Board had no jurisdiction in light of s 173 of the East African Customs and

Transfer Tax Management Act (Cap 27). The Board considered whether it was A
bound by its earlier decision which was overturned by the Tribunal and
whether it had jurisdiction to hear the appeal on merit.

Held:

(1) This is a fresh appeal before this Board as it has been instituted afresh,
and so bears issues which are to be determined on merits afresh, and thus has
no relation to any other appeal before this Board; B

(2) the matter should proceed on merits in order that the matter is resolved
in all fairness; consequently the issue of jurisdiction will be determined
accordingly basing on evidence;

(3) the preliminary objection is accordingly dismissed.

Preliminary objection dismissed.

C

Mr Chabruma, for the appellant
Mr Teemba, for the respondent

16 June 2006:

Mr Teemba, for the respondent: Your Honour, and Honourable members of the D
Board, before you is an appeal by the appellant challenging the decision of the
Commissioner General of the Tanzania Revenue Authority (TRA): first,
challenging a compoundment order made under The East African Customs and
Transfer Tax Management Act (Cap 27) (Laws of the Community) as well as
seeking for refund of a total sum of about more than Tshs 60 million. The
respondent wishes to challenge the appeal against the order of compoundment. E
The compoundment order was made under s 173 of The East African Customs
and Transfer Tax Management Act which essentially has an effect of ousting the
jurisdiction of this Board to entertain any issue in respect of that order. There are
two reasons for that ouster of jurisdiction. One is based on s 173 (1) of the same
law I have just cited. Essentially when talking of a compoundment of this nature
it means that a criminal offence was committed. It is similar or akin to a person F
charged with a criminal offence and pleading guilty and on conviction, sentenced.

The appellants were charged, pleaded guilty, convicted and sentenced
accordingly. The jurisdiction is to be found in s 7 of the Tax Revenue Appeals
Act. Section 173 (1) talks of an offence, and for all practical purposes it has its
origin in criminality. This Board cannot entertain a matter of criminal nature. The
second reason that ousts the jurisdiction of this Board is 173 (2) (*e*). In substance,
s 173 (2) (*e*) talks of a decree and so the compoundment order is a decree in this G
respect. This Board is subordinate to the High Court and cannot entertain a decree
passed by the High Court. For the reasons submitted, this appeal is incompetent
and resultantly it has to be struck out. I accordingly pray so and I pray for costs
as well.

H

Mr Chabruma, for the appellant: Your Honour, I have carefully listened to my
learned friend's presentation. Firstly, I will start by stating that the impression he
is giving this Board is that this matter is new. It is not new, it is three years old.
The first time this matter was heard, it ended with the decision of Honourable
Meela in 2002. It said in effect that this Board has the jurisdiction to entertain the
matter before it, and it was decided that on those grounds the Board will proceed

A to hear the matter. The matter went on appeal to the Tribunal, in which the appeal ended with the ruling by Justice Nsekela on 20 December 2002, which stated that the matter was improper before the Board for the only reason that the documents were incomplete but not for any other reasons.

Secondly, it is a common practice that preliminary objections, in fact all of them, are raised before the hearing of the matter. When this matter was brought
B before the Board for the first time there was a preliminary objection that the matter was of a criminal nature. This time the respondent is raising another preliminary objection that the hearing of this matter contravenes s 173 of The East African Customs and Transfer Tax Management Act. It is not clear why these preliminary objections were not raised at the commencement. They are being brought in piecemeal. It is contrary to legal practice and an abuse of the court
C process to raise preliminary objection in piecemeal.

Thirdly, if one goes through the statement of facts, one will discover that there were peculiar circumstances surrounding the compoundment. The compoundment was done when the director of the appellant company was behind bars. This brought pressure that the matter should be compounded, and in fact the Director was released following the compoundment. What we are saying is that there were
D unusual circumstances which make it look like it was done under duress. That is why we are challenging the compoundment, and we are demanding that the duties paid should be refunded.

On these premises, I am submitting that the preliminary objection be struck out and the matter be heard on merit.

Mr Teemba, for the respondent, in reply: First of all, I am not aware of the
E judgment of Honourable Meela on this matter, and even whether the Chairperson held that the Board had the jurisdiction to entertain the matter under The East African Customs and Transfer Tax Management Act, s 173. The matter went to the Tribunal and the case was thrown out. It was thrown out and we are not barred from raising the preliminary objection. Even if the Chairperson was right, the ruling has not been upheld by a higher authority. This Board is entitled to
F hear this preliminary objection and give out its decision. This is a normal practice in law.

I am pleased that my friend is the one who pleaded with the Commissioner for Customs and Excise informing the Customs that his client was prepared to plead guilty. I think he might have forgotten this (annex TRA A1 collectively) There were no special circumstances. He pleaded himself to the Commissioner. Among
G the documents of TRA 1, is a charge sheet detailing all the offences that the appellant had committed and of which he had pleaded guilty. My friend had a copy of the same. He cannot deny what he had previously admitted. I am once again pleading to the Board that the matter is of a criminal nature with abundant evidence coming from the counsel himself and as such this Board cannot entertain the criminal matter or a decree of the High Court.

H This Board has eyes to see what is on record. So your Honour, I once again submit that the Board has no jurisdiction to entertain this matter, and consequently, the appeal has to be struck out. I pray for costs as well.

Order: (1) The Ruling will be on 20 June 2004 at 9.00 am.
(2) Deliberation will be on 17 June 2005.

RULING

(Delivered 20 June 2006)

The preliminary objection raised by Mr Teemba, respondent's learned counsel, is to the effect that this Honourable Board has no jurisdiction on the following grounds:

(a) Section 7 of the Tax Revenue Appeals Act vests jurisdiction of this Board solely on maters of a civil nature arising from revenue issues.
(b) Section 171 of The East African Customs and Transfer Tax Management Act confers jurisdiction on matters in respect of offences of a criminal nature and as the offence committed by the appellant was of a criminal nature, this Board has no jurisdiction over the present appeal.
(c) As there is a compoundment order by the Commissioner General of which, as per s 173 (2) (*e*) of The East African Customs and Transfer Tax Management Act is final and not appellable and is tantamount to a decree of the High Court, this Honourable Board's jurisdiction in this matter is accordingly ousted.

To add more salt to the injury, in the appeal documents there is evidence of a charge sheet whereby the appellant pleaded guilty, was convicted and subsequently sentenced.

On the other side, Mr Chabruma, learned counsel for the appellant, strongly disputed the criminal charge on the ground that there were peculiar circumstances in this matter as far as the compoundment order was concerned, as it was done under duress.

It was also argued that this matter has been brought before this Board for the second time after an appeal from the Tribunal which ended on only one ground which was in relation to a document and not on matters of jurisdiction.

Moreover, it was reiterated that practically, preliminary objections are raised on the commencement of a matter, but in this case, while the case was before this same Board, the respondent never raised the points of compoundment under s 173 of The East African Customs and Transfer Tax Management Act, but only raised a point of civil jurisdiction *vis-à-vis* criminal, a matter of which according to Mr Chabruma, was decided upon by this Honourable Board.

To start with, we make it very clear that this is a fresh appeal before this Board as it has been instituted afresh, and so bears issues which are to be determined on merits afresh, and thus has no relation to any other appeal before this Board.

As far as the preliminary objection is concerned, if one goes through the submissions of the two parties, it is clear that there are triable issues which need elaborative evidence to be submitted before this Board in order for the Board to satisfy itself on these issues. It is not enough for one to just state the events and documents while the other party is also disputing the events. It is upon the above findings and our feeling that justice should be done, that for the sake of justice, we rule that the matter should proceed on merits in order that the matter is resolved in all fairness. In so doing, the issue of jurisdiction will consequently be determined accordingly basing on evidence.

It follows then that the preliminary objection is accordingly dismissed and we make no order as to costs.

The right of appeal is explained.

Read this day of 20 June 2005 in the presence of Mr Chabruma for the appellant and Mr Teemba for the respondent.

Mr Teemba: Your Honour, we intend to appeal against the decision.

Order: Matter is adjourned sine die pending the respondent's appeal

RUNGWE FREIGHT (T) LIMITED v COMMISSIONER GENERAL (No. 2)

TAX REVENUE APPEALS BOARD

DAR ES SALAAM

(CUSTOMS AND EXCISE TAX APPEAL: NO. 13 OF 2004)

23 December 2005

BR Mutungi, *Vice-Chairperson*, I Dallushi and J Karashani, *Members*

Jurisdiction—Ouster of jurisdiction—Compoundment procedure and order following commission of an offence—Whether the Board has jurisdiction to entertain an appeal on such matter—East African Customs and Transfer Tax Management Act, s 173 and Tax Revenue Appeals Act, 2000, s 7

Compoundment—Compoundment of offence—Ouster of jurisdiction—Whether jurisdiction of the Board is ousted following compoundment order of the Commissioner General—East African Customs and Transfer Tax Management Act, s 173 and Tax Revenue Appeals Act, 2000, s 7

This was an appeal against the respondent over a claim for refund of additional taxes to the tune of Tshs 59,269,814 and fines amounting to Tshs 2,500,000. While the appellant claimed that the additional taxes and fines were illegal having no legal basis, the respondent argued that the additional taxes and fines were legal having arisen because of the appellant's act of making false declaration, his seeking for compoundment of his offence and the compoundment order made by the Commissioner General. That being the case, the order of the Commissioner was final and not appealable. On the evidence adduced the Board considered whether or not it had jurisdiction to entertain the appeal.

Held:

(1) On the evidence it was the appellant who sought for settlement by voluntary admission of the offence of making false declaration;

(2) the respondent had no other way but to proceed with the compoundment procedure found under s 173 of the East African Customs and Transfer Tax

Management Act, which had the effect of turning the whole matter into a criminal affair; A

(3) a decision by the Commissioner General based on a criminal affair and such procedure is final and not appealable;

(4) the extra duties, fines and penalties as imposed by the respondent, were imposed according to the laid down law and the hands of the appellant were tied by that compoundment procedure and so cannot now come before this B Board for any refund of the extra duties imposed, the fines and penalties;

(5) by the mere fact that the whole matter was already a criminal matter, the jurisdiction of this esteemed Board was automatically ousted and hence it cannot question the punitive powers of the Commissioner;

(6) the appeal is incompetent for lack of jurisdiction.

Appeal incompetent. C

Mr Chabruma, for the appellant
Mr Teemba, for the respondent

3 November 2005:

D

Mr Chabruma, for the appellant: Your Honour this matter is fixed for hearing and pleadings are complete. There is also a defence and we do not wish to file a rejoinder and we are ready to proceed.

Mr Teemba, for the respondent: We were discussing with my colleague on the way forward.

E

Issues:

(1) whether the subject goods were under-declared or not declared at all to Customs;
(2) whether the respondent was right in imposing extra duties and taxes; F
(3) whether the appellant is entitled to refund of the extra taxes, fines and other payments made;
(4) whether the compoundment procedure was complied with; and
(5) to what relief are the parties entitled.

Mr Chabruma: I will have five witnesses, but today I have one witness only, and I pray to proceed. G

(For witnesses for the appellant and one for the respondent are called, and are each examined, cross-examined and re-examined.)

Final submissions H

Mr Chabruma, for the appellant: Firstly, I will start with the issue of the effect of compoundment of the offence. Looking at the request of compoundment of the offence, the s under which the charge was levelled against the appellant is s 148 (*b*) of the East African Customs and Transfer Tax Management Act (Cap 27).

A When the compounding order was made it was made precisely on this s and
the fines were paid under this section. After the fines had been paid, the appellant
was required to pay taxes. Following that, the respondent wrote a letter requiring
the appellant to pay taxes amounting to Tshs 591,269,814 on the ground that he
was guilty of under-declaration and non-declaration.

The computation which was being demanded had nothing at all to do with the
B s under which the appellant was charged, because when we talk about non-
declaration we talk about the absence of documents, and when we talk of false
declaration we talk of documents which are defective. Charging somebody for
false declaration where it is non-declaration is wrong and unfair.

Having received the letter on 19 July 2001, the appellant wrote a letter dated
17 August 2001, which indicates that the money was paid under protest.

C After a period of about two and a half years, there was a reply from the
Commissioner of Customs on 12 August 2003, which was levelling yet another
offence against the appellant, the offence of under-valuation. The situation was
that the charge was under s 148 (*b*) but the appellant was directed to pay taxes
which relate to yet another s 146 (*d*) (3). There is no relationship between the
amount which the appellant was forced to pay and the offences under which the
D compoundment was done.

Secondly, it is on evidence (PW2) that on 5 June 2001 the Chairperson of the
Board of the TRA was supervising the exercise of compounding seven containers,
and in fact, according to PW2, officers of the TRA went to the scene on the orders
of the Chairperson. Although it would appear that the compoundment was
done under normal procedures, behind it was a big man. We submit that the
E involvement of the Chairperson in this exercise caused pressure on the officer
who signed the request.

The request was signed on 11 July 2001 that was the time when the managing
director of the appellant company was apprehended in Tanga. Thus this
apprehension was ordered by TRA officers. So in order to release the managing
director from the cell, it was necessary to sign the compound request. This makes
F us submit that the compoundment was done under pressure.

Thirdly, after the compoundment was done, a letter was written by the
appellant's advocate seeking lenience or mitigation but this letter was written
about a week after the compoundment, and usually in legal practice, mitigation is
sought before judgment and not after. So, any mitigation after judgment is of no
effect. Judgment in this matter was passed on 16 July 2001 and mitigation was
G sought after that. That letter has no effect at all in this case, because it was not
acted upon, it came after judgment. The appellant was not satisfied with payments
he had made; therefore he decided to seek refund of the additional taxes which he
had paid. We are submitting that there were no goods which were not declared
because according to the testimony of PW3, the containers which were inspected
at Tanga were eleven in number. Four of these were made port to port, which
H means that they stayed at Tanga port. The contents of these four containers were
squeezed into the other seven and transported to Dar es Salaam. The documents
which were impounded to the customs officials related to the seven containers
only, and the customs officials did not take trouble to know what happened to the
four other containers. So, in fact the contents of the four containers were
documented, and that is why the goods were released from the Tanga port. It is

incorrect to say that the goods, in respect of which the documents were not found, were uncustomed. In addition, it was in evidence (PW3) that the value of goods was uplifted by 100% in Tanga and duties were paid on such basis and the examination of the goods in Tanga was done in collaboration with other state organs such as the police and state security. It was only after these various bodies were satisfied that the goods were released from Tanga port. Unlike the examination which was conducted in Tanga by various bodies, the examination conducted in Dar es Salaam for three consecutive days was done by the custom officials only and no other person was involved. This brings doubt to the outcome of the re-examination, as it was one- sided, and this in turn brings doubt on any computation based on that examination because the purpose of involving several parties including the owner is to remove this kind of doubt. We are saying that the goods impounded in Dar es Salaam were fully paid for in Tanga and any payment made in Dar es Salaam is double taxation. For this reason we submit that the appellant is entitled to a refund of not only the taxes paid but also the fines and parking charges which he paid.

When we submitted our appeal, the question of costs was not included because of the format in which the appeals are described. There is no space for costs but we are adding that the appellant is entitled to costs as well.

Mr Teemba, for the respondent: There is a sixth issue that the claim of refund is time barred and this has cropped up during the trial. I will start with the issue of compoundment. Your Honour, you recall that when this matter came to this Board the respondent raised a preliminary objection that the Board had no jurisdiction to try or question an order made under s 173 of The East African Customs and Transfer Tax Management Act.

We also recall that the objection was dismissed on the understating that the Board felt that the matter should be tried fully on merits and that is why I never raised it. I will come back to it once again. What happened on this compoundment affair? It is now not in dispute that goods belonging to the appellant were seized here in Dar es Salaam on suspicion of being uncustomed. The goods were subjected to a second examination when it was discovered there were under-declaration, non-declaration and under-valuation. This was the evidence of DW1. The witness testified to the effect that it was in the pressure of PW4 and the appellant and he explained that it could not be done in their absence since these had access to the warehouse and held the keys. The only evidence of the pressure of the respondent was the seal on warehouse No. 9. The witness explained to this Board that on close examination of the documents and physical check, he discovered that some of the goods found were not declared in the documents presented to them (non-declaration). He also said that there were other items which indicated a lesser number (under-declaration); and stated that on further examination of documents the value indicated was not correct (under-valuation).

Your Honour, the witness testified to the effect that this amounts to false declaration, as there is falsity in all the three actions. On discovering these differences, the officer of the appellant who gave evidence (PW4) was informed and we were told that he was on a number of occasions acting on behalf of the managing director of that firm. He submitted himself there and was never arrested

A by the respondent. He was told of the offences committed by the company and he told us that he consulted PW1 (director) who instructed him to sign the special forms for settlement, but what we are being told is that PW1 was under arrest in Tanga. We have not been shown any evidence that he would have been elsewhere. PW4 was shown the forms and willingly signed them on behalf of the appellant. Then the normal procedure took its normal course (compoundment of offences).
B The appellant paid the fines and the goods were released to him, but naturally he knew that he had to pay the taxes that he evaded. He chose not to be taken to court and it was settled in a civil manner, and that was the end of it.

Your Honour, it is common knowledge and practice that after being convicted for an offence such as stealing and being fined by the court, does not mean that one should not be told to pay tax. This is what happened to this case; after the fine
C the taxes you pay are evaded.

The only difference is that a Commissioner has no power to send somebody to jail. The company was charged on a criminal offence. The appellant knew the consequences of a criminal offence and it would have landed him in a criminal court. I am submitting that the compoundment procedure was followed to the letter.

D What is the effect of the Commissioner's order under s 173? We may like it or not, but the order shall be final and not be a subject to appeal. It is my humble submission that the presentation before this Board is incompetent as the Board has no jurisdiction to entertain the orders of the Commissioner General. We have a decision of this Board, Simon Steven, which says that this Board has no powers to question the orders of the Commissioner, and whatever took place was
E criminal, so this Board only has civil jurisdiction but no criminal jurisdiction. So the pleading of PW4 should go to a criminal court (equivocal or un-equivocal). Under s 7 of The Tax Revenue Appeals Act, the issue of compoundment is not covered; therefore this Board should not entertain such an issue.

We finally submit that the compoundment procedure was done properly and in accordance with the law. Moreover, even if there were some irregularities which
F I submit that there were none, the issues of irregularity cannot be brought before this Board because they are not of a civil nature. The matter should be struck out as incompetent, and I submit so.

As to the second issue which is framed No. 1, I have narrated to what transpired here in Dar es Salaam, at warehouse No. 9. We have evidence from the respondent's witness who conducted the re-examination of the warehouses, and
G he is the one who discovered the under-declaration and non-declaration. This same witness told this Board that it is quite normal for goods to be subjected to re-examination if any of those are suspected. The goods released at Tanga were suspected of being uncustomed.

Furthermore, it is not disputed that even in Tanga the value was uplifted as there was cheating and this is the reason for the uplift, and I do not see any reason
H as to why PW1 is silent on the uplift in Tanga. One cannot claim that simply because the checking was before various organs of state there cannot be any cheating.

For one business man to be subjected at two places raised doubt and he should provide an answer to this suspicion. The goods were under-declared, under valued and non-declared for the second time.

As for the third issue on extra taxes, this was a natural consequence of under payment. The respondent's witness testified to that effect, and the law is s 117 of The East African Customs and Transfer Tax Management Act. The respondent after discovering mischief can collect the extra taxes underpaid and evaded.

As for the fourth issue, that is the issue of refund, the appellant is not entitled to a single cent as refund, for once he was found to have evaded tax he paid it to the respondent and he was told under s 122 (2) of The East African Customs and Transfer Tax Management Act, that assuming this money was wrongly collected, then this money should have been claimed within one year after the event had taken place. This was explained to the appellant on 12 August 2003 by the respondent. The claim was made 13 months later. I submit that the claim for refund is time barred.

Finally, I submit that this appeal has no merit at all and it should be dismissed with costs.

Mr Chabruma, for the appellant, in reply: As to the arrest of PW1, this was in a pleading and it was not disputed. My friend has talked of uplift of value both in Tanga and Dar es Salaam. The question of uplift is not a matter of agent of clearing and forwarding, the documents are brought by the importers.

As to the refund, this section cannot oust the jurisdiction of the court. The refund is a civil matter and so the law of limitation gives six years.

Order: (1) Deliberations will be on 16 December 2005
(2) Judgment will be on 23 December 2003 at 9.00 am.

JUDGMENT

(Delivered 23 December 2005)

Rungwe Freight (T) Ltd, the appellant, duly represented by Mr Chabruma has preferred an appeal against the Commissioner General, represented by Mr Teemba, legal counsel.

The appeal itself is over a claim for refund of additional taxes to the tune of Tshs 59,269,814 and fines amounting to Tshs 2,500,000. In pursuing the appeal, the appellant preferred to prove the appeal by use of witnesses as follows:

PW1, Jimmy Brown Mwalugelo, testified to the effect that he was the director of Rungwe Freight Company Ltd (the appellant) which does business of customs clearing and forwarding. He further complained that sometime on 4 June 2001 he went and cleared eleven containers at Tanga but as they had shortages in the transporting vehicle, they mixed the containers and forwarded seven of them. On narrating on the procedure at the port, PW1 stated that they started off with COTECNA who go through the documents which they moved to ICS and then to the customs. PW1 explained that they went through the full process and in the end there was 100% uplift on the value which they paid and were issued with a release order. The payment was done on 4 June 2001 at 4 pm. The customs clerk wrote on the receipt 6 June 2001 and issued eleven receipts as they were eleven containers. This was because on 5 June 2001 it was a Maulidi holiday. As they had seven vehicles only, they off-loaded some of the containers and left them empty.

A PW1 further explained that after the full procedure were completed; he left
together with the consignment up to Dar es Salaam at Kiwalani warehouse. As
they got inside the warehouse, a gentleman followed them and inquired on the
documents of which he demanded to go with. On realizing the Gentleman's
intention after introducing himself as an official from customs, PW1 ordered his
employees to lock the gate. The gentleman locked himself in his vehicle (Suzuki)
B and after an exchange of bitter words between the two; the gentleman gave back
PW1 the documents by throwing them at him. PW1 went ahead and stated that
the gentleman came back with a police officer who interrogated him and told
them that the gentleman had refused with his documents. After this, PW1 saw the
TRA Commissioners who came to the warehouse and he came to learn that the
gentleman was actually the TRA Board Chairperson known as one Bukuku.

C PW1 also learnt that the said Chairperson had ordered the closure of the
warehouse of which PW1 asked them to wait for the other vehicles but they could
not listen to him and only two vehicles managed to offload the consignment. PW1
also had learnt that the Chairperson had noticed the difference in the dates. PW1
also informed the Board that as the other vehicles arrived, they had to park in the
government warehouses at Temeke and PW1 had to pay for the parking charges.

D PW1 further narrated that he latter got a phone call from one Setonga (Deputy
Commissioner) informing him to go to Tanga and meet him. PW1 went to Tanga
and actually met Mr Setonga who informed him that they had found out that the
containers were eleven in number and not seven, and the date which was to be
written was 4 June 2001 but it was written 6 June 2001.

PW1 also informed the Board that Mr Setonga has informed him that the
E Board Chairperson was at Dodoma and needed Tshs 15,000,000 as he had
problems. Mr Setonga also advised him to go and meet the Chairperson at
Dodoma, which he did, but after arranging to meet him, things changed as the
Chairperson had to leave urgently due to the fact that the Vice President had
passed away. After this PW1 met one of the Members of Parliament who
promised to help him once in Dar es Salaam, and this was one Mtwina. On arrival
F at Dar es Salaam, Mr Mtwina informed PW1 that the Chairperson had stated that
he knew nothing about the consignment and PW1 should go and see one of the
Commissioners (Mr Lauwo). PW1 did this and Mr Lauwo told him that the
Chairperson was very disappointed.

PW1 then left for Tanga to proceed with his other businesses and was able to
talk to Mr Setonga (Assistant Commissioner), and informed him that he was at
G Tanga on 11 July 2001. The Tanga Regional Revenue Officer informed him that,
he would better leave for Dar es Salaam as he was to be arrested but PW1 refused
and so was later arrested.

After two days in custody, the Customs officials came and took him under
police escort up to Buguruni police station at Dar es Salaam. PW1 explained that
he spent other four days in custody after which the RPC ordered that the TRA
H officials should take him. What he saw was for the TRA officials going round
searching for seals.

Furthermore, in his testimony, PW1 stated that he was to pay Tshs 59,000,000
and he made the payments, but he was dissatisfied to the criteria used as he
did so to save himself as he was in custody. PW1 stated that the process of
seizing his goods was arbitrarily done as the containers which had been

transported to Dar es Salaam were stuffed with goods which had been de-stuffed from four other containers which were port to port containers which remained at Tanga port. These were later intercepted and seized by the Customs officials and without involving PW1 the Customs officials re-verified the goods for being under declared and non-declared and came out with a short collection of Tshs 59,289,814.

According to PW1, as neither he was present nor his agent, the respondent came up with a highly exaggerated account, and so the additional duties which PW1 paid while knowing that he had paid all the duties at Tanga.

On cross-examination, PW1 denied neither to have admitted to the offence nor to have made any admission to his lawyer. PW1 also stated that he did not know if any of his employees or family member had done anything on his behalf.

PW2, Hussein Turingo, testified to the effect that he was an employee of the TRA, employed to inspect consignments at the port after the documents came to the receiving counter, then to the collector who assigns someone to inspect the consignment or cargo. After this, a report is written and given back to the collector. PW2 further testified that on 1 June 2001 he inspected six containers. After having carried out the inspection, the collector on receipt of the report, uplifted the amount by 100% and then forwarded the documents to the Regional Revenue Officer, then to the cashier and later PW2 released eleven containers. On carrying out the inspection, he was together with the customs officials. ICS, National Security officials and the port's auxiliary police.

PW2 informed the Board that after a few days he heard that the cargo had been compounded, and after a few weeks he was suspended from work. Later he was summarily dismissed due to negligence after being established that he had not done a proper inspection.

On cross-examination, PW2 admitted that there was nothing wrong with what the TRA officials had done for declaring under-declaration or non-declaration on the said goods.

PW3, Kileo Shaban Mimsaba, explained that he was one of the watchmen guarding the warehouses in the morning of 5 June 2001. While on duty, he saw two vehicles carrying containers with PW1 escorting them. Immediately as the vehicles passed the gate, a gentleman in a vehicle came from behind and started asking for documents. PW1 gave him the documents and instructed the watchman to lock the gate. As PW2 was locking the gate, he could see PW1 and the gentleman arguing. As PW1 was given back his documents, he ordered PW2 to open the gate for the gentleman. As he left PW1 told him that the gentleman was the TRA's Board Chairperson. After an hour the Chairperson came back but remained outside talking on his phone and suddenly PW3 saw a TRA vehicle and officials get in together with the Chairperson. PW3 informed them that PW1's warehouse was No. 9. All the warehouse customers were summoned after which all the warehouses were sealed. The Chairperson on leaving left with them his phone number so that if customs inquired for their goods he would send someone there.

PW4, Emmanuel Mwakatuma, explained in his testimony to the effect that he was a clerk with the Rungwe Freight Company Ltd (appellant) and that he was informed by PW1 who was by then at Tanga, of the impoundment of the company's goods. He stated further that on going to the scene, he found that the TRA officials and other employees had gone there and were busy counting goods.

A He heard them say that some goods had no tax paid for them. On 10 July 2001 PW1 informed him while at Tanga that he had been arrested in connection with the seized goods.

PW4 then started working on the matter and was told to sign the F 89 form in order for PW1 to be released. PW4 had to admit so as to have PW1 out of custody, and he also signed another form by which they had to pay the tax added. B As the accounts were then prepared by the TRA, these were exaggerated, as no one from the appellant's side was present to witness the whole process. PW4 further testified to the effect that they had to get the assistance of a lawyer.

On cross-examination, this witness explained that he signed the settlement form on behalf of the company and that he was the one who instructed the advocate.

C On the other side the respondent had one witness, DW1, Solomon Kahuta, who testified to the effect that he was an employee of TRA as Customs collector. DW1 further testified that some time in June 2001 he was to go and seize the appellant's goods at Kiwalani after the vehicle carrying goods had been suspected of transporting uncustomed goods from Tanga. DW1 explained that one Mwakatuma PW4 an employee of the appellant was there and that they managed D to seal the warehouse and the appellant, through his agent, also locked it with a padlock and remained with the keys. The inspection was carried on the goods from 6 June to 8 June 2001. In the inspection they were able to discover undeclared goods, under-declared goods and under valued good. They then did a new accounting and the appellant was notified of the new taxes and the offence he had committed, collectively under the cover of false declaration. PW1, as the E Director, preferred the matter to be settled amicably and Mwakatuma, PW4, signed on behalf of the company. After all the necessary documents were signed, the request was taken before the Deputy Commissioner for compoundment of the offence on 16 July 2001. DW1 also saw the appellant Advocate's letter praying for lenience on behalf of his client and the Commissioner was very lenient in his decision by just fining the appellant instead of forfeiting the goods.

F DW1 explained that all that they did was according to the laid down legal procedures in reviewing tax assessed by a subordinate officer.

After the above testimonies, the counsels made their final submission as follows. Starting with Mr Chabruma, learned counsel, he challenged the fact that in charging the appellant, there was no relationship between the amount which the appellant was forced to pay and offences for which the compoundment G was made. The charging section was s 148 (*b*), yet the punishment was under s 146 (*d*) (iii) of the East African Customs and Transfer Tax Management Act.

Mr Chabruma also submitted to the fact that although it seems the exercise was done in the normal official channels, behind it was the TRA Board Chairperson who was masterminding the whole exercise and so putting on pressure over the TRA officials. The appellant's counsel also commented on the H advocate's letter written to the Commissioner which was never acted upon.

He also elaborated as to the issue of the re-examination that was done that it was only the involvement of Customs officials alone which raises a lot of doubt. As a whole, all the taxes involved were fully paid at Tanga and so the appellant is entitled to a refund of all the additional duties, fines and parking charges paid by him.

The final submission by Mr Teemba, legal counsel of the respondent, was to A
the effect that the re-examination done on the appellant's goods was done in the presence of PW4, the appellant's employee. More emphasis on this is that the warehouse could only be opened by the appellant using his keys. The whole procedure was open to the appellant and so after the respondents findings, the appellant was notified and PW4 signed on behalf of the appellant and went ahead
to seek for settlement and PW4 willingly went ahead to sign the forms on behalf B
of the appellant. The respondent had no alternative but to follow the normal course of compounding process which resulted into the appellant paying fines and goods being released while the appellant was also to pay the taxes evaded.

Mr Teemba emphasized as to the effect of s 173 of the East African Customs and Transfer Tax Management Act, in that the Commissioner's order is final and
not appellable. So the Board has no jurisdiction to entertain the same, as what C
took place was all of a criminal nature.

Mr Teemba also mentioned that what the TRA officials did in uplifting of the values at Dar es Salaam was very proper if there was a suspicion of goods being under-declared, under-valued and non-declared, and even if there was any refund to be made, then the claim for refund was time-barred as it was made 13 months
latter. D

The issues that were raised before this Honourable Board are:

(1) Whether the subject goods were under-declared or not declared at all to the Customs;
(2) whether the respondent was right in imposing extra duties and taxes;
(3) whether the appellant is entitled to refund of the extra fines and other E
payments made;
(4) whether the compoundment procedures was complied with; and
(5) To what relief are the parties entitled.

In order to adjudicate upon the present appeal, we had to deal with the paramount
issue which is whether the compoundment procedure was complied with, which F
is issue number four.

It is apparent on record that the appellant was charged with the offence of making false declaration contrary to s 148 (*b*) of the East African Customs and Transfer Tax Management Act and s 46 of the Value Added Tax Act.

It is also very clear on the evidence before us that it was the appellant who
sought for settlement, which was to be done amicably by signing Form C 56. The G
appellant through the evidence availed to us voluntarily admitted to the offences, as the appellant's rubber stamp and a representatives signature appear on the Commissioner's form.

With the above fulfilled, we find that the respondent had no other way but to proceed with the compoundment procedure found under s 173 of the East African
Customs and Transfer Tax Management Act. This in our opinion had turned the H
whole matter into a criminal affair on which the decision based upon, and such procedure of the Commissioner is final and not appellable.

We also find that there was a letter from one Mr Chabruma, advocate, of 16 July 2001 which was praying for lenience from the Commissioner in case of any punishment imposed upon the appellant as his client. We take it that the

A learned Advocate knew the consequences of the compoundment procedure, as the decision of the Commissioner is final and conclusive.

From the foregoing, we finally find that the extra duties, fines and penalties as imposed by the respondent, were imposed according to the laid down law and this brings us to the crucial finding that the hands of the appellant were tied by that compoundment procedure and so cannot now come before this Board for any
B refund of the extra duties imposed, and the fines and penalties.

This also in compliance with s 7 of the Tax Revenue Appeals Act that ties the hands of this Honourable Board, as by the mere fact that the whole matter was already a criminal matter, the jurisdiction of this esteemed Board was automatically ousted and cannot question the punitive powers of the Commissioner.

The big cry by the appellant is that all that was done was done out of pressure
C and malice of the TRA's Board Chairperson one Mr Bukuku. This needed strict proof especially when the matter was at the stage whereby the appellant was seeking for settlement and admitting the offence not just mere suspicions harboured by the appellant. We therefore, from the foregoing reasoning, answer the fourth issue in the affirmative.

Having pondered with the fourth issue we find no reason in going through the
D rest of the issues and it is our settled decision that as the appeal stands before us is incompetent for lack of jurisdiction and we proceed to strike it out.

Each party is to bear its own costs.

The right of appeal is explained.

Read this 23 December 2005 in the presence of Mr Chabruma for the appellant and Mr Francis Mbando for the respondent.

E

COMMISSIONER GENERAL v RUNGWE FREIGHT (T) LIMITED

F

TAX REVENUE APPEALS TRIBUNAL

DAR ES SALAAM

(APPEAL: NO. 4 OF 2004)

G

4 November 2004

A Shangwa J, *Chairperson*, D Kinabo and N Mbise, *Members*

H *Applications—Application for extension of time to give notice of intention to appeal—Reasonable cause should be shown for failure to give notice of intention to appeal or to lodge an appeal within the prescribed period—Tax Revenue Appeals Act, 2000, s 16 (4)*

In this appeal the appellant was appealing against the ruling of the Tax Revenue Appeals Board granting leave to the respondent to file appeal out of

time against his refusal to refund it custom duties of Tshs 59,269,814. The A
Board had granted such leave because the respondent delayed to respond to
the appellant's appeal to the Commissioner General against the refusal by the
Commissioner for Customs and Excise Duty to refund his money until the
expiration of the appeal period.

The Tribunal made some pertinent observations regarding the proceedings
that took place in the Board in relation to preliminary objection. B

Observed:

(1) Raising of preliminary points of law at the hearing of the application
without prior notice was contrary to good practice and procedure; the Board
should not entertain any preliminary objection to the appeal or application as
the case may be where prior notice to raise it has not been filed; the rationale
for such notice is to avoid taking the opposite party to the appeal or application C
by surprise;

(2) it was not proper for the Board to hear and determine the preliminary
objection simultaneously with the application; the preliminary objection must
be heard first and determined before hearing the appeal or application which
is objected to;

(3) it was contrary to good practice and procedure for the applicant's D
application to be filed without being supported by affidavit as was the case
before the Board; any application to the Board should be by way of chamber
summons supported by affidavit which is a simple procedure that can easily be
followed;

(4) it was not proper for the Board to design a form to be used by any
person who wishes to file an application before it; the only appropriate E
authority which is empowered to design any form to be used by the appellants
or applicants in the Board or Tribunal is the Minister responsible for Finance.

Held:

(1) a taxpayer who intends to appeal against the decision of the
Commissioner General who has failed to give a notice of intention to appeal F
or to lodge appeal within the specified period of time under s 16 (4) of the Tax
Revenue Appeals Act, 2000, has a legal right to apply to the Board for
extension of time within which to give a notice of appeal or to lodge an appeal;

(2) under the same provision the Board is given discretionary powers to
grant or refuse to grant the application depending on whether or not the
applicant taxpayer has a reasonable cause to show for his or her failure to give G
a notice of appeal or to lodge an appeal within the specified period of time;

(3) in this case the respondent's failure to lodge an appeal to the Board was
occasioned by the fact that when the respondent's managing director appealed
to the Commissioner General against the refusal by the Commissioner for
Customs and Excise to refund his money he did not get a response before the
expiration of the appeal period; H

(4) as the respondent fell out of time to lodge its appeal to the Board
while the its managing director was waiting for the response from the
Commissioner General, whom he thought could intervene so that he could
get his refund which he claims to have paid to the Commissioner for
Customs and Excise under great pressure and protest, we think there was

reasonable cause by the respondent for its failure to lodge an appeal within the specific period of time;

(5) in a tax application for leave to appeal out of time, it is not necessary to show or disclose as to whether the intended appeal will have chances of success in order to proceed; rather what is required to be shown by the applicant is reasonable cause for failure to lodge appeal within time.

Appeal dismissed.

Case referred to:
Rungwe Freight Tanzania Ltd v Tanzania Revenue Authority Commissioner General (App 1/2002), unreported

Mr Primi, for the appellant
Mr Chabruma, for the respondent

15 October 2004:

Hearing of appeal opens:

Mr Primi, for the appellant: My lord and Honourable members of the Tribunal, this is an appeal against the ruling of the Tax Revenue Appeals Board dated 20 June, 2004 in which the ruling granted an application for leave to file an appeal before it out of time.

In that application, the respondent had argued that the Commissioner General had not replied or responded to the application for refund. In other words, the Commissioner General had not made a decision in the matter. On the strength of that, the Board granted the application for leave to file an appeal before it out of time. In this appeal, the appellant has raised four grounds of appeal namely:

1. The Board erred in fact and law in holding that the failure of the Commissioner General to avail the respondent with essential documents or decision for appeal purposes was wrong.
2. The Board erred in law and fact in failing to note that the Commissioner General had since 12 August 2003 determined the respondent's refund application as per law and issued his decision thereon vide a document or letter with ref. no. TRA/CE/F.10/1 dated 12 August 2003 in which case Commissioner General became functus officio on the matter.
3. That the Board erred in law and fact in granting respondent's application for leave to file appeal out of time. The application was not supported with any reasonable cause or lawful justification.
4. The Board erred in law and fact by ignoring the arguments raised by the appellant herein, that in substance the respondent's application violated procedure as it was brought without notice and there was no disclosure of valid circumstances justifying the grant of extension to file appeal.

On our first ground of appeal, we submit that the Commissioner General did receive the respondent's application for refund way back on 17 August 2001. Since the said application was not complete, the Commissioner General did on 19 March 2002 write a letter to the respondent to furnish the original receipts which the respondent had made payments to the Commissioner General and reasons and grounds for application for refund. Unfortunately, the respondent failed to reply our letter as soon as possible. He delayed to reply it. He replied after about 13 months after the date of our request. He replied by way of a letter dated 7 April 2003 with ref. no. RFC/CCE/01/03. A copy of this letter is attached to our statement of appeal. It was addressed to Commissioner for Customs and Excise and it was received on the same date. After the said letter was received by the said Commissioner, by virtue of the powers invested in him under s 122 of the East African Customs and Transfer Tax Management Act, (Cap 27), he was supposed to look into the application for refund and determine it. He did look into the application and on 12 August 2003. He determined it and conveyed his decision to the respondent. He did convey his decision by his letter with ref. no. TRA/CE/F.10/1 dated 12 August 2003. A copy of this letter is attached to the statement of appeal before the board. It is also attached to the statement of appeal before the Tribunal and it is signed by the Commissioner for Customs and Excise himself. According to s 3 of the Tax Revenue Appeals Act, 2000 the Commissioner General is defined to mean Commissioner General appointed under s 15 of the Tanzania Revenue Authority, 1995 and includes any person appointed as Commissioner in respect of any tax. I submit that for customs under which this matter relates, the Commissioner General is the Commissioner for Customs and Excise because he is duly appointed under the relevant law. In this matter therefore, the Commissioner General had made a decision refusing to refund vide a letter quoted above. Therefore, the holding of the Board that the Commissioner was the problem for failing to avail the respondent with essential document or decision for appeal purposes is not correct.

On ground two my lord and Honourable members of the Tribunal, we submit that after the Commissioner General had determined the refund application vide the letter dated 12 August 2003 the Commissioner General became functus officio. In other words, the Commissioner General had discharged his duty and in case of grievances, the respondent had all rights to lodge an appeal to the Tax Revenue Appeals Board under the procedure envisaged under ss 14 (1) (*b*) and 14 (3) of the Tax Revenue Appeals Act.

In other words, the respondent was required within 30 days after receiving the decision by the Commissioner General to give a notice of intention of appeal to him.

My lord, under s 16 (2) (*a*) and (*b*) of the said Act, the respondent was supposed to appeal against the Commissioner General within 45 days from the date of service of that decision.

As it appears the respondent failed to lodge an appeal to the Board within the time prescribed by law. Instead of lodging the appeal, the respondent wrote a letter of grievance to the Commissioner General dated 29 September 2003; it appears the Commissioner General made no reply. It is our argument that the respondent had all the necessary documents to lodge an appeal in time. The grant of its application on grounds that the Commissioner General was a problem and did not avail it with the decision is wrong. The respondent had the decision of the Commissioner General with it. When the letter of grievance was served on the Commissioner General his decision had already been passed and he was functus officio.

My lord and Honourable members, on ground number three, we submit that the respondent did not show reasonable cause and lawful justification for delay in lodging the appeal to the Board in time as the respondent was physically present in Dar es Salaam, was not sick and was throughout represented by Advocate Mr Chabruma who is very conversant with customs procedures having worked in this department for a number of years. So, the respondent had no reason for the delay and the Board erred in law and fact in granting the application.

My lord and Honourable members, on ground four, we submit that the Board erred in law and fact in entertaining the application before it whilst knowing that the said application was not properly lodged before it because there was no notice served on the Commissioner General regarding the filing of the appeal before the Board. Also, the reasons in support of the application did not disclose as to whether the intended appeal will have chances of success or not. In other words, the statement supporting the application was devoid of merits. For this reason, therefore, the application before the Board was incompetent in itself and the Board ought not to have entertained it. Given the above reasons therefore, I humbly pray the Honourable Tribunal to grant this appeal with costs.

19 October 2004:

Mr Chabruma, for the respondent: My lord and Honourable members, I did carefully listen to the submissions by my learned friend for TRA. First of all, I wish to point out the legal provisions which govern the lodging of appeals in the Tax Revenue Appeals Board. Secondly, I wish to give a brief history of the matter which is before this Tribunal. Thirdly and finally, I wish to address myself to the grounds of appeal filed by the appellant.

My Lord and Honourable members of the Tribunal, before I start with the first part of my submission, I think it is proper to make some observation with regard to the title of the Commissioner in this case. He is not the Commissioner for Exercise as some people sometimes pronounce it. It is the Commissioner for excise. After making this observation, let me now start with the first part of my submission. The legal provisions which govern the lodging of appeals in the tax Revenue Appeals Board are the following: Section12 (1), s 12 (2) and s 12 (4) of the Tax Revenue Appeals Act, 2000 (15 of 2000). The next provision is s 16 (1) and (2) and (3) of the Tax Revenue Appeals Act. That is as far as the legal provisions are concerned.

As regards the history of this matter, it can be traced back to a letter of assessment which was written by the Acting Zonal Tax Investigation Officer on 19 July 2001 and referenced TRA/DCTI/CE/OFF/11/2000-2001 and addressed to the respondent. It is a letter of assessment of taxes. I wish to produce a copy of this letter for reference purposes.

Mr Primi, for the applicant: My lord, no objection.

Tribunal: The said letter is received and filed for ease of reference by the members of the Tribunal.

Mr Chabruma, for the respondent: As a reaction to that letter, the respondent wrote a letter dated 17 August 2001 protesting against the assessment and since he had paid the taxes which were demanded after receiving the assessment, he was protesting against the assessment and claiming the refund of taxes paid. I have a copy of that letter written by the respondent. I also wish to file it for ease of reference. A

Mr Primi, for the applicant: My lord no objection.

B

Tribunal: The said letter is received and filed for ease of reference by the members of the Tribunal.

Mr Chabruma, for the respondent: In reaction to that letter that is a letter of 17 August 2001, the appellant wrote a letter dated 13 March 2002 with Ref. No. TRA/CE/F.10/F.11. I wish to produce this letter for ease of reference. C

Mr Primi, for the appellant: No objection.

Tribunal: The said letter is received and filed for ease of reference.

Mr Chabruma, for the respondent: Having received the said letter written by the appellant, the respondent wrote another letter dated 7 April 2003 to the appellant which is in fact an annex to the statement of appeal. It is annex TRA 1 of 7 April 2003. Having received the said letter, the appellant wrote a letter of 12 August 2003 which is annex TRA 1. D

My lord and Honourable members, in between, that is on 22 February 2002, the respondent filed a notice of intention to appeal in the Tax Revenue Appeals Board. That marks the end of the second part of my submission. E

My Lord and members of the Tribunal, if I come to the first ground of appeal, we dispute the allegation that the Board erred in fact and law in holding that the Commissioner General was the problem for failing to avail the respondent with essential documents or decision for appeal purposes. My Lord, I have already said while recounting the history of this case that on 22 February 2002, the respondent filed a notice of intention to appeal. That is appeal No. 1 of 2002. In that appeal, the present appellant Commissioner General raised a preliminary point of objection that the Board had no jurisdiction to try the matter because the issue filed was of a criminal nature and was therefore improperly before the Board. The Board decided that it had the jurisdiction to try the matter and therefore the matter was properly before it. The appellant was dissatisfied in that appeal with the Board's decision and decided to appeal to this Tribunal that is Appeal No. 3 of 2002. The appeal was allowed not because the issue was of a criminal nature but because the respondent had not annexed a copy of the Commissioner's refusal to refund the taxes paid. The letter of refusal could not be annexed to the statement of appeal simply because it had not been written by the Commissioner. F G H

As it turned out, the letter we are talking about was written on 12 August 2003. So, it is obvious that a letter which should have been written in the year 2001 was written in the year 2003 and it is this letter which caused the respondent to lose the appeal. So, to answer the first ground of appeal, the Commissioner General was a problem in failing to arm the respondent with a letter of refusal.

A If I may now go to the second ground of appeal, the only portion which is not disputed in that ground is that a decision by the Commissioner of Customs and Excise was the decision of the Commissioner General. But, this decision was issued some 17 months after the respondent had filed a notice of intention to appeal and after the respondent had protested against the assessment. Under s 16 (2) (*a*) of the Tax Revenue Appeals Act, the respondent had only 30 days to B respond. So if the respondent was to file the notice of appeal properly, he had to do so within those 30 days and that notice of appeal which had been filed could not be followed with a statement of appeal in the absence of the Commissioner's letter. So, it was necessary for the respondent to seek extension of time. Furthermore, under s 16 (2) (*b*) of the Act, the respondent had to file the notice of appeal within 45 days from the date he received the assessment. The appeal C could not be filed in the absence of the Commissioner's letter. So, we have a situation here where the notice of appeal was filed on 22 February 2002, the Commissioner's letter was issued some 17 months after and that notice is still valid to date. Therefore, in the absence of extension of time, the respondent is bound to lose his appeal like he did in the Tribunal Appeal No. 3 of 2002.

My Lord and members, I now come to the third ground of appeal which says D the Honourable Board erred in law and fact in granting the respondent's application for leave to file an appeal out of time. The application was not supported with any reasonable cause. We are refuting this ground and in view of the history which I have tried to recount, the Commissioner's decision which was delayed had the adverse effect of tying the hands of the respondent, in that no appeal could be lodged without a copy of the Commissioner's decision, and E because there is a time limit for lodging appeals, the only way an appeal can be accepted at this juncture is by seeking extension of time.

My Lord and Honourable members let me now turn to the fourth ground of appeal. I wish to say that we are denying this ground because it was the Commissioner, who blocked the whole appeal process by delaying his decision up to 12 August 2003. That was the only time the respondent could switch on the F appeal process and he did not have to file another notice of appeal because the parties were still the same, the issue was still the same and both parties had full knowledge of the facts of the case. So, the respondent had all the reason to seek extension of time and the Commissioner's delay in making a decision is enough reason to seek extension of time. I wish to conclude by praying that the appeal be dismissed with costs.

G

Order: Rejoinder to be heard tomorrow at 2 pm.

20 October 2004:

Mr Primi, for the appellant, in reply: My lord and Honourable members, H Mr Chabruma's submission only covered a portion of applicable laws of filing appeals to the Board relating to assessments of duties and taxes. But the Act also provides for disputes arising from other matters. For instance, s 14 (1) (*b*) of the Tax Revenue Appeals Act, talks of the refusal by the Commissioner General to make a refund whereby a taxpayer can directly appeal to the Board pursuant to the procedure highlighted under s 16 (2) of the Tax Revenue Appeals Act. Under this section, such a person is required to lodge a notice of intention to appeal to the Board against that refusal and serve that notice to the Commissioner General within a period of 30 days failure to which the Honourable Board will not entertain the appeal. And the substantive appeal against the refusal to refund is to be filed or lodged within the period of 45 days from the date of service of the decision of the refusal to refund by the Commissioner. That is a procedure in case the taxpayer wishes to appeal against the Commissioner General's refusal to refund. A B

My Lord and Honourable members, I wish to say that the notice of intention to appeal against the Commissioner General's refusal to refund becomes valid only when that decision by the Commissioner General is issued to the taxpayer and the taxpayer is aggrieved by that decision and lodges that notice of intention to appeal to the Board and serves it upon the Commissioner General within a period of 30 days. A notice of intention to appeal is not a notice if it is lodged C to the Board before the Commissioner General issues his decision to refuse to refund.

My Lord and Honourable members, it is my submission that the submissions by Mr Chabruma on the history of the matter is basically partial and misleading. Learned counsel Mr Chabruma started with a letter dated 19 July 2001 with ref. no. TRA/DCTI/CE/OFF/11/2001 which was signed by one J O Manyanga, D Acting Zonal Tax Investigation Officer and the said letter was demanding payment of taxes and duties. According to Mr Chabruma, this was the first step to the matter. It is my submission that, that is not true. The truth of the matter is that this matter originated sometimes in June 2001 when the respondent's goods were seized by the appellant and subjected to custom investigation. The respondent was found guilty of false declaration contrary to s 148 (*b*) of the East E African Customs and Transfer Tax Management Act and relevant charges were raised against the respondent. After the said charges were served on the respondent, he requested the matter to be compounded and on 16 July 2001, the respondent's Advocate wrote to the appellant a letter of ref. no. PLC/C/MISC/2/2001 in which advocate for the respondent submitted as follows:

F

> "In order not to further jeopardize the interests of their customers my clients are pleading guilty to the charges preferred against them and they have signed the request for settlement of the case with a view to having the seized goods released to them upon payment of such additional duties, fines and penalties as may be determined by the compounding officer".

Prior to the Advocate's letter, my lord, the respondent had already pleaded guilty G to the charges and requested for compoundment and this request was made on 11 July 2001.

My lord, thereafter pursuant to s 173 of the East African Customs and Transfer Tax Management Act and s 48 of Value Added Tax Act, 1997, the Commissioner for Customs compounded the matter on 16 July 2001 and made the following order: H

> "That the respondent pays a total of Shs.2, 000,000 in respect of offences committed under s 148 of the East African Customs and Transfer Tax Management Act, plus Tshs 500, 000 in respect of offences committed under s 46 of the VAT Act, 1997. And the Commissioner made a further order that the goods be released to the owner after proper taxes and penalties are paid".

A My Lord and Honourable members, after these compoundments orders were made by the Commissioner, taxes were assessed and additional taxes and duties were discovered to the tune of Tshs 59,269,814 plus the penalties which amounted to Tshs 2,500,000. Hence on 19 July 2001, the respondent was duly informed of the additional taxes and the relevant compoundment.

My Lord, according to the provisions of s 173 (2) (*e*), particularly subs (2) (*e*)
B an order of compoundment made by the Commissioner is final and not subject to appeal. Therefore, the matter which was brought before the Board was essentially generated by the compoundment orders made under s 173 of the East African Customs and Transfer Tax Management Act, orders which were made before the respondent lodged its application for refund or indicated any protest. And indeed the respondent did pay all taxes plus penalties without registering any protest to
C the appellant as the said payments were made on 20 July 2001. And there was made only that after a month that is on 17 August 2001. The respondent did lodge an application for refund of Tshs 59,629,814 and in that letter the respondent only indicated that the said payments were made under protest. There were no reasons attached to the application for the refund. After having received the application for the refund, the Commissioner General did on 19 March 2002 request the
D respondent to give reasons and grounds of their refund claims because the Commissioner were unable to process the refund application as there was no reason or ground in support of the refund claims.

My Lord and Honourable members, before the Commissioner decided on the refund application, the respondent lodged a notice of intention to appeal in the Tax Revenue Appeals Board on 22 February 2002 and the substantive appeal was
E also filed in the Board as Appeal No. 1 of 2002. This appeal did not only challenge the additional taxes assessed that is Tshs 59,269,814, but also challenged the penalties that were imposed amounting to Tshs 2,500,000. It was basically an appeal which is different from what is contemplated in this appeal. This appeal relates to an application for refund and the refusal of that application by the Commissioner General. For the sake of clarification, I invite the Tribunal
F to go through the Board's record in *Rungwe Freight Tanzania Ltd v Tanzania Revenue Authority Commissioner General* (App 1/2002), unreported. The notice of intention to appeal in respect of that appeal certainly cannot be applied because of the following reasons:

1. The said notice of intention to appeal had been struck out by the dismissal of
G the substantive appeal by the Tribunal in Tax Appeal No. 3 of 2002.
2. That notice of intention to appeal related to assessment and penalties that were imposed by the Commissioner General.

Due to these reasons, the notice dated 22 February 2002 no longer exists.

My Lord and Honourable members, on the first ground of appeal we wish to
H reinstate our position that the Commissioner General was never a problem because if at all there was a delay in reaching a final decision that delay was contributed by the respondent himself for the following reasons:

1. The respondent failed in his application to disclose the reasons for the refund.

2. The respondent took more than a year to submit the reasons for the refund A after having been requested for by the Commissioner. As it can be seen the said reasons were submitted in April 2003 and the Commissioner after receipt of his reasons did deliver his decision within a period of four months in August 2003.

My Lord and Honourable members, according to the East African Customs and B Transfer Tax Management Act there is no time limit for the Commissioner General to process the refund application. However, there is time limit set for the taxpayer to lodge an application for a refund. That time limit is 12 months from the date when the payment is made, see s 123 of the Act. The applicant did submit the reasons in support of the application in a period which was more than 12 months. In a way that defeated the intention of the law because under s 122 (2) C of the East African Customs and Transfer Tax Management Act, the person claiming for the refund is required to present his claim within a period of 12 months. The presentation of the claim has to be complete with reasons so that it can be processed. The filing of incomplete claims results into problems of delays in the processing of the applications. The Commissioner was not a problem in this case. D

My lord and Honourable members, I maintain my position and say that the Board did err in law and fact. Counsel for the respondent has failed to give reasons as to why extension should be granted.

On ground three, I submit and insist that the notice of intention to appeal dated 22 February 2002 is no longer valid as it was dismissed by the Tribunal in Appeal No. 3 of 2002 after the Tribunal dismissed the substantive appeal in respect of E that notice. The Commissioner did not delay his decision. He acted within a reasonable time and also the law does not prescribe a specific period for the Commissioner to give his decision. The respondent had no sufficient reasons to warrant a grant of his application to appeal out of time. Given the above reasons, I pray the Tribunal to allow our appeal and quash the Board's decision. I also pray for costs of this appeal. F

Order: The Tribunal members will meet in chambers tomorrow 21 October 2004 and the day after tomorrow 22 October 2004 to go through the Board's proceedings and ruling together with the submissions made by learned counsel for the parties before the Tribunal. Thereafter, we will meet in chambers on 2 November 2004 for recording the opinions on the matter between the parties. G

Judgment on 4 November 2004 at 2.00 pm.

JUDGMENT

(Delivered 4 November 2004) H

A Shangwa J, Chairperson:

In this appeal, the Commissioner General of Tanzania Revenue Authority is appealing against the ruling of the Tax Revenue Appeals Board delivered on 30 June 2004 granting leave to the respondent Rungwe Freight (T) Ltd to file an appeal out of time against his refusal to refund it custom duties of Tshs 59,269,814.

The appellant was represented by Mr Primi advocate and the respondent was represented by Mr Chibruma. Both of them represented the parties in this case ably.

Four grounds of appeal were raised by the appellant. However, it is only two out of four that are pertinent to this appeal. These are as follows:

1. That the Board erred in law and in fact in granting the respondent's application for leave to file appeal out of time. That the application was not supported with any reasonable cause or lawful justification.
2. That the Board erred in law and fact by ignoring the arguments raised by the appellant herein, that in substance the respondent's application violated procedure as it was brought without notice, and there was no disclosure of valid circumstances justifying the grant of extension of time to file appeal.

Before going into the merits of this appeal, we wish to point out what we have observed from the Board's record and make some comments and guidance to the Board below.

Our first observation is that at the hearing of the application some preliminary points of law were raised by Mr Haule for the Commissioner General without prior notice to raise them. This was contrary to good practice and procedure. The Board should not entertain any preliminary objection to the appeal or application as the case may be, where prior notice to raise it has not been filed. The requirement for such notice is to avoid taking the opposite party to the appeal or application by surprise.

Our second observation is that the Board heard and determined the preliminary objection simultaneously with the application. That was not proper. Whenever there is a preliminary objection on a point of law or fact raised against the appeal or application, the preliminary objection must be heard first and determined before hearing the appeal or application which it is objected to.

Our third observation is that the applicant's application was filed without being supported by affidavit. This was also contrary to good practice and procedure. Any application to the Board should be by way of chamber summons supported by affidavit which is a simple procedure that can easily be followed. In this case, however, we do not intend to invalidate the applicant's application which was filed without being supported by affidavit. Doing so is likely to create a delay of justice in the matter between the parties. Our fourth observation is that the Board has designed a form to be used by any person who wishes to file an application before it. That is as well not proper. It should be noted that the only appropriate authority which is empowered to design any form to be used by the appellants or applicants in the Board or Tribunal is the Minister responsible for Finance. Such powers are generally vested in the said Minister under s 33 of the Tax Revenue Appeals Act.

We now start to consider the two grounds of appeal which we said are pertinent to this appeal out of the four grounds raised by the appellant. Generally speaking, a taxpayer who intends to appeal against the decision of the Commissioner General who has failed to give a notice of intention to appeal or to lodge appeal within the specified period of time under s 16 (4) of the Tax Revenue Appeals Act, has a legal right to apply to the Board for extension of time within which to give a notice of appeal or to lodge an appeal.

Under the same section, the Board is given discretionary powers to grant or A
refuse to grant this right. It entirely depends on whether or not the applicant taxpayer has reasonable cause to show for his or her failure to give a notice of appeal or to lodge an appeal within the specified period of time. In this case, the Board was satisfied that Rungwe Freight Company's failure to lodge an appeal to the Board was occasioned by the fact that when the said company's managing director Mr J B Mwalugelo appealed to the Commissioner General against the B
refusal by the Commissioner for Customs and Excise to refund his money vide his letter with ref. no. RTC/CCE/01/04 of 29 September 2003, he did not get a response before the expiration of the appeal period. In a way, the Board found this to be a reasonable cause for his failure to lodge the appeal within time. We think the Board did not err in so finding.

For us, we believe that when Mr J B Mwalugelo appealed to the C
Commissioner General after receiving a final response from the Commissioner for Customs and Excise on 12 August 2003, he must have thought that his problem could still be solved by him due to a very clear fact that the Commissioner General is the Chief Executive Officer of the Tanzania Revenue Authority.

As the respondent fell out of time to lodge its appeal to the Board while the D
aforesaid managing director was waiting for the response from the Commissioner General, whom he thought could intervene so that he could get his refund of Tshs 89,269,814 which he claims to have paid to the Commissioner for Customs and Excise under great pressure and protest, we think there was reasonable cause by the respondent company for its failure to lodge an appeal within the specific period of time. For this reason, the first ground of appeal fails. E

We now turn to the second ground of appeal. We have examined this ground of appeal and the submissions made by Mr Primi for the applicant on this ground, and we have come out with a settled view that the applicant's application did not violate any procedure.

In the Board below, Mr Haule submitted on behalf of the Commissioner General that Rule 4 of the Tax Revenue Appeals Boards Rules was not fulfilled, F
as Rungwe Freight Company Ltd did not serve a copy of the notice of intention to appeal on the Commissioner General. In his own words, Mr Haule stated as follows, and we quote:

> "We did not get a notice. We only got a summons for this application".

Now, you may try to imagine, how could Rungwe Freight Company Ltd serve a G
notice of intention to appeal without having been granted leave to file an appeal to the Board out of time and when he was actually waiting for the intervention of the Commissioner General himself, and upon whom the notice of intention to appeal had to be served by this company? We think therefore that a summons which was sent to the Commissioner General requiring him to appear and reply to the application for leave to file appeal out of time was sufficient for that H
purpose.

We wish to point out at this juncture that in a tax application for leave to appeal out of time, it is not necessary to show or disclose as to whether the intended appeal will have chances of success in order to proceed. What is required to be shown by the applicant is reasonable cause for failure to lodge appeal within time. This ground of appeal has also failed.

A Due to the fact that the period of time within which to lodge the appeal which was ordered by the Board has already expired, we order that Rungwe Freight Company Ltd should give a fresh notice of appeal to be served on the Commissioner General within 30 days from today; and should lodge the appeal to the Board within 45 days from today.

Finally, we dismiss this appeal, but we order that each party should bear its
B costs.

Delivered today at Dar es Salaam in the presence of Mr Chabruma advocate for the respondent and Mr Mwakandege legal counsel for the appellant.